THE SCALE M(

The Scale Model does one thing: makes it easy for business owners and entrepreneurs to grow their businesses. Using a proven methodology that is easy to understand and implement, business teams can learn how to diagnose and solve barriers to growth.

The Scale Model equips CEOs and leadership teams with a framework to assess where the pain points lie in their business, and easy-to-use templates to help them work out the solutions to enable growth. The Model has been used by high-growth companies around the world to achieve industry-beating growth in sales and profits, with engaged and aligned teams. In a complicated business environment, the straightforward advice and practical structure of the Scale Model provides clarity for business planning.

When you're busy running your business, you want just one place to go to fix it. This is that place. Pick up The Scale Model today, work through the tools inside, and watch your business grow. That's how easy it is.

Andy Clayton is an award-winning entrepreneur, having founded four companies: one failed, one sold, and two going strong. Andy has a skill for identifying and clarifying key concepts that has helped him to succeed as a business teacher and author. Andy is an autistic entrepreneur, a passionate sportsman, and supporter of climate change causes.

Dear Alex,

Would love to hear your thoughts on the enclosed?

Best,

Antony
x

THE SCALE MODEL

How to Set Up and Run a Successful Enterprise

Andy Clayton

Routledge
Taylor & Francis Group
LONDON AND NEW YORK

Designed cover image: © Getty Images / Mykyta Dolmatov

First published 2024
by Routledge
4 Park Square, Milton Park, Abingdon, Oxon OX14 4RN

and by Routledge
605 Third Avenue, New York, NY 10158

Routledge is an imprint of the Taylor & Francis Group, an informa business

© 2024 Andy Clayton

The right of Andy Clayton to be identified as author of this work has been asserted in accordance with sections 77 and 78 of the Copyright, Designs and Patents Act 1988.

All rights reserved. No part of this book may be reprinted or reproduced or utilised in any form or by any electronic, mechanical, or other means, now known or hereafter invented, including photocopying and recording, or in any information storage or retrieval system, without permission in writing from the publishers.

Trademark notice: Product or corporate names may be trademarks or registered trademarks, and are used only for identification and explanation without intent to infringe.

British Library Cataloguing-in-Publication Data
A catalogue record for this book is available from the British Library

Library of Congress Cataloging-in-Publication Data
Names: Clayton, Andy, author.
Title: The scale model: How to Set Up and Run a Successful Enterprise / Andy Clayton.
Description: Abingdon, Oxon; New York, NY: Routledge, 2024. | Includes bibliographical references and index. |
Identifiers: LCCN 2023032602 (print) | LCCN 2023032603 (ebook) | ISBN 9781032472287 (hardback) | ISBN 9781032481265 (paperback) | ISBN 9781003387558 (ebook)
Subjects: LCSH: Small business—Growth.
Classification: LCC HD62.7 .C53 2024 (print) | LCC HD62.7 (ebook) | DDC 658.02/2—dc23/eng/20230818
LC record available at https://lccn.loc.gov/2023032602
LC ebook record available at https://lccn.loc.gov/2023032603

ISBN: 978-1-032-47228-7 (hbk)
ISBN: 978-1-032-48126-5 (pbk)
ISBN: 978-1-003-38755-8 (ebk)

DOI: 10.4324/9781003387558

Typeset in Joanna
by codeMantra

This book is dedicated to the amazing team at Scale, and all our Members that we've been on the journey together with. Creating the content of this book has been a team effort, and draws on the collective experience of the coaching team, in particular, our inspiring lead coaches, Antony Enright and James Summers, who have tirelessly shared their experience, tested the tools, and enriched this content over the years.

Also, a special thanks to Claire Butcher who so patiently pulled all the content together for publishing.

CONTENTS

Foreword xiv

PART I
Getting started 1

1 **Introduction to the Scale Model** 3
   Summary 3
   Scale members 3
   Let's talk about scale 4
   The barriers to scale 9
   How to break through? 10
   Commit to change 12
   Get support 14
   How to use this content 14
   Where do the ideas come from? 15

2 **Key principles** 17
   Summary 17
   Mindset 18

Accelerating growth	19
Investment required	20
Your role	22
Vision and belief	23
Commit to a rhythm	25
Que sera, sera	27

3 The Scale Model checklist — 29

Summary	29
Key concepts	31
Worksheet	33
Understanding the checklist items	34
Exercise – how to use the Scale Model checklist (SMC)	37
Tips and guide	38

PART II
Strategy — 41

4 SMC 1 – Scale Strategic Plan — 43

Summary	44
Introduction	44
Getting it into one place	45
Getting it on to 'one page'	48
Components of a Strategic Plan	48
Strategic Plan worksheet	50
The 'how' of it: a practical guide to preparing your strategy	51

5 Strategy 1 – The core — 59

Summary	59
Purpose	60
Vision	69
Culture – Core Values	75

6 Strategy 2 – Commercial strategy — 85

- Summary — 85
- Introduction to commercial strategy — 86
- Building out your commercial strategy — 91
- Core customer — 91
- Market positioning — 97
- Choosing the right axes — 101
- X-factor — 105
- USPs — 111
- The 1-minute strategy — 119
- The 1-minute strategy exercise — 121

7 Strategy 3 – Base camps — 124

- Summary — 124
- What do we mean by 'base camps'? — 125
- A clear picture of 3–5 years — 126
- Annual initiatives — 130

PART III
Checklists – Diagnosing bottlenecks — 139

8 SMC 2 – Meeting effectiveness — 141

- Checklist item — 141
- Summary — 141
- Concepts — 142
- Solving your meeting problems — 144
- Worksheet — 147
- Meeting best practices — 148
- Two key meetings — 151
- Weekly management meeting — 152
- Daily huddle — 157
- Key concepts — 157
- Worksheet — 161
- Exercise — 162

9 SMC 3 – Accountability and team structure — 163

- Checklist item — 163
- Summary — 164
- Tools and exercises — 164
- Accountability — 164
- Team structure — 172

10 SMC 4 – We're too busy! — 181

- Checklist item — 181
- Summary — 181
- Key concepts — 182
- Worksheets — 188
- Exercise — 190

11 SMC 5 – Executing strategy – quarterly planning — 194

- Checklist item — 194
- Summary — 194
- Key concepts – the 'QPD' (Quarterly Planning Day) — 195
- What is a QPD? And why are they important? — 196
- When to do QPDs? — 197
- Why a quarter? — 197
- Where to have QPDs? — 198
- Workshops virtual vs. in-person — 199
- Who should attend QPDs? — 199
- Cascading QPDs — 199
- QPD agenda — 200
- The QPD process — 202
- On the day — 203

12 SMC 6 – Team leadership — 214

- Checklist item — 214
- Summary — 215
- Concepts — 215

	Team dynamics	218
	Key concepts	218
	Personality profiles	226
	Coaching	231
	Guide and pitfalls	237
	Leadership characteristics	239
	Giving feedback	243
13	**SMC 7 – Profitability**	**252**
	Checklist item	252
	Summary	252
	Key concepts – profitability	253
	Power of One	258
	Pricing	263
	Key concepts	263
	Cost control	276
14	**SMC 8 – Cash**	**278**
	Checklist item	278
	Summary	278
	Dials of cash flow	279
	Key concepts	279
	Cash conversion cycle	285
15	**SMC 9 – Organisational culture**	**292**
	Checklist item	292
	Summary	292
	Bringing Core Values to life	293
	Talent assessment chart	301
	Key concepts	301
16	**SMC 10 – Systems and processes**	**307**
	Checklist item	307

	Summary	307
	Process accountability	308
	Key concepts	308
	Worksheet	310
	Exercise	311
	Process resolution	312
	Key concepts	312
17	**SMC 11 – Collecting customer feedback**	**320**
	Checklist item	320
	Summary	321
	Key concepts	321
	Worksheet	326
	Exercise	327
18	**SMC 12 – Sales and marketing functions**	**328**
	Checklist item	328
	Summary	328
	Brand map	329
	Key concepts	329
	Worksheet	333
	Exercise	334
	Marketing channels	334
	Key concepts	335
	Worksheet	338
	Exercise	339
	Sales Playbook	340
	Key concepts	340
	Sales Playbook	344

PART IV
Bonus tools — 351

19 Maximising company value — 353
Summary — 353
The problem — 353
How to fix it? – The shareholder value checklist — 355
Worksheet — 356
Exercise — 357
Pitfalls, guidelines, and FAQs — 358

20 Planning survey — 360
Welcome page — 360
Survey questions — 361

FOREWORD

Is this program for you?

If you relate to the description below, then this book may help you to transform your company (and your life).

If not, you may find your time best spent elsewhere.

- You **run a business**. Maybe you started out as a 'practitioner' – an expert in a specific field who does not view business or being an 'entrepreneur' as your primary vocation, you are something else first. Maybe business was never your first interest, or focus of your academic interest.
- You **read business books**, and find them useful, but they contain a lot of unnecessary terminology and breathless promises of the world, without being a practical guide on what to do.
- You **have a good team** but haven't been able to get them to fully step up to take the business forward and through to the next level of sales.
- You're constantly hitting **bottlenecks** to further growth and getting frustrated with them.
- Maybe you've **had an insight**, an idea on how the business might grow, or a knowledge of your market and industry that you could use to drive growth, and you want to scratch that itch, to see if you can really make it work.

- You have friends or people in your network that have **sold their companies** and made good money from it, and you're wondering how to achieve this for your business. Not that that was your primary motivation in setting up the company, but as time passes, you realise that it may be important for you too.

What happens next

If that does describe you, then let me share what will happen if you put in practice the tools laid out here.

Firstly, things won't suddenly change overnight. That might be promised elsewhere, but not here. You and the team will derive short-term energy from setting a new direction and creating new strategies, but it will feel difficult to maintain the habits and disciplines necessary to see them through. You will have to get into the habit of constantly referring to a new source of insight – this program. Maybe you'll hire someone, like a coach, to help keep you on track, to make the journey easier.

You will find that, in the first few quarters, you will still be stuck clearing out some of the issues of the past. Maybe you need to free up capacity to focus on change projects, or get key processes un-gummed. Maybe you realise you have some missing spots in the team that take time to fill.

Whilst making these changes though, you will simultaneously narrow your plans down to just one or a few key projects that you know will deliver real growth, and get the team focused on delivering them. At times you will doubt whether you can see it through, or whether it will achieve the outcomes you want. But, deep down, you'll know you're on the right track, and you will have wonderful moments where you can see the end in sight, and know you've got it in you.

Then you'll have some kind of launch. Maybe a new product set, or a pivot to a new market. Maybe you'll expand, opening new offices, functions, or departments. Even then, it might not go as planned, at first. Sales and orders may take time to come through, some of the people hired will turn out not to be the right ones, and at those times you and the team just have to keep the faith, and carry on tweaking till you get it right.

And then, like the engines of a plane opening on the tarmac, you will feel it. Growth will start to power through the organisation, generating a momentum all of its own. People who've been around a while will come to believe it, newer people will take it for granted, and all around you you'll see new faces.

What the future looks like

In 2 – 3 years' time, this is what life will look like:

- You have the intense pride and pleasure of listening to plans, proposals, and solutions from a team of people, many of whom are new to the business, that genuinely impress you. This growth in the team has been funded by growth in your business.
- Your role has changed. You're no longer involved in those day-to-day tasks that frustrated you, but working on the key area where you add value.
- You have a leadership team around you who are aligned, working well together, and driving real change. You realise they're actually doing a better job of key functions than you could.
- You're able to go on holiday, and the phone doesn't ring.
- There are clear schedules of meetings to set and manage growth plans for the business. Sometimes, you cannot make it to them, but they carry on and deliver great outcomes regardless.

It's not all perfect in this new world though, new problems and emotions have emerged:

- You look at the P&L and cashflow forecast, and though everything is fine, it's scary to see how large some of the numbers have become.
- You're having to seriously consider what your exit from the business looks like, which feels like a weighty decision. Dealing with actual or potential investors may be beneficial, but is changing how you feel about the business.
- The team still has a strong culture, which you've worked hard on, but it's lost some of the former intimacy. Elements of corporate life have crept in, and pressure is sometimes required to ensure teams work well together.

- You reflect that it's been several years of challenge, with stressful periods, tough decisions, and a lot of hard work.

So, before you read on, think carefully. Growth is a laudable objective, but is it what you're really looking for? There will be trade-offs to be made. Much as I want to make it easy, there will be late nights, early starts, difficult conversations, and moments of doubt and discomfort. Only read on if you're really game.

Final thought

One final thing to bear in mind. As you go through that journey, you will have dark moments. You will doubt yourself, question the sanity of the undertaking, face fears and risks. In those moments, you may feel like you're the only person who could make such a mess of things.

Please trust me when I say: **you are not alone**. Choosing the path of being an entrepreneur is not easy. Maybe there is a mythical version of us out there that wears it like a light garment, but I've yet to meet them. Never let yourself believe that it is easier for others in some way, we continue to choose to experience those tough moments.

If it was easy, everyone would do it.

Part I

GETTING STARTED

Part 1

GETTING STARTED

1

INTRODUCTION TO THE SCALE MODEL

Summary

Most companies remain small, because growing a business is hard. It requires both managing day-to-day activities well *and* focusing on change projects to drive growth. Few teams pull this off. In this chapter, we share some of the key tools and techniques to understand how to focus the business on such change initiatives.

Scale members

This is a book about forward-thinking, purpose-driven, entrepreneurial companies, committed to providing a great life to their team members, real value to their customers, and having an impact on the world.

THIRDWAY

Take ThirdWay Group – www.thirdway.com – (TWG). By 2022, they had become the United Kingdom's leading office space design and build company, just 13 years after they were founded. In that time, they outpaced their competition, and won awards for their products and services, how they treat their staff, and innovation in the industry. They are now expanding across the country, are well-funded, growing rapidly, and highly profitable.

But it hasn't all been smooth sailing. They experienced some serious setbacks and stalled badly in their growth in 2018. Several crises came one after another, and they realised they were suffering from the issues of growth.

They knew they needed to make big changes, so they got their team together and committed to a new system to manage the business. Since that time, quarter by quarter, they have cumulatively built up improvements that have culminated, 4 years later, in becoming the #1 company in their industry.

They have used the Scale Model.

They're not alone. The Scale Model is working for companies across industries and geographies. These companies have expanded to global markets, won prizes for their impact as excellent employers, and achieved ambitions, such as acquisition by global leaders. Many of their stories are included in this book. We hope you can see a link between where you are and where you would like to be – and how you can take practical steps to get there, through the following pages.

They all have a few things in common:

- A desire to **have an impact** on the world
- An **openness to new ideas**, to be 'coachable'
- A willingness to stick to some **hard disciplines**
- A desire to **do things differently** – different from the competition, and different from how they used to be done.

This book brings together for you the collective learnings and best practices from this extraordinary community. Above all, it will show you where and how to apply focus, and to stick with that focus.

Let's talk about scale

Scaling a company is hard, few companies get there. Of the 5.5 million companies registered in the United Kingdom, just 1.4 million actually employ people, and of those, just 7,700 have more than 250 employees. Did you know that if your company passes 50 employees, it makes you one of just 0.7% of companies in the country?

5.6 million (total number of U.K. businesses in 2021)

Type	# Employees	# Companies	% Companies
Self-employed/sole traders	0	4.17 million	74.7
Micro	1–10	1.16m	20.8
Small	11–49	210,295	3.8
Medium	50–249	35,600	0.6
Large	>250	7,700	0.1

Source: Companies House, % of types of businesses in the United Kingdom.

Most people are surprised to learn this, as we are much more aware of those 7,500 large companies, either as clients, employees, or suppliers. They account for about a third of employment and GDP of the country, but there are actually very few of them.

On a chart, it's even clearer what big jumps these are. The number of companies decreases by orders of magnitude with each tier. Each is approximately 20% of the previous (i.e. there are about 20% as many small companies as micro ones). This is a **negative exponential curve** – a constant, compounded rate of decline.

Distribution of UK companies by size

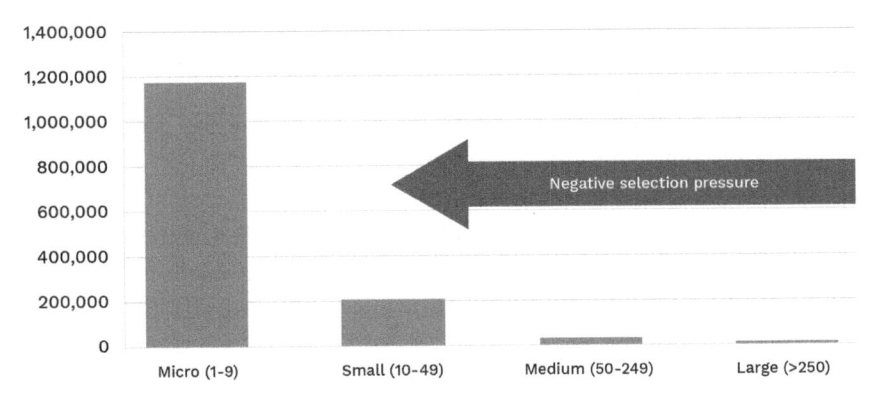

(Bar chart showing Micro (1-9) ~1,200,000; Small (10-49) ~210,000; Medium (50-249) ~35,600; Large (>250) ~7,700. An arrow labelled "Negative selection pressure" points from large to micro.)

It's easy to say 'of course there are fewer large companies than small ones', it seems somehow obvious. But why should it be so? From the perspective of ideal organisational size, is there a reason that dictates that within an economy it is inherently more efficient for most companies to be small?

In theory, company size could follow a **normal distribution,** like so many other population groups.

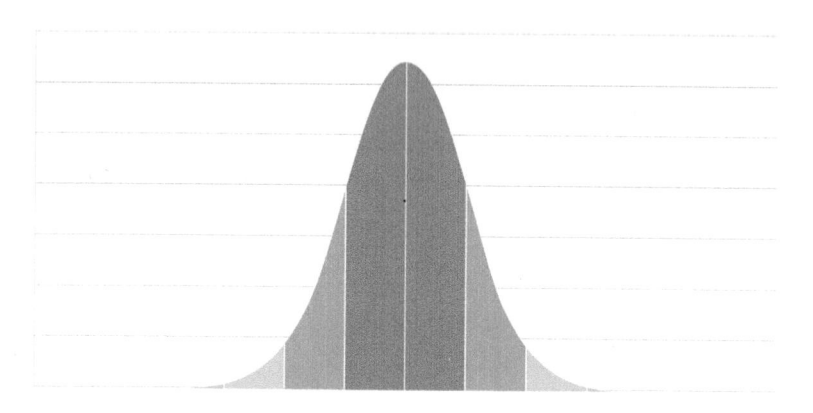

Normal distribution

The fact that it doesn't, implies that there is some strong selection pressure against companies growing to scale. Why might this be the case? It could be because of...

- **Preference**. Maybe most company owners do not want to own a large company and the stress that comes with it.
- **Team effectiveness**. Human beings operate together optimally in certain small group sizes. Once you pass those limits, team dynamics start to erode and fail, naturally slowing growth.
- **Growth of complexity**. An organisation is full of 'nodes'. Each person, point of communication, IT system, product, department, and so on, is a node. Linear increase in # of nodes leads to quadratic increase in # of connections between those nodes, which becomes **complicated**, becoming harder and harder to manage. Prevalent is the effect on **decision-making**, and how this slows with growth. This is called 'Metcalfe's law'.

Metcalf's Law

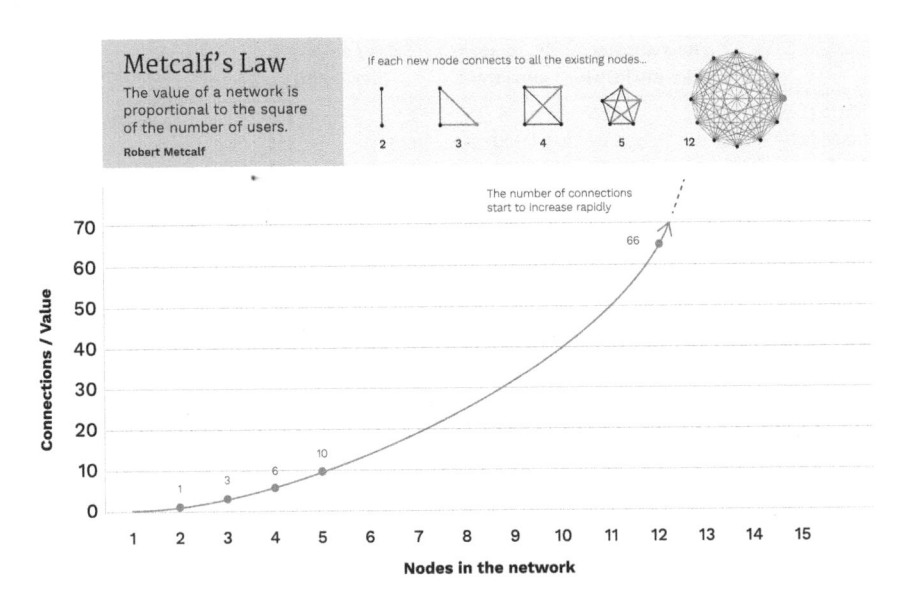

The value of a network is proportional to the square of the number of users.
Robert Metcalf

Metcalfe's law.

- **Limited lifespan**. Founders cannot run companies forever, and when handed over to second generations or new owners, the focus, insight, and drive that grew the company often fades. Average company lifespan in the United Kingdom is just 8.5 years, and they generally start from zero sales, so there's a limit to how far you can go, and how fast.
- **Investment**. Growth requires cash, therefore the limited pool of capital caps growth to a small number of companies.

But there is a problem with these arguments. The data show considerable **benefits of scale**. Something happens as companies get larger that leads to **larger companies being more efficient**. Look at the average sales and sales per employee for companies of different size (U.K. Companies House data for 2021):

Large companies are almost 30% more efficient than micro ones when measured by sales per employee. This is the principle of **economies of scale** at work. So what are the benefits of scale?

- **Network effects**. Some business models benefit intrinsically from scale, especially those where a network effect is at play (e.g. a social

	Av. company sales (millions)	Av. company employees	Sales / employee (thousands)
Micro (1-9)	£ 0.55	4	£ 151
Small (10-49)	£ 3.09	20	£ 158
Medium (50-249)	£ 20.23	98	£ 207
Large (>250)	£ 279.47	1,390	£ 201

Medium-sized companies generate almost £50,000 more revenue *per employee* than Small ones.

NB. Where do you benchmark with respect to these figures? Are you above or below these benchmarks?

Sales per employee for different company sizes.

media network, or a car share platform). The larger the network becomes, the more valuable it is to each node within the network.

- **Ability to invest.** Areas such as research and development, international expansion, product development, branding, and attracting talent all benefit from a critical mass in investment. Larger budgets give an advantage, creating **positive snowball effects**.
- **Brand.** Once a brand accumulates credentials and recognition in a market, it accrues many benefits, such as preferential selection by customers and employees. Legacy and scale often accrue brand benefit over time.
- **Access to capital.** Capital flows not to where it is needed the most, but to where it is viewed as being most secure. This leads to the counter-intuitive reality that **capital chases capital**, that is, investors are more likely to put more money into large organisations with considerable existing resources.
- **Cost economies.** If a large pool of people can share resources and support functions, such as IT systems, HR, and Finance, there is a cost per unit saving that increases with scale.

Combined, these forces can create powerful **flywheel effects**, whereby each contributes to the other, with increasing velocity, complementing increasing scale.

These are common flywheel effects:

Flywheel effects

Examples of flywheel effects, where scale can have direct benefits.

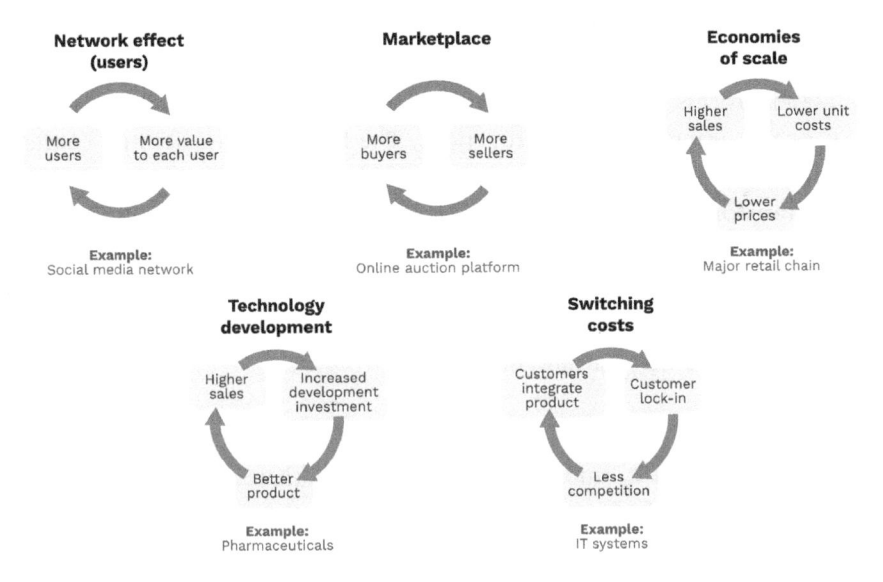

Network effect (users)
More users → More value to each user

Example: Social media network

Marketplace
More buyers → More sellers

Example: Online auction platform

Economies of scale
Higher sales → Lower unit costs → Lower prices

Example: Major retail chain

Technology development
Higher sales → Increased development investment → Better product

Example: Pharmaceuticals

Switching costs
Customers integrate product → Customer lock-in → Less competition

Example: IT systems

Common flywheel effects that can drive the growth to scale.

The barriers to scale

So, if scale accrues such benefits, why is it so rare, and hard to attain? Having worked with many companies over the years, and observing those that grow and those that don't, it's clear to us why growth is so hard. It's because it requires you to **do three things at once**:

- Day to day operation — **RUN IT**
- Deal with bottlenecks to growth — **IMPROVE IT**
- Create and deliver growth strategy — **TRANSFORM IT**

Three key barriers to scale — you have to do these at the same time:

- **Run it**. No matter how good your recruitment and delegation skills, managing the day-to-day tasks of a business consumes time, such as serving clients, managing the team, and making sure everyone gets paid on time.
- **Improve it**. As a company grows, many issues become bottlenecks that have to be *actively solved* in order to maintain growth, such as systems and process improvements, training and development of the team, or recruiting senior new functions. The functions and abilities of the business need to be constantly upgraded.
- **Transform it**. Really reaching scale requires constantly reinventing what you do. This is the hardest of all is to focus time and resources on, but where step-change growth comes from. Examples include developing a new product set, moving to new markets, or changing your business model in a substantial way.

It is the ability of the leaders of the business to focus efforts on the 'Improve it' and 'Transform it' initiatives that determines their ability to scale. It's about working *on* the business, not *in* it.

How to break through?

The key to breaking through this barrier to growth can be summed up in one word: **change**. If you want to make a change in your life, such as lose weight, get sober, or change a career, you have to set aside time to focus on, and apply energy to, that project.

Change in a business works the same way. If you think of the time that you (and your team) have as being like space in a jar, day-to-day activities that currently fill that time are like sand, they easily move to fill all the space.

INTRODUCTION TO THE SCALE MODEL 11

Prioritising your life

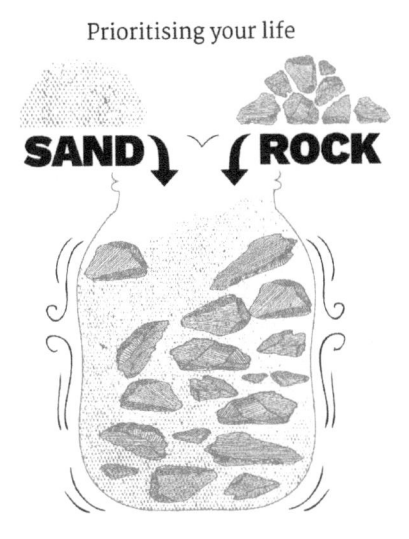

Rocks and sand – making room for the important stuff.

Think of change projects as rocks. How are you able to fit both rocks and sand into the jar? There is only one way: *put the rocks in first*, and the sand will fill the rest of the space.

This is how change works; you must **force focus**. Change projects need to be prioritised over day-to-day work, for example by diarising regular team off-sites to focus only on change projects. It will not happen by itself.

An organisation's capacity for reaching scale is directly linked to its ability to **focus** effort away from day-to-day running (whilst ensuring that it still happens) and on to projects to both improve on the current model and, crucially, update the business model.

One key habit to achieve this is to bring the leadership team together every 2–3 months for strategic review, and to set key **sprint projects** to drive change in the business; Chapter 11 covers how to structure these sessions.

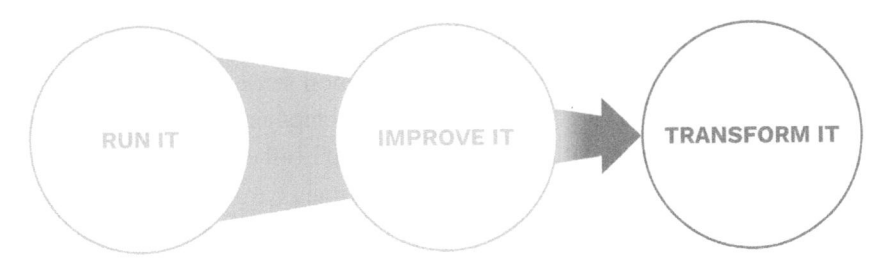

RUN IT → IMPROVE IT → **TRANSFORM IT**

The direction of travel – where to focus your time and energies.

We make this easy for you by introducing two key tools that drive this priority-setting process:

- The Scale Model checklist. A simple, easy-to-use diagnostic tool to work out where you need to apply focus to continue growth. It links to over 30 exercises and worksheets to solve your bottleneck.
- The Scale Strategic plan. An easy-to-understand and follow framework to create a strategic plan that will inspire the team, win commercially, and is easy to execute.

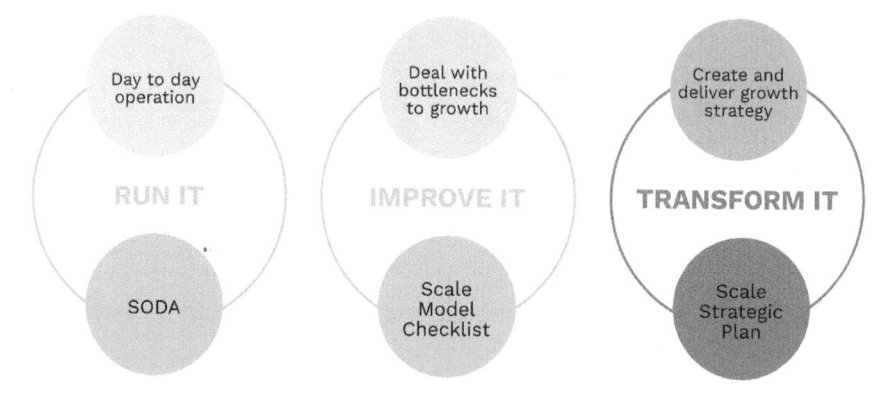

RUN IT — Day to day operation — SODA

IMPROVE IT — Deal with bottlenecks to growth — Scale Model Checklist

TRANSFORM IT — Create and deliver growth strategy — Scale Strategic Plan

The tools to use to help in these three key areas.

These two tools: the **Scale Model checklist**, and the **Scale Strategic plan**, distilled over many years of what works and doesn't work in actual high-growth companies, will ensure, with the right work and discipline, that your business grows, and reaches the aspirations you have for it.

Commit to change

This book will describe for you, in some detail, the specific steps to take to grow your business. It's practical and helpful. There will be insights that may be new, and some will be familiar common sense. But it can't make the change for you. The Scale Model process helps make it easy, but the journey to scale is hard work, often stressful, and full of pitfalls.

If you're serious about achieving the outcomes we describe, then you need a strong motivation to make change. I have observed several common drives among the many entrepreneurs with whom I have worked through this journey:

- **A sense of purpose.** Often with entrepreneurs, you don't have to scratch far below the surface to find a motivation to change the world in some way. This is often married with the mindset that the more this positive impact can be expanded, the greater the benefit to the world.
- **Legacy.** At a certain stage in life, it becomes a powerful motivation to realise the value of a lifetime's insight and work and leave behind something that outlives your direct involvement in it.
- **For the team.** Some entrepreneurs feel a strong sense of commitment to their team and want to expand the platform of the business in order to bring in more people and provide greater opportunities for them.
- **Make money.** We use many terms to describe it, such as 'ambitious', 'commercial', or 'growth-focused', but the desire to get richer is a strong motivation for many entrepreneurs. Sometimes, we observe friends or competitors 'running ahead', and want to catch up.
- **Insight.** Timing is everything. Sometimes a particular opportunity appears in an industry, or you become aware of an insight that could lead to growth in the market, and a sense of a ticking time clock to capitalise on that opportunity.
- **Frustration.** Running a smaller business can be very frustrating. You often can't employ the kinds of people you'd want to work with, it can be hard to delegate away functions you do not enjoy, and it can all feel like 'groundhog day'.

Maybe some of these may appear at odds with each other, or there are multiple drivers that apply to you. That's ok. For example, it's fine to be motivated by a strong sense of purpose to change the world, *and* a desire to personally make money. These can exist as 'ands' rather than 'ors'. Popular business author Jim Collins speaks about **'the power of the and'**, and avoiding the **'tyranny of the or'**. Life is rarely black and white (though our interpretation of it often can be), and a theme of this book is about getting comfortable with such apparent contradictions.

Think about what your motivations are for wanting to scale up your company. Do any on that list resonate with you? Is it enough to be willing to deal with the stresses and strains that growth will bring?

Get support

The best approach is to have someone on this journey with you. My best marathon time occurred when I hired a coach, Natasha. Natasha brought expertise, such as on how to train, and was an important accountability partner to ensure that I actually got my training done. It's the same with growing a business. It may be a new shareholder, a co-founder, a key team member, or an external coach or consultant. You will stand a much better chance of delivering the changes you desire if you work with someone together on this journey.

For most people, insight (e.g. a book like this one) is not enough. I have observed many businesses that have, at some point, felt the need to describe changes they want to make, and then not followed through with them. They make plans that gather dust, or worse still, pay someone else to make plans that get left in a drawer somewhere. Having another human being to fully accompany you on this journey will have an enormous impact on the likelihood of you achieving what you're looking for. Also, compensating that person will have a big impact on the chance of you doing what is necessary to achieve your goals.

The process will run more quickly, and you will be more likely to see it through with the help of a coach. Either introduce this book and methodology to your existing coach or visit www.scalecoach.co.uk and get in touch with our team if you're looking for help with the implementation of anything from this book.

How to use this content

This is a manual. It's intended to be practical, to be used rather than just read. Here's how to get the most out of it:

- **Trust the process**. Some of the teams we work with don't like to hear this phrase, and none of us are comfortable with blind faith. However, leaning on one system and sticking with it has tremendous benefits:

It works. It's tried and tested with dozens of high-growth companies that have achieved major growth.

- It's been deliberately made **simple and easy** to use, with no confusing terminology, so it's accessible to the whole team.
- **It all fits together.** This is an integrated system, using one tool as a diagnostic, which guides you to others for resolution.

- **Start at the beginning**. Start by reading the intro chapters, then get familiar with the Scale Model checklist. Avoid the temptation to jump into specific tools before understanding this one.
- **Big bang**. Begin the process with a 2-day team away. Kickstart a deliberate commitment to change and growth.
- **Repeat each quarter**. Growth takes time. It requires persistence and the development of certain habits and routines. Plan for 2–3 full-day meetings to stay on track each quarter.
- **Share with the team**. The extent to which your team can be educated on the principles, concepts, and tools here will decide how your life will be made easier as part of this process. Make this required reading at least for the whole leadership team.
- **Appoint a champion**. Regardless of which tools you decide to work on first, appoint a champion to lead the process.

The book starts with key principles and mindsets to prepare yourself to enable growth. Then it introduces the diagnostic tool the Scale Model checklist which will allow you to diagnose your bottlenecks to growth, and guide you to the tools to solve them. The rest of the book then consists of over 30 **worksheets, tools, and guides** that you will use to solve those bottlenecks.

In each case, I share stories, examples, and key concepts, then introduce the worksheet to be used in the relevant workshop, as well as a clear guide on how to run that session. Some of the sections also include guides, pitfalls, and FAQs associated with those workshops.

Where do the ideas come from?

All the tools in this book are ones that work effectively with our member companies and have helped them significantly. We have chosen what works. Many of the tools originate from other business books, often with our amendments and improvements. This is a book of books. Very few of the ideas are original; this is about what works, not about what's shiny and new. In all cases, authors and sources are referenced and suggested reading provided.

2

KEY PRINCIPLES

Summary

This is a book about **change**: identifying, designing, and delivering the change you want in your organisation to hit important objectives for your life. To prepare yourself for this change, there are several key principles and mindsets you must take on board to make this journey work for you:

- Growth depends on adding **quality people**, which feeds a positive 'flywheel effect'
- **Growth demands investment**
- You will need **confidence** in your vision
- Establishing a **rhythm** of execution is the key to success
- To avoid being the bottleneck, you must progress from running and managing the business to being the **owner** (*on and not in*)
- Never take yourself too seriously, or forget the huge impact of **luck and timing**.

Mindset

If you're serious about scaling, there is a critical mindset that you have to develop, and again it hinges upon a concept with the **power of the and** at its heart. Let's take an example.

A team that we work with, as part of a key project, was debating whether or not to set a target for staff recruitment over the upcoming year. The team wanted to grow as a business, and associated this with an increase in headcount (HC), particularly in the sales team. They identified a correlation between the two statements: 'Grow business' and 'Add people'.

The debate was as to whether growing HC itself was in fact a legitimate target, or whether it was the outcome of other growth-related activities. Some people held that the relationship between these two statements was:

Grow Business –> Add People

This is an example of 'linear causality', one thing leads to another. An equivalent statement might be 'When I become a senior leader, then I will hire a PA'.

Others were making the counterargument that, if they increased capacity in their sales team, this would in fact drive growth

Add People –> Grow Business

Also a linear statement, but in reverse, much like 'people become senior leaders because they hire executive help early, which helps them to progress faster'.

The answer lies in understanding that the relationship between the statements above is circular, not linear. With **circular causality**, the relationship between the two original statements looks more like this:

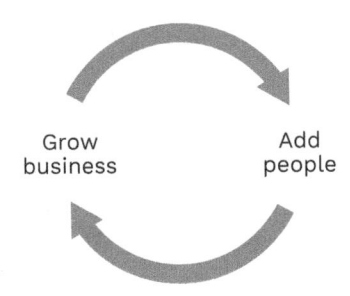

The circular relationship between adding people and growing the business.

A better term to describe this might be **complementarity**. It is an AND statement, rather than a THEN statement. One reinforces the other, with no distinct start or end point.

So where did that leave the team looking to set HC targets? In this case, they did set HC as a target for the sales teams. They took the view that each person and each team they added would drive revenue-generating capacity over the medium term for the business, which would drive growth. They chose to force the wheel to turn faster by adding people.

Accelerating growth

This concept of circularity is important to the related principle of **the flywheel** (also popularised by Jim Collins). At first, running a business takes a lot of energy to make any progress. As it grows, with each incremental improvement (e.g. new customer, team member, system/process, or improvement in financial standing), the system starts to move ever quicker, gaining momentum, until it ends up pushing you forward.

So how do you accelerate this flywheel? There are many things that can contribute to the speed of rotation, such as having high enough prices and margins to allow reinvestment, having a tight rhythm of meetings and communications, and maintaining consistent direction of strategy. The one thing that most tangibly accelerates it though is **adding and retaining quality people** to the team. The heart of company growth therefore often

The flywheel.

comes down to *how quickly can we get quality people in place*, to focus on the challenges we face, and grow the business.

For many entrepreneurs (but not all), our default setting again tends to be cautious. Having experienced existential cash crises, or dealt with the consequences of hiring the wrong people, it's easy to become conservative about hiring decisions and to hold back. To grow, however, you have to find an optimum speed for growth. It's like a rally car drifting through a corner. Go too slow, and you won't win the race, go too fast, and you'll spin out…

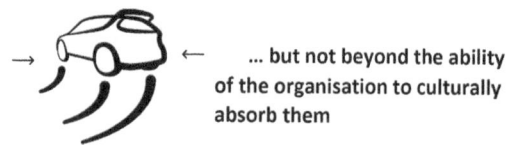

Push against the discomfort of the expense of new hires → ← **… but not beyond the ability of the organisation to culturally absorb them**

Cornering at the right speed.

As you truly progress and start to think like an investor in your own business, you realise that growth is often limited by the **speed at which you can generate and deploy capital**. Let's look more at the relationship between business growth and investment.

Investment required

All entrepreneurs have experienced failure, it comes with the territory. At some point, this has almost always included running out of money. These events can be traumatic, the pain of them stays with us and affects our decision-making and approach throughout our careers. This is a healthy trait; however, it can cause entrepreneurs to become conservative and risk-averse.

Growth requires in us a desire to take risks, and **growing a business takes investment**. It's hard to avoid this fundamental law. Engrain these words in your mind, as it's key to everything that follows.

Please do not assume that 'investment' immediately means looking for external sources of funding. It simply means that if we want to grow in the future, we will have to apply resources today; there is simply no escaping this. 'Investment' can take different forms, most of them revolving around two key (semi-interchangeable) inputs: time and money.

- **Your time**. The single most valuable resource in the company.
- **The team's time**. This may 'cost' more than just the expense of their paid time, such as time away from other projects (opportunity cost), or fee-earning time, so lost client revenue.
- **Company funds**, including reinvesting retained profits, or using company reserves.
- **External funds**, including debt (such as a bank loan or mortgaging the house), and raising external equity investment.

One CEO with whom we work, when discussing a key priority project for the business, described the issue as follows: 'If this was a client project, we wouldn't be discussing whether we can hit timelines, we would just resource it, plan it, and get it done'. This is an **investment mindset**, it's an understanding that, in the long run, change projects such as the one being discussed will generate more value than a current client project.

The key challenge you face in making these commitments is that it requires taking on **certain costs now** and committing them to **uncertain future outcomes**. This asymmetry profoundly affects decision-making in strategic discussions.

Amongst Scale members, many have found external funding an accelerant to growth, while others have managed to find internal sources of cashflow to fund growth.

Your role

Looking back at the growth model introduced at the start of the book, we can also use it to think about the stages of development of the entrepreneur:

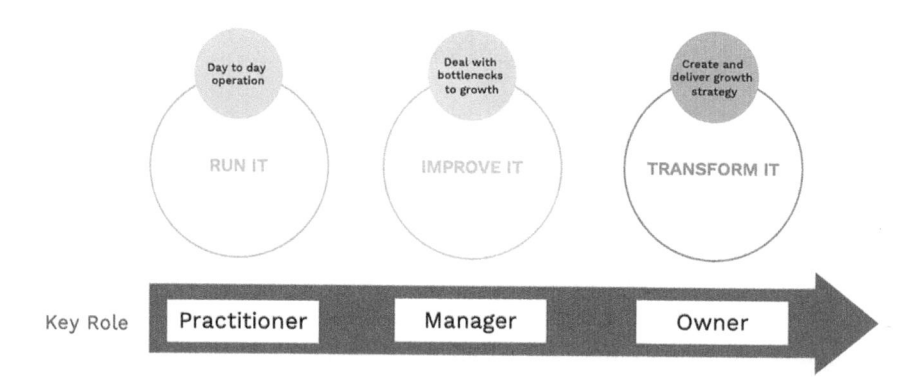

	RUN IT	IMPROVE IT	TRANSFORM IT
	Day to day operation	Deal with bottlenecks to growth	Create and deliver growth strategy
Key Role	Practitioner	Manager	Owner

Each bottleneck corresponds to a key role.

Practitioner. In many scaling businesses, the founder(s) are also the ones who originally provided front-line service to customers. This makes them practitioner-experts, maybe skilled in a vocational area, such as dentistry, psychology, construction, or hospitality. This subject matter expertise is of value in designing the development of the business, but involvement in front-line practitioner work takes away from activities to grow the business.

Manager. As a business evolves and grows, the capabilities of the organisation need to be constantly upgraded and improved, in order to avoid the inevitable bottlenecks that come with growth. The knowledge required for this work is much more 'general business', covering specialist business functions like operations, finance, and HR. This requires importing or developing such skills, often from outside.

Owner. Although we have this role from day 1, it's often strangely backseat, and the voice of shareholder value is often drowned out by more urgent day-to-day concerns. Over time, as entrepreneurs grow and develop, they start to think increasingly like investors in their own business. The development of this mindset is key to really achieving scale.

Or, to take an example:

1 **Practitioner**. 'I am an architect'.
2 **Manager**. 'I run an architecture practice'.
3 **Owner**. 'We transform green buildings'.

This matches with the well-known '3 stages of developing wealth' often shared amongst entrepreneurs:

- **Stage 1**. Use your time and efforts to make money.
- **Stage 2**. Use other people's time and efforts to make money.
- **Stage 3**. Use your money to make money.

Understand clearly: **you are the bottleneck to the growth of your business**. The extent to which you can accelerate your progress up the curve from Practitioner to Owner will unlock growth.

Vision and belief

The path to achieving growth requires courage, mostly in the form of belief in our own visions.

Everything is conceived twice – once in the mind, and then again in reality. Entrepreneurs are people for whom the first conception must be strong enough to ensure that the second follows. This requires **confidence**

in vision, and a willingness and ability to bring others on board with it. For some entrepreneurs, this is a natural strength, they exude a force or willpower that compels others. Sometimes, it can border on delusion, a conflation of fantasy and reality.

> Everything is created twice.
> First in the mind
> and then in reality.

What is more common though is **self-doubt**. Do you have the correct insight, idea, or vision to merit investing considerable resources – your own and those of others – into it?

The answer lies in **experience**. If you've been doing what you do for more than 2–3 years, you probably have as good an idea as anyone in your industry as to where the opportunities and threats lie. More than 4–5 years and you are an industry expert. However, a quirk of human psychology works against us here.

The **Dunning–Kruger effect** is a common human bias. It is common to see an irrational surge in confidence at an early stage of competence. When I first started learning to windsurf, I believed I would be riding huge waves in no time. It took time to learn just how far down the curve I was, and how hard that would be. When you start to gain expertise, however, you're more likely to question yourself. After having spent 15 years in China, I ended up having almost nothing to say about it, beyond 'it's a big place' because I was overwhelmed by the complexity of what I had come to understand.

Dunning Kruger effect

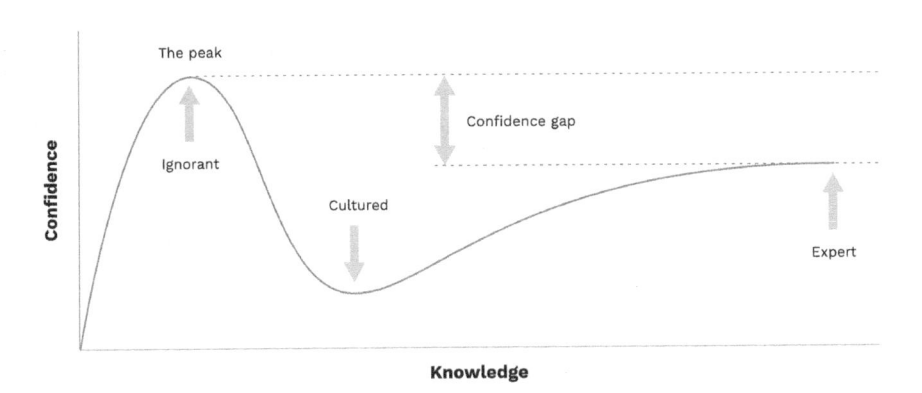

The Dunning–Kruger effect — when confidence means ignorance.

At this stage of knowledge, what holds us back is not false hubris, it is either lacking confidence in our own ideas or being overwhelmed at the complexity of potential things that could go wrong. So, as you consider going on the path and journey towards scale, if you have years of experience in your field, **calibrate towards taking a chance**, chasing a dream, and making leaps of faith. You are far more likely to be held back by fear of failure or error than you are by actual failure.

Commit to a rhythm

"The message of the Kaizen strategy is that not a day should go by without some kind of improvement being made somewhere in the company."
                                                                        Masaaki Imai

Delivering change, getting difficult things done, scaling a business, all these take time and require harnessing the compound effect of rhythms and habits to achieve. The concept of small incremental improvements compounding to huge changes over time is a key part of the 'Kaizen' philosophy.

The commitment to scaling is not just to a single-shot project or one-off planning session, it is to a **new way of working over a sustained period of time**. Be aware of the nature of how benefits accrue when you start making changes and improvements. Adding a 1% benefit each day is barely noticeable at first. When all the 1% start to compound, over time big improvements become clear. In the early stages, it takes grit and perseverance to keep going, and get through 'the valley of disappointment'.

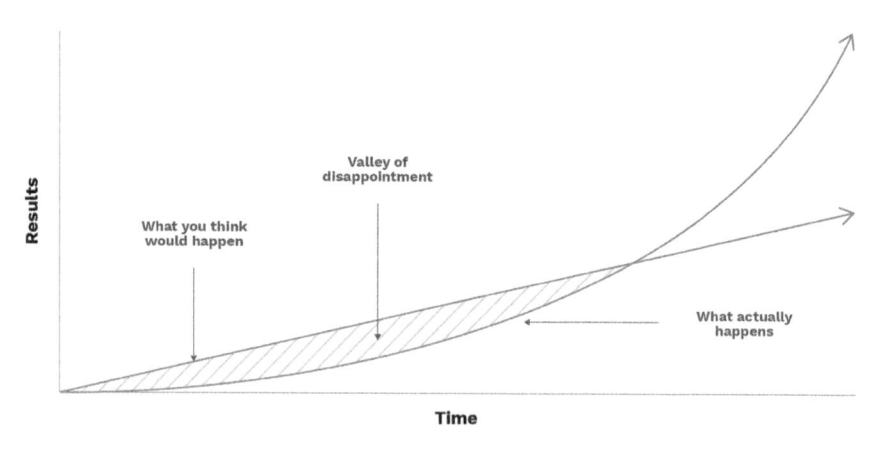

The valley of disappointment – incremental gains take time to hit (then get big fast).

One team with whom we work has been growing at 50% per quarter now, but it took it 3 years to reach that point. As the saying goes: *'It's amazing how long it takes to build an overnight success'*.

One of the keys to maintaining this is to **have a rhythm**. Be intentional about how you design the daily, weekly, monthly, quarterly, and annual meeting rhythms, and *stick to it*. Have a bias to rapid, short meetings so that you batch ad hoc communication and maintain pace. This is explained in more depth in Chapter 8.

Que sera, sera

This book provides a formula for how to grow a business that has been used many times for success. It rests on the concept that a business is a complicated, but ultimately controllable, system. The same cannot be said for the markets in which businesses operate. I was asked once by the CEO of a member company: 'Do you believe it is better to have great people in a bad market, or bad people in a great market?'. Much as I wanted to answer the former, I had to share with him the story of The Cambridge Mask Company (www.cambridgemasks.com).

CAMBRIDGE MASK CO
EST. 2015

Cambridge Mask Company has been in the business of high-filtration masks for consumers since 2015. For most of that period, it experienced slow, steady growth, and all the normal problems growing companies face. Then, at the start of 2020, the COVID-19 pandemic hit. What followed was insane. It experienced 10× growth within 3 months, and almost the same again in the next 3 months. It was a crazy, dizzying rollercoaster ride.

Was it foresight or strategy that allowed this business and team to prosper so much, whilst others in other industries faced devastation? Sure, they put themselves in the right place at the right time. But their CEO would be the first to admit that the major factors were **luck and timing**.

So, the final mindset I leave you with comes from a community that has come to mean a lot in my life – Alcoholics Anonymous – the serenity prayer:

Does this situation require?

Acceptance — **Wisdom** — **Courage**

Grant me the serenity to accept the things I cannot change,
The courage to change the things I can,
and the wisdom to understand the difference.

3
THE SCALE MODEL CHECKLIST

Summary

A healthy business has problems (This short phrase has brought me great comfort over the years).

Israeli business professor

Running a company can feel like the proverbial boy with the fingers in the dyke – there are always numerous problems to be fixed and multiple opportunities to be pursued.

So, **where to apply focus**? That is always the question.

The Scale Model checklist is a simple tool that allows you to regularly diagnose and identify these bottlenecks and guide you to the solution.

It's an amazing tool to see in action. Teams naturally align on their key issues for resolution and get so much energy from being able to quickly and

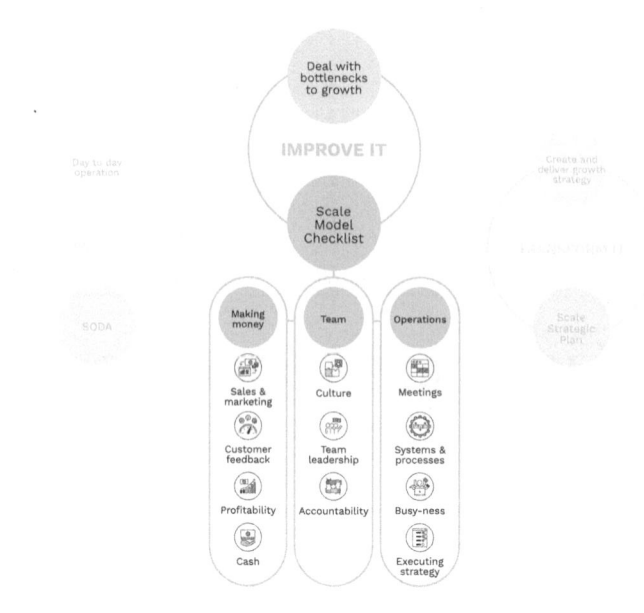

'Improve it' – the key tools for overcoming bottlenecks.

'boy with finger in dyke'

easily overcome them. Everything is laid out in simple, easy-to-understand terms, with no jargon. You just share it and get on with it.

Sales and marketing functions

Realising a great strategy requires great performance in these two areas:

- Map key marketing channels to communicate with the market
- Develop essential communication and branding messages
- Distil your sales best practices into a manual, to maximise conversions.

If this is your key issue, go here: Chapter 18.

Exercise – how to use the Scale Model checklist (SMC)

The SMC should be done as a diagnostic exercise once every quarter (for more details on planning and running a Quarterly Planning session, see Chapter 11). It should be the first exercise in a QP session, and follow these steps:

1. Provide all the participants with the orange checklist, and ask them to read and reflect on what they believe are the key issues and challenges to address in the business
2. Emphasise the question of 'which issue, if solved, would make everything better for everyone?'
3. Collect the answers on a spreadsheet report (the online survey tool below can help).
4. Review and share the report with the team before your team planning session.

Online survey tool

Scale's coaching team have developed an automated online survey tool with a simple link to share with the team to fill out the SMC survey. Use the QR code below to fill out a simple form to share a survey link with your team, and receive a compiled report.

Results

The results should look like this:

SCALE **The Scale Model Checklist**		3	3	3	3	3	3	3	3	27
** CHOOSE ONLY 3 OF THE ISSUES BELOW **	Manifestation	James	Warrick	Rob	Andy	Poppy	Peter	Claire	Anais	Antony	TOTAL
We don't have a commonly agreed **strategy** and direction.	• Lack of growth • Confusion or disagreement on direction • The team can't state our strategy clearly					x					1
Our **meetings** are not effective enough.	• Time in meetings is not used well • Meetings are not delivering the changes and results we need										0
Accountability & team structure. We're not fully clear on who's accountable for what, or our team structure is creating silos.	• Confusion or dropped balls due to lack of accountability and who's measured on what • Silo's are hindering teamwork and customer service • Turf-building or politics creeping in			x			x	x	x	x	5
Busy-ness. Everyone is too busy, with not enough time.	• We don't have enough time to focus on key projects • The team is overworked and stressed out						x				1
Executing strategy. We're not delivering on our agreed strategic plans.	• Our strategic plans are gathering dust on the shelf • We're not seeing plans through to actual change	x									1
Team leadership. We have problems within our teams, stemming from how they are led.	• Teams with poor dynamics, or even conflict (overt or implicit) • Poor staff engagement and/or retention • Micromanagement and lack of delegation										0
Our **profitability** is too low, or trending negatively.	• Net profitability is at, or trending towards, <15-25%	x	x		x	x	x	x			6
Our **cash** position is too weak, or trending negatively.	• Cash reserves at, or trending towards, <3 months expenses • More growth is leading to less cash							x	x		2
Organisational culture. People not behaving or performing in line with the culture or performance we desire.	• Inconsistent behaviours across the organisation • Individuals are creating drama or dispute, or having issues with performance • Poor team retention and / or engagement								x		1
We have **systems and processes** letting us down.	• Key processes and/or systems are causing excessive cost, delay, drama, or lack of clarity and communication		x								1
We're not collecting **customer feedback** effectively.	• We lack usable data on customer satisfaction, or how we're delivering on our customer promises					x					1
Our **sales** and/or **marketing** functions are underperforming.	• Not generating enough leads (of the right quality), or • Not converting them consistently enough to support growth	x	x	x	x			x	x	x	8

Example of a Scale Model checklist output report:

1   You can now use this data to decide which areas of the business to focus on. Pick as few items to work on and resolve as possible. At most, choose 1–3 items to work on.
2   Use the rest of the book to work through the relevant tools, based on the area you chose. For example, if the team feels that 'Busy-ness' is a key issue, then go to Chapter 10 and work through the exercises listed there.

The first time you do this exercise, unless you have explicitly done a lot of strategy work recently, I suggest that you ensure that item 1. on the checklist – having a strategic plan – is one area that you choose to focus on. If you're serious about getting the business to scale, then it is critical that the team has a commonly agreed and aligned strategy to go after.

Tips and guide

Learn to stargaze

Every time a team fills out the Scale Model checklist, their answers cluster in a few areas, as they all see the same issues and opportunities in the business. However, the cluster for each team is different, as well as for the same team at different times.

Over time, you start to spot certain regular clusters. For example, 'Busyness' often clusters with items such as 'Meetings' and 'Processes and Systems'. There are certain natural correlations that appear again and again. Understand these correlations in order to drill down to the heart of the problem.

Repetition

The SMC is not a tool to be used once and discarded. It is a constant, repeated process that will continue to drive improvement.

It's also not a linear process. Each time you execute one of the tools you learn more, both of the theory, and the business, which then informs the next diagnosis. We call this iterative process simply 'Think + Do'. Another example of a flywheel in motion.

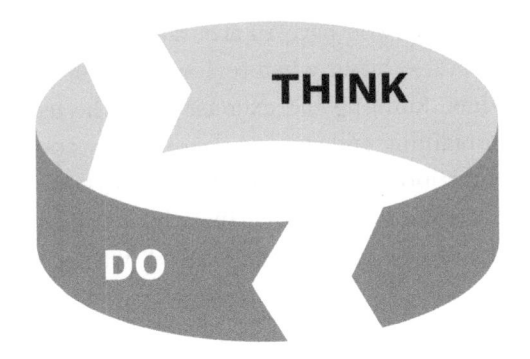

'Think and Do' – *an iterative process.*

Which headaches can you live with?

An implicit consequence of focusing efforts in certain areas is that others will be left unresolved. Get comfortable with the fact that there will always be unresolved problems and unmet opportunities. You may not welcome that fact, but must make peace with it. It's OK to say, 'We understand that that is an issue, but we have other more pressing priorities at the moment'.

One of our Members calls this 'The headaches we are prepared to live with'. The key to success with respect to the outcome of the checklist tool is not choosing as many items to resolve, it is in choosing as few as necessary to have the maximum impact.

Points to bear in mind

The Scale Model checklist is a great tool, but you must learn how best to use it:

- **System complexity.** Making a change in one part can have significant and unforeseen consequences elsewhere, for example, increasing pricing to improve profitability may make life harder for salespeople, or impact the cash conversion cycle. Consider the impacts that changes will have, and be prepared for necessary trade-offs.
- **Inputs = Outputs.** The checklist is perception-based. It does not crunch data for you, interview staff, or do market research. The knowledge of the team is the key limiting factor in the accuracy of your outputs, so the extent to which you can include rigorous review of data prior to doing the exercise will decide the quality of your conclusions.
- **Biases.** Individuals will disproportionately select items that affect them, so be sure that you have an accurate cross-section of the team, and account for these biases when reviewing results.
- **The inside view.** Running the exercise with the team gives you an inside view. Obtaining and sharing data from customers, the market, and about competition will improve your own view of how you think you're doing. Spending time on business books and with other entrepreneurs will also give you a better view of 'what good actually looks like'.

Diagnosis and solution

The SMC allows you to achieve focus on what needs to be worked on. You then need to apply the right tool for the job. The rest of the book contains all the tools and concepts required for this. Please note that in many cases there are multiple tools/exercises, or a sequence of them in order to resolve the issue. Some of these items require significantly more input and work than others. For example, the item Team Leadership has several tools associated with it, whereas 'Customer Feedback' links to just one.

Part II

STRATEGY

Key concepts

Complicated vs complex

A complicated system is one in which "the components can be separated and dealt with in a systematic and logical way that relies on a set of static rules or algorithms." It may be hard to see, but there's a fixed order in something that allows you to deal with it in a repeatable manner. For example, making an electric car and a reusable rocket are complicated problems, but once you figure out how to do these things, you can keep doing them at will.

On the other hand, a complex issue is one in which you can't get a firm handle on the parts and there are no rules, algorithms, or natural laws. "Things that are complex have no such degree of order, control, or predictability." A complex system is much more challenging—and different—than the sum of its parts, because its parts interact in unpredictable ways.

Rick Nason, 'It's not complicated'

It may not feel like it, but by this definition, a company is a **complicated** (but not complex) **system**. It has many interacting components, and external factors that affect it, but companies generally adhere to common sets of rules and principles, that you can learn and spot over time.

The nature of complicated systems is that they develop **bottlenecks**. In a manufacturing plant, for example, a bottleneck causes components to build up before the bottleneck, and unused capacity sits idle below it. You see this effect when you pass roadworks on a motorway. Before the roadworks (bottleneck), traffic backs up and is slow (which is inefficient), and after the roadworks, there is lots of unused road space (enjoyable, but also inefficient).

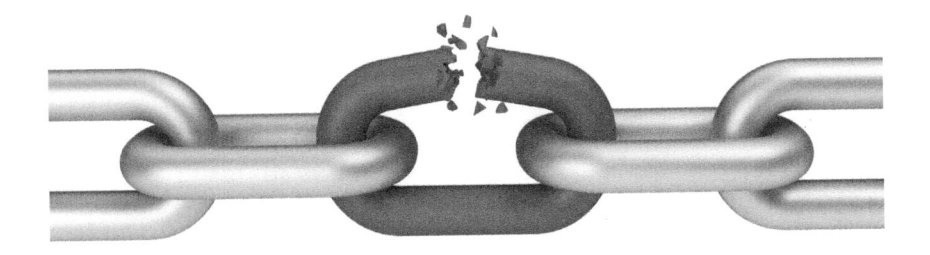

The approach of improvement through the identification and elimination of bottlenecks is known as the Theory of Constraints. Running a company successfully requires a constant diagnosis and resolution of constraints.

It's easy to think that your problems are unique to you and your business. Nothing could be further from the truth. Companies hit the same, predictable challenges as they move through the growth curve.

Lean on the collective wisdom of those that have gone before you, and work with your team to use the Scale Model checklist to run a diagnosis. The key question is: *which issue, if we solve it, will make everything else better for everyone else?* If you really explore this question, you will narrow down to one or a few items that really need to be addressed.

It's common in business literature to hear that a certain area of business is 'the #1 thing', as in 'People are the #1 thing', 'Culture is the #1 thing', or 'Strategy is the #1 thing'. The fact is that they are all important, but *at any given moment in time, they cannot all be most important.* There's no point in having great people if you run out of money or an amazing strategy if internal processes keep failing. What's required is an understanding of what needs to be solved now.

The checklist

The Scale Model checklist helpfully summarises common growth bottlenecks into these key areas:

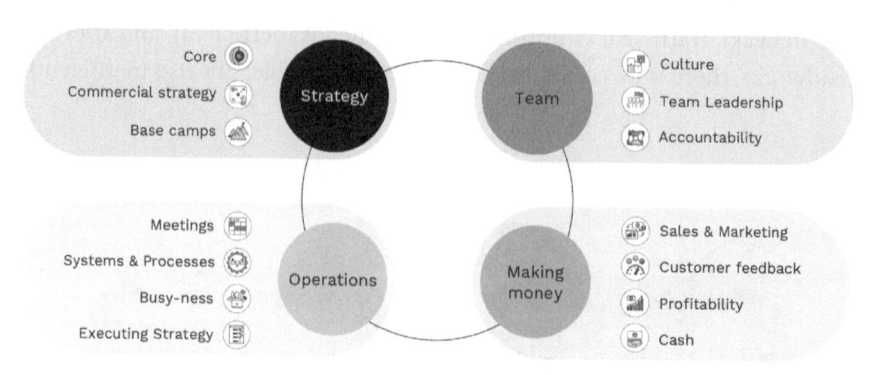

The Checklist Model.

THE SCALE MODEL CHECKLIST   33

This book is a practical guide. It contains worksheets that you need to work through with the team. Each key chapter contains a worksheet to work through, here is the first:

Worksheet

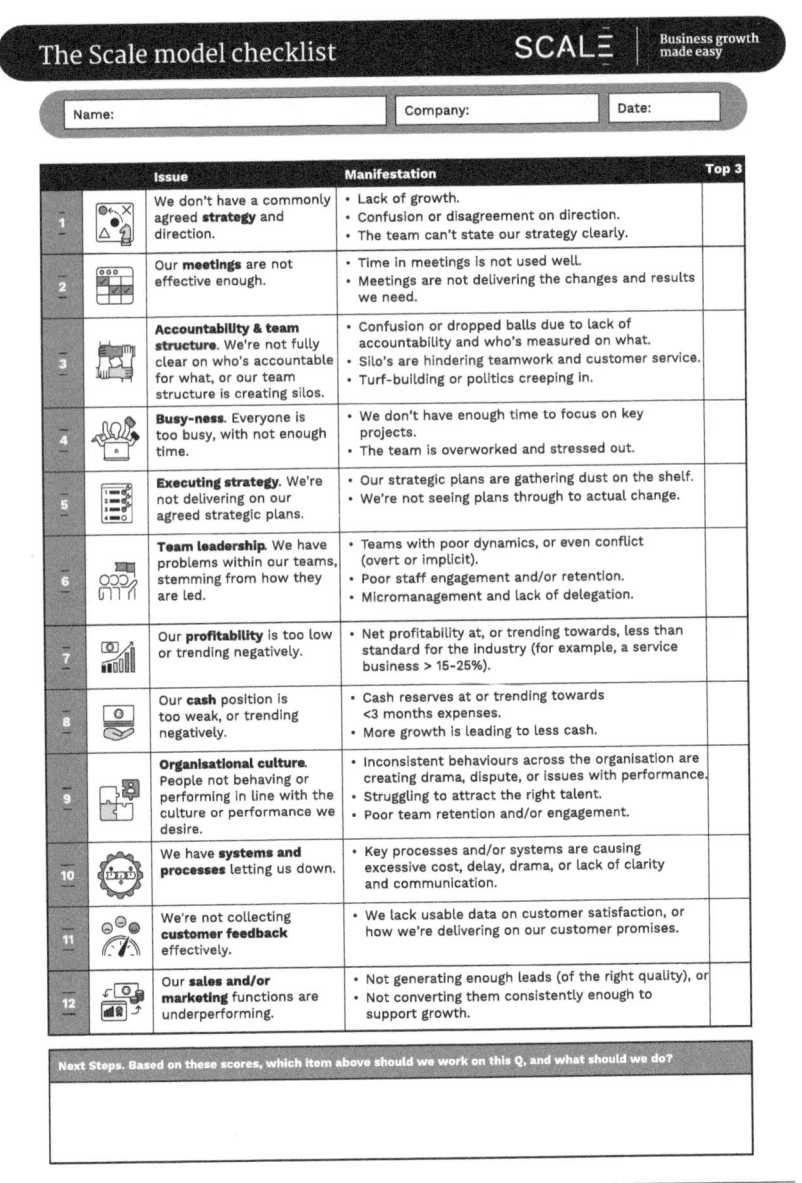

The Scale model checklist — SCALE | Business growth made easy

Name: _____   Company: _____   Date: _____

#	Issue	Manifestation	Top 3
1	We don't have a commonly agreed **strategy** and direction.	• Lack of growth. • Confusion or disagreement on direction. • The team can't state our strategy clearly.	
2	Our **meetings** are not effective enough.	• Time in meetings is not used well. • Meetings are not delivering the changes and results we need.	
3	**Accountability & team structure**. We're not fully clear on who's accountable for what, or our team structure is creating silos.	• Confusion or dropped balls due to lack of accountability and who's measured on what. • Silo's are hindering teamwork and customer service. • Turf-building or politics creeping in.	
4	**Busy-ness**. Everyone is too busy, with not enough time.	• We don't have enough time to focus on key projects. • The team is overworked and stressed out.	
5	**Executing strategy**. We're not delivering on our agreed strategic plans.	• Our strategic plans are gathering dust on the shelf. • We're not seeing plans through to actual change.	
6	**Team leadership**. We have problems within our teams, stemming from how they are led.	• Teams with poor dynamics, or even conflict (overt or implicit). • Poor staff engagement and/or retention. • Micromanagement and lack of delegation.	
7	Our **profitability** is too low or trending negatively.	• Net profitability at, or trending towards, less than standard for the industry (for example, a service business > 15-25%).	
8	Our **cash** position is too weak, or trending negatively.	• Cash reserves at or trending towards <3 months expenses. • More growth is leading to less cash.	
9	**Organisational culture**. People not behaving or performing in line with the culture or performance we desire.	• Inconsistent behaviours across the organisation are creating drama, dispute, or issues with performance. • Struggling to attract the right talent. • Poor team retention and/or engagement.	
10	We have **systems and processes** letting us down.	• Key processes and/or systems are causing excessive cost, delay, drama, or lack of clarity and communication.	
11	We're not collecting **customer feedback** effectively.	• We lack usable data on customer satisfaction, or how we're delivering on our customer promises.	
12	Our **sales and/or marketing** functions are underperforming.	• Not generating enough leads (of the right quality), or • Not converting them consistently enough to support growth.	

Next Steps. Based on these scores, which item above should we work on this Q, and what should we do?

_____

Feb23 · © Clarity Strategy Ltd DBA Scale 2023   www.scalecoach.co.uk

The Scale Model checklist.

Understanding the checklist items

The rest of this book contains tools to solve each of these bottlenecks. Here is a summary of these solutions, and where to find them in the book:

Develop a strategy

Create a strategic plan that the whole team is aligned behind including:

- A Core, consisting of a Purpose, Long-term Vision, and description of Culture
- A Commercial Strategy to create a unique positioning to deliver growth
- Milestones to the achievement of the long-term Vision
- A brief, easy-to-remember form for the whole team to use.

If this is your key issue, go here: Chapter 4.

Meeting effectiveness

Make your meetings great:

- Understand and stick to the golden rules of effective meetings
- Set a rhythm to ensure team engagement, productivity, and alignment with strategy
- Work on two key meetings: the Daily Huddle and Weekly Management meeting.

If this is your key issue, go here: Chapter 8.

Accountability and team structure

As an organisation grows, it's vital to ensure that everyone is clear about who is accountable for what:

- Set accountability for key functional areas with KPIs and metrics tracking
- Create a team structure optimised for teamwork, client service, and agility.

If this is your key issue, go here: Chapter 9.

Busy-ness

Solve over-work and stress in teams by thinking about how time is used effectively:

- Ensure everyone is productive and working in their 'Sweetspot'
- Remove demotivating and low-value activities.

If this is your key issue, go here: Chapter 10.

Executing strategy

Ensure that your strategic plan actually gets executed:

- Use Quarterly Planning sessions to set key Sprint Projects to drive change
- Use a weekly rhythm to execute against these Projects.

If this is your key issue, go here: Chapter 11.

Team leadership

The measure of leaders is the effectiveness of their teams:

- Understand and account for different working styles and personalities
- Overcome common team dysfunctions
- Improve team leaders in seven key traits of Leadership
- Avoid micromanagement by using training coaching skills.

If this is your key issue, go here: Chapter 12.

Profitability

Profit is essential to fund growth and create a business to stand the test of time:

- Identify which key levers to pull to improve profitability
- Improve your pricing, the #1 way to improve profitability.

If this is your key issue, go here: Chapter 13.

Cashflow

Ensure that growth generates, rather than depletes, cash:

- Understand the '5 dials' to manage your cash
- Improve your cash conversion cycle, so you get paid before having to pay out.

If this is your key issue, go here: Chapter 14.

Organisational culture

Use Core Values as a tool to attract, support, and retain staff:

- Bring your company culture to life
- Attract and select talent
- Assess and guide staff based on performance and behaviour.

If this is your key issue, go here: Chapter 15.

Systems and processes

Upgrade and maintain the efficiency and accuracy of key processes:

- Use the 80:20 rule to prioritise processes for improvement (+ assign accountability)
- Apply mapping and checklist tools to hugely improve those processes.

If this is your key issue, go here: Chapter 16.

Customer feedback

Collect customer feedback in a way that is easy for customers to use, and provides proofs that can be used in sales and marketing.

If this is your key issue, go here: Chapter 17.

4

SMC 1 – SCALE STRATEGIC PLAN

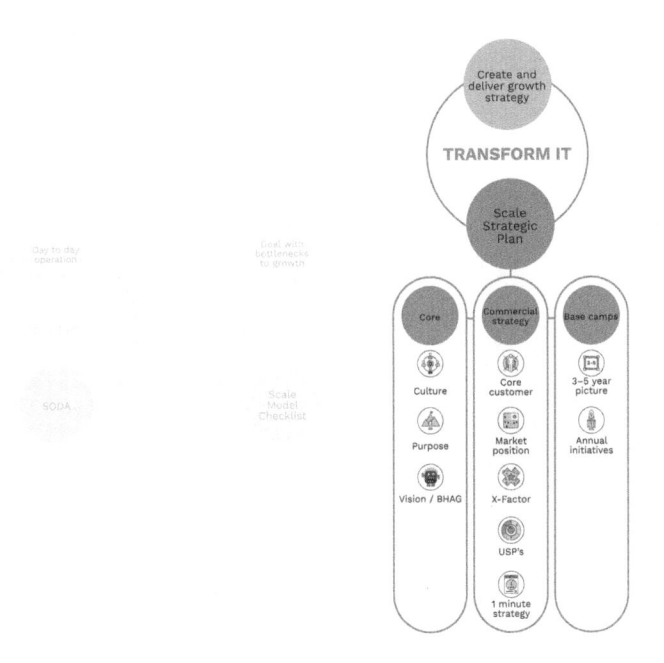

The key elements of creating a Strategic Plan.

DOI: 10.4324/9781003387558-6

Summary

Creating a Strategy for a business sounds like a big, complex thing, but it can be broken down into its component parts, easily created, then put to good use. Getting the right answers for your business may not be easy, but learning how to do it and the process to follow can be. This chapter shows you how to build the key components of a business strategy so you can get the team on the same page, and start to drive growth.

Introduction

Developing a strategy for a business can feel like an overwhelming task. Breaking it into its component parts makes it much easier to build up.

The elements of a Strategic Plan range across two axes:

- **Emotive vs. rational**. Some parts are there to motivate, inspire, and include; others to make difficult tactical decisions, and turn ideas into plans and actions.

- **Temporal**. Some elements remain fixed over time; some change on a more regular basis.

Across these two axes, a Strategic Plan can be broken into three parts:

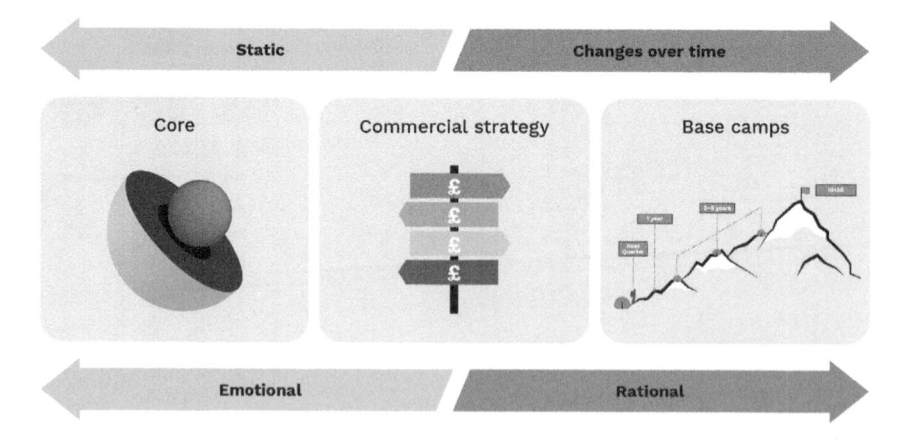

Understanding the three key components of a company strategy.

- **Core** (Strategy 1 – The Core). Several key concepts about why the company exists, what long-term aspirational goal it has, and beliefs around how the team wants to work.
- **Commercial Strategy** (Strategy 2 – Commercial Strategy). How you plan to win in the marketplace. Based on target customer groups, how will the company differentiate from the competition for growth?
- **Base Camps** (Strategy 3 – Base Camps). As we plan out the strategy, what are the key milestones and targets we pass along the way? They allow us to plot a course from here to there.

Having these elements of strategy figured out, agreed, and clearly communicated is one of the key roles of the CEO of the organisation. This is not something that can be delegated or avoided. If you are serious about scaling your organisation, you will have to take time to research, define, and communicate each of these elements of your Strategic Plan. This will allow you to:

- **Recruit and motivate** people to your cause, from staff, to partners, customers, investors, the media, and even the general public.
- **Align the team**. Something to work towards in strategy and planning work. Also affects not just large projects, but filters to everyone's everyday decision-making too.
- **Clarify your thinking**. As entrepreneurs and people ourselves, we want to understand and feel the difference we can make in the world. You will feel better about yourself if you have a clear vision.

None of this will happen if you don't do the work on this.

Getting it into one place

Let's look at two simple examples where teams have pulled together key elements of their Strategic Plans in ways that make them easy to absorb and understand.

LNP China

In the early 2010s, I had established a small business in China, helping Western companies to run their operations there. I was motivated by a desire to level the playing field for smaller Western businesses, by allowing them to sell more easily into the Chinese market, and thereby balance trade.

The business was expanding, so I chose to recruit a General Manager, and started scouting candidates. At this time, I had just put together a summary of my strategy, and presented it on one colourful slide. Here's a subsequent version of it:

LNP China Message Stack

Mission 使命	Make business in China easy and secure, for the worlds best small companies to thrive. 让在中国做生意变得既简单省心又安全低风险，让来自全世界的小型公司在这里繁荣发展！					
Vision 远景	By 2020, complete aggregate >US$100m of foreign SME turnover in China. =>=>年前在中国完成超过累计D亿美金海外中小企业的销售					
Core Values 核心价值观	Trust 信任	East meets West 东西方结合	Solution to Execution: 超前，挑战 执行	Entrepreneurial 企业家	To Serve 一切为了服务	Teamwork 团队配合
Positioning statement	"We are experts at **company back office management in China**, providing easy, secure, and scalable operations for our clients"					
Value Proposition	We make it: easy (no government registraHons; start immediately; low upfront and fixed costs), and secure (total control and transparency) to get started in China. This allows our clients to test the market at low risk (easy out if it doesn't work), grow more quickly (they focus on their core business), and avoid piUalls and crises through having an experienced back office.					
Tagline	Business in China can be easy.					

An early version of a one-page strategy at LNP China.

As I met with each candidate, I presented my simple strategy to them. I felt self-conscious about it, almost ridiculous, wondering if anyone would 'believe' or take my little vision seriously. And indeed, two of the candidates were polite but muted about what I shared. But one candidate – Alex – had a reaction I shall never forget. His words were: 'How did you know that's what I want to do with my life?' Guess who I hired, and proved to be one of our most valuable and loyal team members throughout the life of that business?

The business ended up growing well, almost hitting that US$100m of foreign turnover target mentioned above, before we sold it to our largest competitor several years later. Much of that success can be traced back to that moment where I actually put my 'vision' down on a page, and had the courage to share it and recruit around it.

It shows the difference that even a small, simple start can make.

Metasphere

metasphere
make data count

Metasphere (www.metasphere.co.uk) are a U.K.-based supplier of telemetry and monitoring systems to water utilities.

They are currently doubling their revenues approximately every 6 months, and increasing their profitability by 100% year-on-year. This is because everyone in the team at Metasphere is clear on a few key elements of their strategy, and for the past 3 years, they have met every Quarter to deliver this strategy through actionable **sprint projects** (see Chapter 11).

One of the key things they look at is:

OUR FOCUS & CULTURE

Our Manifesto

We believe in
Using telemetry to drive sustainable use of the world's natural resources

With our own unique way of working

CLOSER TO THE CUSTOMER | INTUITIVE INNOVATION | CHALLENGE CONSTRUCTIVELY | BE HONEST, BE SINCERE DO IT RIGHT | WIN TOGETHER

Whilst striving towards
By 2040, 10% of the world's population benefit from our solutions

To deliver No Escapes
No leakage
No spillage
No shrinkage
No pollution

Key headlines of Metasphere's strategy.

Their full strategy is a long deck with many slides. This is a core component of it, one they come back to again and again in daily decision-making and project planning.

Getting it on to 'one page'

The 'Message stack' and 'Manifesto' slides above are examples where key components of a Strategic Plan have been pulled together in one place so that other people, including internally and externally, can easily understand and retain it. You can see that they both contain key elements from the model for a full Strategic Plan, particularly from the 'Core' and 'Commercial Strategy sections':

Components of a Strategic Plan

Let's have a more detailed look at what each of these sections typically contains, and what the constituent components of a complete Strategic Plan are:

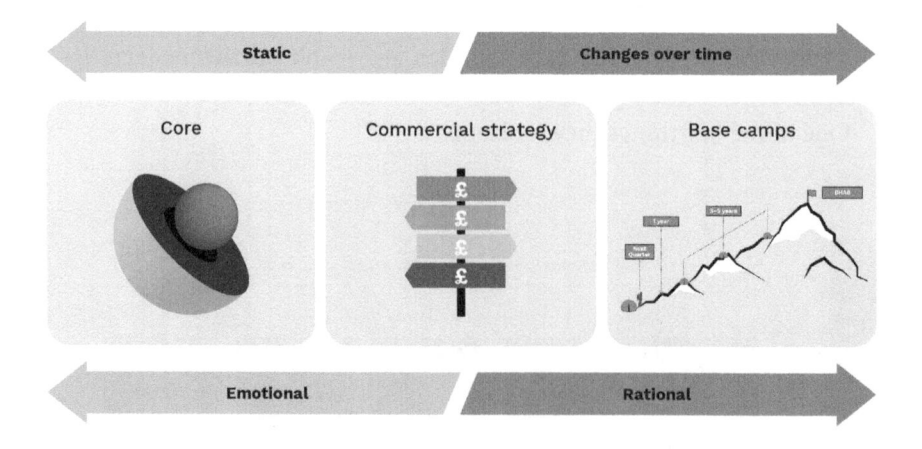

	Key component	Common terms	Description
Core	Statement of **Purpose**	Core purpose, mission, mission statement	A statement of why the company exists, what common calling or belief the team has that motivates them to continue and to grow.
	Vision of the future	BHAG, Vision	A distant, ambitious, and inspiring objective of how the business will change the world in some way.
	Culture	Core Values, Culture code.	The special or unique way of working within the organisation. Key statements on 'what it's like to work around here'.
Commercial Strategy	Definition of **customers**	Core Customer, Target customer, customer avatars	Detailed description of target customer group(s), including demographics, personalities, and needs.
	Market **positioning**	Market, Niche, competitive positioning	Where the positioning of brand sits, relative to the competition, and what niche or category it occupies / owns.
	Critical **insight**	X-Factor	A market opportunity (trend, bottleneck, technology, regulation, customer need...) the solving of which would lead to 10x growth.
	Differentiation	USP, Brand Promise, Positioning Statement	What the business delivers that is unique or differentiated in a way that is of value to target customers.

The worksheet below allows you to record each of these elements, simply called the 'Strategic Plan'. The rest of this section shows you how to create all these key components of your Strategic Plan.

Strategic Plan worksheet

Strategic plan
SCALE — Business growth made easy

Name: _____ Company: _____ Date: _____

Core

Core values / culture
-
-
-
-
-

Purpose
-

Vision / BHAG
-

Commercial strategy

Core customers
-
-
-
-
-

Market niche or category

X Factor

Essential question

USPs
-
-
-

USP KPIs
-
-
-

Differentiating activities / Key capabilities

USP guarantee

One minute strategy

Base camps

3-5 year picture

Targets	Descriptions	Initiatives
•	•	•
•	•	•
•	•	•
•	•	•

Annual initiatives

Feb23 · © Clarity Strategy Ltd DBA Scale 2023   www.scalecoach.co.uk

The 'how' of it: a practical guide to preparing your strategy

Terminology

As you can see from the previous table, there is a lot of overlapping and different terminology used to describe each element of a Strategic Plan. It varies in different countries and in different books and systems. Follow these two key principles regarding terminology:

1 **Concepts matter, not titles**. We have given each of the tools in this section a name. They are a helpful guide, but not intended as a mantra for you to follow. The key is to understand the intent and concept of each one, so focus on the descriptions of each item, rather than assuming you know what something is from its name.
2 **Put things in your own words**. Reviewing Metasphere's, 'Manifesto' document, look at the terminology they use in their Strategic Plan:

OUR FOCUS & CULTURE

Our Manifesto

We believe in
Using telemetry to drive sustainable use of the world's natural resources

With our own unique way of working

CLOSE TO THE CUSTOMER | INTUITIVE INNOVATION | CHALLENGE CONSTRUCTIVELY | BE HONEST, BE SINCERE, DO IT RIGHT | WIN TOGETHER

Whilst striving towards
By 2040, 10% of the world's population benefit from our solutions

To deliver No Escapes
No leakage
No spillage
No shrinkage
No pollution

You can see that they've used their own words. Each element of this plan was discussed using different terminology, for example, what they've called 'Whilst striving towards' comes from an exercise called 'BHAG'® (Big Hairy Audacious Goal). They prefer to use terminology that's meaningful for them, and it is much stronger for it. They haven't even used the term 'Strategic Plan', to them it's their 'Manifesto'.

Pulling together a full strategy is a process of expansion followed by refinement. You spend time working through many details, but end up with something concise.

Getting started – when and how

If you've decided you want to go ahead and develop a strategy for your organisation, the first thing to do is find **2 days out with the leadership team** (we call it a **Kick-Off** session) and put it in the diary now.

To create the right environment for change, away from the distractions of home and the office, arrange these meetings **off-site** and ideally all **in-person** (though virtual meetings can work if you have no alternative). In order to prepare for the kick-off session:

- **Length and location.** Plan on 2 full days, with the leadership team, away from the office.
- **Communicate** with the team that:
    - To commit to growth, you are meeting to align together on strategy
    - Every quarter you will meet to define the sprint projects to deliver that strategy
- **Prepare** for the session by sharing
    - Performance data, such as financial targets and metrics, so everyone is on the same page on the performance of the business
    - High-level agenda of what you're going to cover
    - The Scale Model checklist, and collate answers in advance of the session

- **Team learning**. Provide everyone attending with a copy of this book, and the expectation to read at least the introductory and 'Strategic Plan' sections.

Kick-off agenda

How best to use these 2 days? The focus and objective of each day is different:

Day 1 – Strategy	Day 2 – Quarterly planning
Strategic Plan. Annual initiatives.	Set and plan key priorities for the Q.

Day 1 – Strategic Plan. You will not be able to complete an entire Strategic Plan in 1 day. Read through the Strategic Plan section in advance (this chapter), and pick three to five of the elements that are most important to you. Always make sure you include Annual Initiatives by the end of the day, to pull together your ideas

Day 2 – Quarterly Planning Day. This is covered in detail in Chapter 11. In short, you will review the Strategic Plan to create and plan out sprint projects for the quarter. Always make sure it concludes with planned-out specific projects.

How to record and present your strategy?

Before starting on strategic planning, one small but important detail to get right is where to record the output. The trick is to have the outputs in formats that are both usable and keep the strategy alive. In practice, we see it done in these ways:

1 **Task management platform**. When doing detailed project planning, it's vital to use a professional project or task management software (covered in more detail in Chapter 11). You can record all the elements of the Strategic Plan in the same platform, so that when doing detailed

project planning, everything is in one place for easy reference. Here is a demo example of how that can look, using the 'text widget' function on a 'dashboard' board on monday.com:

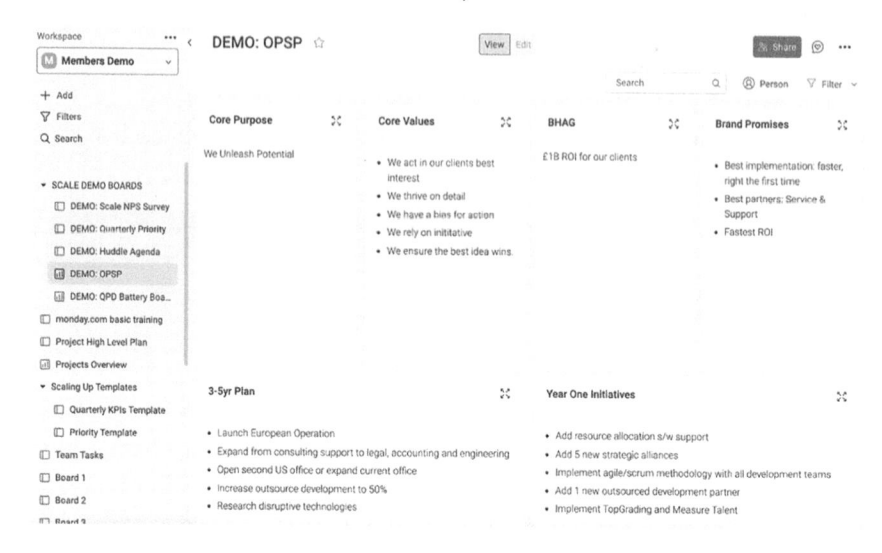

Example of the key elements of a strategy recorded on one page on monday.com.

2 **Presentation**. You will have to present and repeat your strategies and plans over and over, such as to the team, clients, investors, partners, or at industry events, and for this, you will need to compile them into an attractive presentation format. This may be a ppt, a sales deck, or investor memorandum, depending on the context.
3 **Sales and marketing materials**. Your outputs will inform and guide key sales and marketing materials, such as the company website, sales decks, product designs, and investor manifestos. It can be quite a job to keep this stable updated as strategies evolve.
4 **Team visuals**. It's vital to ensure that the team has full visibility of company plans and strategies, so finding creative ways to keep the members informed and involved is important, such as these postcards, which were distributed to the team of Workstories, a London-based furniture company. You can see it includes key elements of 'Core' and 'Base Camps'.

workstories...

Inspiring people to create

Core Values
- Care about people
- Invested in our journey
- We help each other to be the best we can be
- Own it

Core Purpose
Inspiring people to create

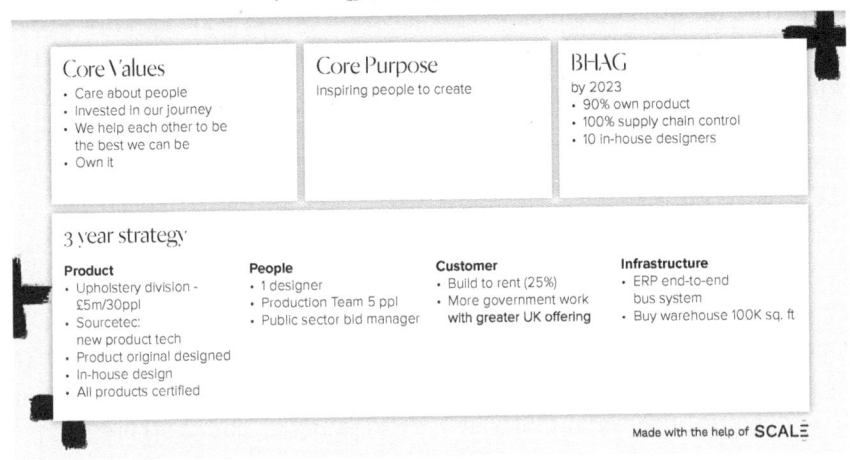

BHAG
by 2023
- 90% own product
- 100% supply chain control
- 10 in-house designers

3 year strategy

Product	People	Customer	Infrastructure
• Upholstery division - £5m/30ppl • Sourcetec: new product tech • Product original designed • In-house design • All products certified	• 1 designer • Production Team 5 ppl • Public sector bid manager	• Build to rent (25%) • More government work with greater UK offering	• ERP end-to-end bus system • Buy warehouse 100K sq. ft

Made with the help of SCALE

Workstories 'Strategy postcard' shared with the whole team.

Experience has shown that the quicker you actually start using your new strategic outputs in these ways, by sharing them with the team and the outside world, the quicker you will refine and update them to the point where you are fully behind them. It's common for the first pass, the kick-off, to reveal what might feel like the 80% right answer. Nonetheless, it's better to roll it out and use it, rather than waiting for the perfect answer. People are tolerant of an evolving strategy, and the more times you repeat what you have, the quicker you will get to that 100% answer. It's so much better than no strategy.

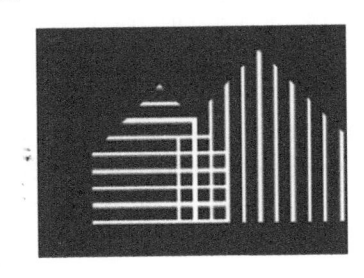

Take, for example, Christoph, CEO and Founder of The Hamlet (www.thehamlet.com), a luxury boutique apartment chain, based in Geneva, Switzerland. After setting his new strategy for the first time, he had to pull his outputs together to present to landlords and investors to secure more properties for growth. He picked the answers he was happiest with at the time, even though in the back of his mind, he thought he might come up with better ones in time, and just got on with it.

The outcome for him was that he was able to secure funding and a great new location for his second building, a huge and vital step in the development of the business.

Stages of development

Once you've created a strategy and start executing it, what can you expect next? It takes time for that strategy to reach fruition. You may find that you have to go through certain intermediary steps before you get there:

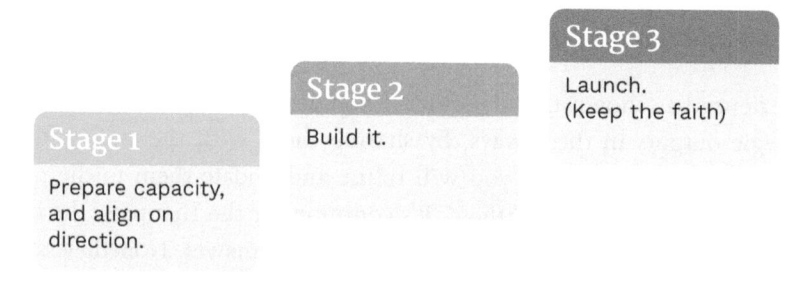

Stage 1
Prepare capacity, and align on direction.

Stage 2
Build it.

Stage 3
Launch.
(Keep the faith)

Stages of execution of your commercial strategy.

1. **Capacity**. Once you've decided on a strategy, the first step may be to establish the resources and capacity to deliver it. This might include securing financing, clearing diaries, hiring new people, or shutting down other non-critical projects.
2. **Build it**. The planning and delivery of projects to deliver that on your strategy. This may be where the bulk of time and resources are spent.
3. **Launch**. It takes time for systems to adapt to change. Sometimes results are immediate and noticeable. More often though, they take time to deliver results, and this period can require patience and determination.

Earlier in this chapter we looked at Metasphere, the telemetry supplier. Over the course of 2–3 years, they went through these phases in this way:

Stage 1. Before starting work on their new strategy, which involved the creation of a new generation sensor technology, the first thing they had to do was clear out their gummed development pipelines. It took 1-2 quarters before they were even able to start executing their new strategy.

Stage 2. Building the actual product set took 2 years and required the recruitment of specialist resources.

Stage 3. Once the solution was ready, it took 9 months of customer interaction before the first order came in. Throughout this period, the business was under considerable pressure, in terms of profitability, cashflow, and team workload. They really needed to 'keep the faith'.

The outcome was that that first order alone represented a 50% increase in the size of the business. Each quarter, the business has been increasing by the same amount again, and they are over 100% more profitable than when they started the process. The process to get there though was experienced as a tough time. Hard work, internal strain, and a sense of having to rapidly focus on many moving parts at once.

Communicating your strategy

Once you have your strategy complete, remember that it's predominantly for internal communication, to guide and motivate the team and decision making. The statements that you create are not necessarily the terms you will use to present yourself to the outside world.

For example, we worked with a consulting company that has the Unique Selling Promises (learn more about these in chapter 6.):

- **Effective**. Their solutions change behaviour in provable ways.
- **Democratising**. Their solutions can cover the entire population within organisations, not just a few leaders at the top.

However, these are not the words they use for communicating their positioning with the outside world. They have slogans, such as 'Deeper Difference' and a series of external communication scripts and images that do this job.

This is explained further in Chapter 18 where you can work through a process to translate strategies into messages. Remember, when your strategy is ready, the work is not quite done; you must expect to spend some time (probably with branding experts) on translating it into messages that will resonate with your target market.

Now let's move forward with the details of putting together each element of your Strategic Plan:

Strategy 1 – The Core
Strategy 2 – Commercial Strategy
Strategy 3 – Base Camps

5
STRATEGY 1 – THE CORE

Summary

The Core sits at the heart of your stratey, it drives everything else. It encapsulates why you do what you do, your fundamental motivations, and how you expect to have impact on the world. It's divided into three key sections:

- Purpose. A statement on why the organisation exists, that drives everything else.
- Vision/BHAG®. An ambitious and motivating long-term goal for the organisation that becomes a constant 'north star' reference point.
- Culture/Core Values. Developing a set of 'Core Values' – a code that defines the behaviours and beliefs of how the team works together.

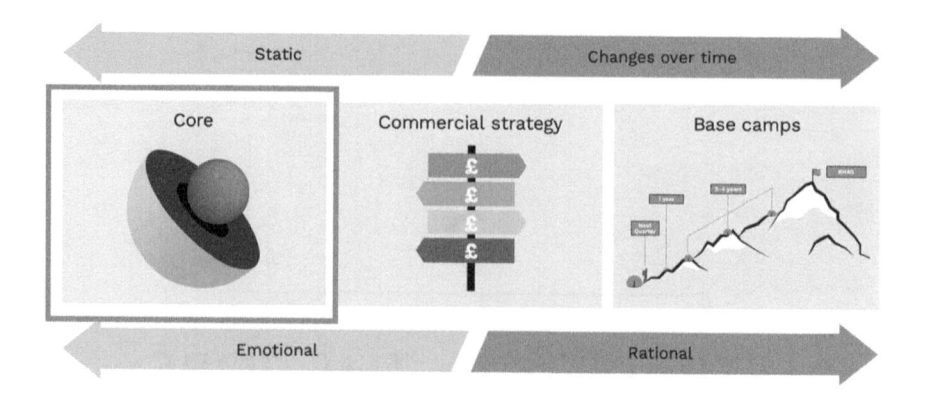

Purpose

Summary

The best description I have heard for working in a team that has a strong, common sense of Purpose is that it's 'like cycling down-hill'. Human beings have a powerful capacity to support one another (or not) on any given venture, and this agency to a large extent dictates the pace and ease with which progress is made.

It's personally immensely more fulfilling to work on an enterprise that you believe in. During those regular moments when darkness sets in and it all seems too hard, this is the bedrock that keeps you going. You do it because it's important.

The role of the entrepreneur, at its heart, is about bringing people together behind a common cause. There is a good reason why we do this exercise first; it is the taproot from which everything else grows. Defining it requires answering: 'why do you do what you do?'

Key concepts

What is a 'Purpose'?

'Purpose' is a statement used to define the key belief or motivating factor behind an organisation. For example, for Tesla's is:

Tesla's mission is to accelerate the world's transition to sustainable energy.

Source: tesla.com

Its function is primarily to align and motivate the team and provide a context for decision-making.

Purposes like these can be motivated or driven in several ways, such as setting right some wrong, or a point of inspiration or belief. Often, they originate from a personal experience or story we have had (positive or negative) that has driven a desire to change something in the world.

For example, a college co-alumnus of mine, Dr Sheri Jacobson, runs Harley Therapy (https://harleytherapy.com), an online platform that connects people to quality therapists across the country. As a trained therapist herself, and the beneficiary of therapy, she believes strongly in the ability of therapy to improve people's lives, and she and her team are highly motivated to allow more people to benefit from it. Their belief is:

We believe that therapy can help anyone to transform their life.

Source: harleytherapy.com

harley
THERAPY

Every time I see Sheri, I am impressed by her energy. She tirelessly goes from event to event, meeting to meeting, with a constant positive energy, because she *believes in what she's doing*, And the same is true of her team. This is the heart of a great business. At its heart, a company is a group of people who share a common purpose and want to change the world in some way in which they all believe.

It can be easy to be cynical about 'Purpose Statements', particularly when they are presented by large corporations which we may feel are paying lip service to them. This conflates two issues though: the benefit of having a clear Purpose, with the sincerity of such a statement. The fact is that running a company is hard – hard for the founders, and for the teams that run them. To a surprising extent, entrepreneurs are people that are motivated by a sense of Purpose, and you often don't have to scratch far under the surface for them to show it to you.

What's it used for?

A Purpose is both a practical and deeply emotional tool in a business. It has a vital **motivational** role to play. I run a biotech company working on deep tech solutions to reduce the costs of protein production for food. Businesses like this are challenging because science R&D is expensive, so I often have to fund-raise, which can be a demoralising task. Some days, it's only the Purpose ('Biology solving the climate crisis') that keeps me going. One morning, facing another day of draining investor pitches, I saw a speech by Al Gore at Davos, a blistering clarion call regarding the climate crisis, and it got me immediately back to the mindset of: 'Why would I not do this? This is the most important thing I can be doing with my life. Keep going, I will be fine'.

Above all, a Purpose should drive **decision-making**. A friend of mine in the United States, Ryan Shortill, runs a team-building activities agency called https://www.onyxteams.com. His Purpose is 'Giving Back', and it guided him to take steps that ended up both delivering on his Purpose and growing the business. Reflecting on how he might better 'give back', he chose to support local charities by offering them US$2,000 vouchers. The charities would sell the vouchers at raffle events to corporate supporters, who would then use the vouchers for their team-building events. These events would often require extras, such as extra attendees or activities, so Ryan would still get paid something for putting them on. It created a win-win-win, providing financial support to the charities, low-cost quality team-building events for the companies, and a great marketing channel for Ryan, all through acting on his Purpose.

Where to start?

Below I explain how to go about developing a clear statement of Purpose together with the team.

Before diving into such group work, it is worth reflecting for yourself why you are leading this venture. What is it about it that motivates you? Is there a problem in the world you care strongly about that this solves? The extent to which you can reflect on these questions in advance will help you when hashing out the exercise with your team.

Worksheet

Core foundation — SCALE | Business growth made easy

Name: | Company: | Date:

Core purpose

WHAT
Every organisation on the planet knows WHAT they do. These are products they sell or the services.

HOW
Some organisations know HOW they do it. These are the things that make them special or set them apart from their competition.

WHY
Very few organisations know WHY they do what they do. WHY is not about making money. That's a result. WHY is a purpose, cause or belief. It's the very reason your organisation exists.

WHY
HOW
WHAT

The 'Golden Circles' concept and imagery is taken from **Start With Why** by Simon Sinek

Consider the questions

| What was the Founders' original passion or purpose? | What motivates you & the team everyday? (Why this rather than something else?) |

Now create your Core Purpose statement – what is your why?

BHAG

- If you live your CP every day, where could it take you?
- Not a linear projection of current growth.
- Inspires you and others; will require a breakthrough.
- Think about purpose and impact.

Specify a date (e.g. 'Dec 2030')

What is your BHAG?

Exercise

Session basics	
Name	'Core Purpose/Find your Why'
How to Communicate	'We're going to identify what motivation we have in common in this venture, and clarify why we do what we do'
Time	90 minutes (may require follow-up sessions to refine)
Attendees	Senior leadership, especially anyone involved in the foundation of the organisation

Preparation	
Objective and outcome	One short statement that defines the 'Why' of the organisation. What motivates us; what do we exist to do?
Learning and reading	
Watch the Simon Sinek video 'Start with the why' (https://www.youtube.com/watch?v=u4ZoJKF_VuA)	
Materials	• Draw up a flipchart with the three circles • Requires Post-It notes and sharpies

Exercise	
Confirm agenda and objective	Each person to share/write down the objective of the session. Define the objective of the exercise: to land upon a short statement that defines your 'why'
The Concept	Discuss and agree on the understanding of the concept of a Core Purpose. Pick and review some favourite examples
Brainstorm	Each participant fills out their ideas on Post-It notes, one idea per Post-It

Idea sharing	Share the ideas by adding the Post-It notes to the three circles, agree together on whether each statement fits into the 'What', 'How', or 'Why' circles
Clustering the Why Statements	Review only the statements in the Why circle. Place ones that relate to similar concepts together, in order to create clusters
Select/Decide	Discuss and decide which of the clusters represents the concept that is closest to the Purpose of the organisation
Example	Say, for example, that you run a hospitality business, and you have two clusters of statements, one around 'being of service' and another around 'experiences of freedom for our guests'. You must now decide which of these is the primary motivation for the business
Wordsmithing	You now need to craft a short (max 15 word) statement that represents the concept in a way that is memorable, unique, and compelling

Tips, pitfalls, and FAQs

Statement wording and length

Getting the specific words right is often the most time-consuming part of the task. People have a general shared sense of the concept to be conveyed, but struggle to find an actual wording that sounds both specific and inspiring.

Regarding the **length** of the statement, it should be one short sentence. People cannot remember statements above about 15 words, so that is a natural limit to how long it should be. The best ones are usually **not longer than five words**.

For example, The Chartered Institute of Waste Management is the leading membership organisation in the United Kingdom for companies in the waste industry. They had previously created numerous long 'Purpose Statements' that included lengthy sets of words of what they did, why it was important, and how it grew their business. However, the Purpose Statement that stuck was 'A world beyond waste'. It's easy to see why. It flows off the tongue, sounds good, and is easy to remember. Anything beyond this will not be remembered or used by the team.

Who decides?

It's interesting and helpful to get a sense of where the team is at, and sometimes teams like to have votes and polls. This is an area though where we often see the founder of the company come into their own, as it's a question they've been thinking about, sometimes for many years.

Sometimes, the right words come from team members. Eudelo (https://eudelo.com) is a London dermatology clinic, providing treatments to improve people's skin. Having discussed the question for some time, one of the managers just came out with the sentence that stuck for them: 'Changing Skin, Changing Lives'.

eudelo

As a further note on the potential power of a good Purpose Statement, the following day, the wider team assembled and shared this Core Purpose for the first time. One of the team members was moved to tears by the statement, as she had received a letter from a young patient who had thanked her for 'changing her life' and this statement made her think of that young lady.

Generic vs specific

There is a spectrum that exists which runs from 'have a better widget in this specific market that benefits a certain customer group' all the way to 'save the world'.

The trick to getting Purpose Statements right is to land somewhere that is specific enough to have meaning with regard to what it is that you do and is inspiring enough to feel that it has wider benefit.

Divide people

Like many such statements, Purpose and BHAG® actually become less valuable if they could apply or appeal to anyone.

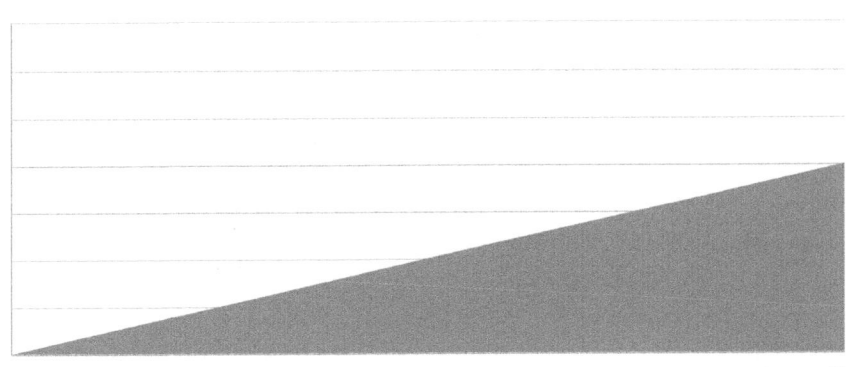

**Specific benefit for
a particular group**   **Save the world**

I like to call this the 'Nissan Cube' effect. Look at this car. You will have one of only two reactions: 'Oh dear that's awful' or 'I love it!'. Very few people sit in the middle. That is the mark of something that is well-designed – it elicits a reaction, an opinion, balanced between fanatics and rejecters.

And so it must be with your Purpose Statement. The point is not to appeal to everyone, just to the right people.

Internal vs. external facing

Teams sometimes find it hard to avoid the trap of 'slogan thinking', that the Purpose Statement needs to sound like something splashed on an advert. Be clear – the Purpose is principally there to motivate you. Some teams do choose to share their Purpose with the outside world; many don't.

If in the discussion you find yourself, like ad men, coming back to slogan statements, or asking what customers or the market might like to hear, then re-focus yourself. Ask 'what would get us excited' or 'what would we like to hear?' and don't worry about how it would look on the website, or what the rest of the world might think.

Jargon and business speak

For some reason, this exercise seems to cause people to come out with a certain type of business speak where the intent is to sound professional or business-like, but ends up sounding flat and jargon-ey. The tip here is to **use your own word**s. Whatever language or terminology you use from day to day, the words of the shopfloor, use those. There is no list of right and wrong words of course, but be careful if you find ones such as these crop up:

- Solutions
- Holistic
- Compelling
- Robust
- Empower
- Inspire.

Getting stuck

Some teams find this exercise challenging and get stuck in a doom loop of competing ideas, versions, and wordings, the outcome of which is no Purpose Statement at all. The advice in this situation is very simple. **Pick one and use it**. Within 3 months, if it's not the right one, you will know, and you'll adjust accordingly. It's better to go out with the 80% right version and update it later, than to leave the job unfinished. The best feedback you'll get is when you start to use it from day to day. If it's the right one, it will help in the following situations:

- When faced with a decision, has it helped you to clarify your thinking around it?
- When recruiting for the team, is it helping to find people with common motivations?
- Has it picked you or the team up at a time when things were tough?
- Have you found yourself using it in contexts such as 'Here, we believe in/love/are driven by…'?
- Have you used it to preface an important email, statement, proposal, memo?
- Have you canned a project, initiative, or product because they didn't fit with it?

If not, then keep tweaking; if so, then good job, you may go far.

What if I don't feel a sense of Purpose for what I'm doing?

Sometimes, there are individuals or teams who find, as a result of exercises like this, that they don't really believe in what they're doing. What to do if this is you?

The answer is as simple as it is drastic: do something else. Take time out, go on a retreat, pursue the burning passion that's been at the back of your heart for years. Life is too short and precious to be spent on things you don't care about.

Vision

Summary

Once you understand your Purpose – your 'why', it's time to think where it could take you. Setting a Vision is about defining a specific and ambitious goal for the future that will motivate you and the team, and provide a clear direction for day-to-day decision-making.

Concepts

This tattoo appears over the heart of the founder of Ceramic Design Labs, a Brighton-based dental laboratory. It's the date by which he will have left his current life behind and set up a mobile dental laboratory to treat patients in Third World countries.

There's no shirking from a tattoo over your heart (Jon likes to joke that the only way to change it would be to change the '6' to an '8' – let's hope he doesn't have to). It's a clear, specific line in the sand. No one has told him to do this; it's his own Vision for the future.

What's interesting is to reflect on what needs to happen for this Vision to become reality. It's not just a question of closing-up shop and setting off. He needs to grow his business to a certain size, find an acquirer to purchase it, complete a hand-over, and invest the proceeds in the mobile unit. Each of these steps is a challenging process. The Vision itself isn't just one action, but the *cumulated result* of a long sequence of difficult things.

Most importantly, it's *emotive*. It challenges Jon and his team to achieve things they otherwise might leave for another day. It reminds them what they're striving for, and why.

What is a 'Vision'?

'Vision' is a description of what could be achieved or changed in the world if the Purpose were to be lived day in and day out over a sustained period of time (typically many years hence).

A great Vision acts like a force of positive gravity, dragging the team out of the day-to-day and towards building something great and ambitious. It forces us to dare to dream, and stay focused on that 'North Star'.

It's also important that a Vision is *specific* – a date-able target that you know if you've hit it or not. The only thing better than setting a great Vision is achieving it. For example, at my old company, LNP China, we achieved the Vision of helping foreign companies operate US$30m of sales in China 1 year before our target.

The term 'BHAG® – Big Hairy Audacious Goal' (a term coined by Jim Collins and Jerry Porras) is often used to describe this – an ambitious statement that describes a clear goal for the future.

Famous examples of these include:

- Microsoft's Vision to have 'A PC on every desk'
- John F Kennedy's goal to 'put a man on the moon and bring him home safely before the decade is out'.

BHAGs® generally fit with the following criteria:

- Linked to a specific date (e.g., '30 Dec 2040')
- State a clear goal or objective (e.g., Red Balloon to have provided '1m experiences')
- Ambitious.

Example

We have discussed Metasphere several times. Their BHAG® is for 10% of the world's population to be protected by their solutions and services. Their CEO, Tim O'Brien, has been steadily calculating the combined population served by the networks into which they've sold.

Worksheet

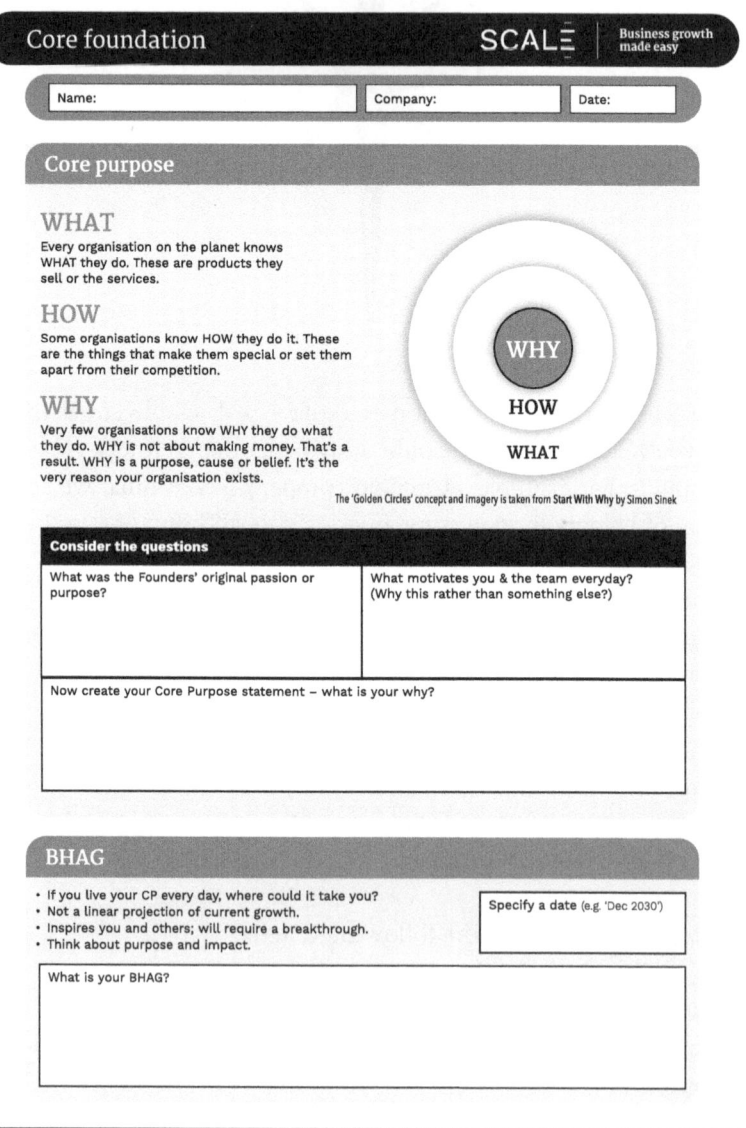

Core foundation

SCALE | Business growth made easy

Name: _____ Company: _____ Date: _____

Core purpose

WHAT
Every organisation on the planet knows WHAT they do. These are products they sell or the services.

HOW
Some organisations know HOW they do it. These are the things that make them special or set them apart from their competition.

WHY
Very few organisations know WHY they do what they do. WHY is not about making money. That's a result. WHY is a purpose, cause or belief. It's the very reason your organisation exists.

(Golden Circles: WHY / HOW / WHAT)

The 'Golden Circles' concept and imagery is taken from *Start With Why* by Simon Sinek

Consider the questions

What was the Founders' original passion or purpose?	What motivates you & the team everyday? (Why this rather than something else?)

Now create your Core Purpose statement – what is your why?

BHAG

- If you live your CP every day, where could it take you?
- Not a linear projection of current growth.
- Inspires you and others; will require a breakthrough.
- Think about purpose and impact.

Specify a date (e.g. 'Dec 2030')

What is your BHAG?

Core foundation sheet.

STRATEGY 1 – THE CORE

Core Purpose and BHAG® share a worksheet, due to the connected nature of these two exercises. They can be covered in one longer session, or as separate sessions, using the same worksheet.

Exercise

Session basics	
Name	'Vision/BHAG®'
How to Communicate	'We're going to set a Vision for what the organisation can achieve in the future that we will use to guide our work and planning over the following years'
Time	90 minutes
Format	Workshop session
Attendees	Senior leadership, especially anyone involved in the foundation of the organisation

Preparation	
Objective and outcome	One short statement that defines a long-term, ambitious goal of the organisation
Learning and reading	Read The Collins/Porras article 'building your company's Vision' (https://hbr.org/1996/09/building-your-companys-vision)
Materials	Post-It notes and sharpies for each person

Exercise	
Confirm agenda and objective	Each person is to share/write down the objective of the session. Share and agree the objective and write it on the wall
The Concept	Discuss and agree on understanding of the concept of a BHAG®/Vision. Pick and review some favourite examples
Set a time frame	Set a nominal period in which you want to achieve your BHAG®, e.g., 5 years, 10 years, or even 30 years out. State it as the future date (e.g., '1 Jan 2040')
Visualisation and Brainstorm	Have each person write down ideas for what significant objective the organisation may have hit by that time. Helpful ways to visualise this include: a news story written about you on that date. A big press release/statement you issue on that date. A big thing you're telling your children that you've achieved, on that date. Each person is to record each idea on a separate Post-It

Share and discuss	As each statement is shared, stick them to the wall, and have the presenter describe the scenario. Stick similar statements together on the wall, to create clusters
Select/Decide	Discuss and decide which of the clusters represents the statement that meets these criteria: does it make the hairs on your neck stand up? Is it motivating and powerful enough to get you up in the morning? Is it an extension of your Core Purpose? Does one lead to the other? Do you believe it? Could there be a real path between here and there?
Wordsmithing	Craft a short statement that represents the concept in a way that is memorable, unique, and compelling

Guidelines and pitfalls

Types of BHAG® statement

We generally see BHAGs® falling into certain types (some of which overlap):

- **Impacting a certain number of people**. If you have a Core Purpose around helping people to achieve something, for example, then a BHAG® of helping a certain number of people would be an good fit.
- **Proxies for people**. Other metrics can provide an approximate measure of people impacted, such as widgets sold, miles of network covered, households covered, or events held. For example, Red Balloon in Australia have had BHAGs® around a number of experiences enjoyed by their clients.
- **Moonshots**. The achievement of a huge goal or milestone, such as establishment of an institution, earning a prize or award or even (and yes, we have seen this) establishing a presence on the moon. Well crafted, these can elegantly imply the achievement of multiple other goals or milestones to achieve.
- **Comparatives**. E.g., #1 in a certain industry or field, or being recognised as 'the gold standard' for something. These can be hard to measure objectively unless linked to an explicit list, ranking, or metric of scale or performance.
- **Financial**. Hitting a certain revenue, profit, valuation, or other financially measured goal. (Explained and discussed further below).

These are not exclusive categories; the key thing is that it is meaningful and motivating to you and the team. The only right answer is yours.

Quantity vs value

Remember, the specific way that you state your BHAG® will affect how you position your products and services. For example, if you sell services that change behaviour or benefit employees in organisations, you could either measure the number of people affected, or the value of engagements sold. The former would encourage you to adopt strategies and positionings that favour ease of adoption, such as lower pricing. Emphasising the value of a clear BHAG® makes these kinds of trade-offs and decisions easier to call.

Should I set a financial target?

Sometimes, teams do set financial targets as BHAG®; we've seen such aims as 'to become a billion £ company'. These can be effective for the right teams; some people are motivated by the concept of growth, impact, and financial reward.

This approach does come with a health warning though. Human beings are complex, and their motivations often stretch beyond financial impact.

Ultimately, there is no right or wrong answer, but we do see more teams progress from financially motivated targets to ones of impact in areas such as human, social, or environmental well-being.

Culture – Core Values

Summary

No matter what you do, even in the most technologically automated business, the heart of the organisation still always revolves around **people**. When people work together, they generate their own particular ways of communicating and getting things done – a collective 'culture'. 'Core Values' describe a particular set of behaviours, usually driven by certain beliefs and characteristics, that hold your team together.

Introduction

Sometimes, it only becomes obvious how particular a team's way of working is when they mix with another team. A friend of mine in The Netherlands acquired another software company a few years ago and was working to merge the two teams. It was a difficult process. Take, for example, a small habit such as lunch. One team liked to order in fresh food every day and eat lunch together at a large table. The other team were used to eating fast-food huddled over their desks. Neither is objectively the right or wrong way to do it; they're just different sets of habits. And each behaviour set to some extent alienates the other, creating feelings of exclusion.

I learned this the hard way when I sold my company. During the acquisition process, our team visited the acquirer's offices several times, to get to know them. Several of our team members opted out at that stage, preferring to leave than make the move. The rest moved over, but within 6 months, none were still working for the company. It's not that either company had a 'right' or 'wrong' way of working; they were just different, and much of it came down to small behaviours, collective characteristics of each time that could have either positive or negative impacts on people, depending on their preferences.

For example, our team used to have a fairly high pace of work. We were dependent on quite a wide range of small customers and had to move fast in order to attract and retain new business. A positive spin on this type of environment might be 'dynamic' or 'entrepreneurial'; a negative one might be 'stressful' or 'overwhelming'. Our acquirer, on the other hand, had a clutch of large, stable clients with whom they had worked with for a long time. Their working pace could positively be described as 'relaxed' or 'un-stressful', and negatively as 'boring', 'unmotivating', or even 'lazy'.

So, when our team went to the new offices, they noticed things like people watching TV in the office (specifically, basketball matches), or people regularly turning up late for work. They felt things weren't 'well organised' and that 'people weren't getting things done'.

No doubt, if things had been the other way round, and we had acquired their business, their team would have railed against the stress, the high expectations, and late nights. This is not a comparison of good or bad working practices. The point is that they were different, that it can be hard to appreciate that you have a particular way of working as a team until it gets cast into sharp relief against another team's way of working.

What are 'Core Values'?

It's difficult to solve the issues described above, and most days you are not managing consequences of a merger or acquisition. However, you do have to constantly select and integrate suitable people into the teams. To do this, it's vital to be able to describe clearly for people: '**What's it like to work around here?**'

This is the purpose of what we call 'Core Values' – a series of short headlines, distinctive, and easy to remember – that describe and guide the collective behaviours of the team.

A good set of Core Values that guide day-to-day culture and influence behaviours across the team are particularly important at times like recruitment and onboarding and can be drawn upon as highly practical tools in contexts such as team assessment and conflict resolution.

> **WORDS FROM A CORE VALUES SCEPTIC**
>
> I have personally never liked the term 'Core Values' as I find them uncomfortable, for two reasons:
>
> - There's something moralistic about the concept of 'values': it feels like 'ethics' or 'commandments'
> - It's easy for teams to confuse with other uses of the word 'values' such as 'brand values'
>
> However, the term is now so widespread that there is benefit in using it, as long as people are clear on what it means.

You know when Core Values are in place and working, as you hear these terms echoing around the place, particularly in situations that are strongly positive (such as recognition and reward) and negative (such as tough feedback or dispute resolution).

For example, one of our Core Values is 'Got Your Back'. In the past week alone, we have had one team member catch COVID-19, another with a family bereavement, and in each case, others have willingly stepped in to fill the gap and support them. In many cases, it's the same people helping each other. Every time, there is enthusiastic support from the group, with much reference to 'having each other's back'. They are actions that are natural to the people in the team (otherwise they would not have been selected or survived in the team), and are given a specific name and encouraged.

→ Natural + explicitly encouraged ←

This is the dual nature of Core Values. It both is and isn't social engineering. It's 'not', because it's about attracting and developing a group of people who naturally want to work in certain particular, common ways. And it 'is', because you are encouraging certain aspects of their behaviours and personalities and discouraging others. You also sometimes have to eliminate people entirely from the group if they are not the right fit for the behaviours expected. This may sound slightly sinister, but the fact is that if you want to scale an organisation, getting a commonly agreed set of behaviours right is crucial.

Let's have a look at how to set them.

Worksheet

Core values

SCALE | Business growth made easy

Name: Company: Date:

Mission to Mars

Who are the 5-7 passengers you would send on a Mission to Mars rocket to best represent your culture?
- Represent what it's like to work around here.
- Models of the behaviours you want to encourage.
- Would re-hire in a heartbeat.

A — Pick examples of real people in the team

Who? Real people	Why? Attributes and traits

Core values criteria
- Must WANT them, and HAVE them (desirable and existing).
- Divide people; pick values where the opposite would also have merit.
- Use the real language of the team.

B — Our core values

#	
1	
2	
3	
4	
5	
6	

Exercise

Session basics	
Name	'Mission to Mars'
Time	Typically 90 minutes
Format	Workshop session
Attendees	As well as the Leadership team, it can help to have a selection of people who have been in the organisation for a while and represent the culture well

Preparation	
Objective and outcome	A series of short statements that describe our working culture — what it's like to work around here
Learning and reading	- *The Culture Code* - *The Values Compass*
Materials	Printed worksheets, Post-It notes, sharpies, and pens

Exercise	
Confirm agenda and objective	Each person to share/write down the objective of the session. Define the objective of the exercise: to land upon a short statement that defines your 'Why'
The Concept	Discuss and agree on understanding of the concept of Core Values. Share some favourite examples
Pick your people	Request each participant to think of several people who they feel exhibit the actions and behaviours that represent the best of the culture of the organisation
Describe them	Have everyone write out, on separate Post-It notes, key characteristics of the people they have identified in step 3. Pick key behaviour words and examples
Clustering	Invite everyone to share their examples (can be done anonymously, or naming who they're describing) and stick the Post-It notes on the wall one by one. Cluster those that describe similar characteristics

Select/decide	Discuss and decide which of the clusters represent characteristics that are both desirable and extant in the organisation
Wordsmithing	For those decided, pick a few words or a short sentence that best describe that aspect of the culture, in words that the team uses every day
Record	Once you have your Core Values agreed, record them

Tips and pitfalls

This guide will help you get Core Values that you love and use all the time.

Reality vs aspiration

The Core Values that you choose must meet both of the following two criteria:

You have to:

- **Have them**
- **Want them**

That is, your Core Values must be both present in the organisation, and traits that you wish to maintain and encourage. It cannot be a list of aspirational traits that are not real and live within the team. If you take that approach, you will not derive any benefit from them. Similarly, they must not describe behaviours that you don't wish to promote.

Sometimes, teams do allow themselves one Core Value which is a 'work in progress' or 'under construction'. For example, in 2021, we were strongly influenced by the book *Reinventing Organisations*, and the practices of 'Teal-level' organisations described therein. As a result, we created a new Core Value (called 'Go Teal') in our organisation in order to drive us to embed these ideas and practices into our team. For several quarters, this was the value on which we scored lowest, and had to focus our efforts to make deliberate changes to our daily behaviours in order to improve.

> **UNDER CONSTRUCTION**

How many Core Values?

It can be tempting to want to define and record all the many ways that make your team special. This can lead to 'core value inflation' where new values keep appearing, and the office wall soon starts looking very full.

The sweetspot we observe with Core Values is that they tend to be between **four and seven items**. Anymore than this: people simply don't remember them; fewer than this: they can't quite represent the breadth of the culture of the organisation.

Divide people

This point was made in the description of Purpose Statements, and here again, as it's so important: your Core Values statements should not appeal to everyone. Disney is an example. They have a Core Value related to 'control'. As they deal with content for children, they demand careful control over their work and output. However, a culture that emphasises control is never going to be for everyone.

Here is another example from London-based office design and building company ThirdWay group:

One of their Core Values is 'Drive it like you stole it'. The intent here is to describe and encourage a culture where people will take risk and ownership over projects that they manage, not to be afraid to push boundaries. The wording is deliberately provocative though; it wouldn't resonate with everyone. To some people, it might imply a culture that might feel reckless, or aggressive (another perspective to the Core Values

STRATEGY 1 – THE CORE

[Photograph of an interior space with a slot car track and a wall sign reading "DRIVE IT LIKE YOU STOLE IT."]

is covered in more detail at the start of the section Core Customer in Chapter 6).

In the example earlier from our team of 'Got your back', there is an element that not everyone welcomes. 'Having each other's back' is not about unconditional support. It does not mean carrying others' bags. If someone is not doing their job well, the way to have everyone's back is to tell them so, not to do their job for them.

So, one of the objectives of Core Values is to avoid going through the pain of bringing people into the team who won't fit. For example, if you have a culture that is big on details and processes, celebrate that and emphasise it, even though it's not going to appeal to everyone, it will appeal to the right people.

'Core Values' does not mean 'brand values'

It can be quite common when teams are discussing Core Values for people to suggest and discuss options that sound like customer-facing slogans, like 'committed to service excellence' or 'always on your side'. These options are not bad per se, it's just important to be clear on the purpose and intent of Core Values:

Core Values are intended principally for internal use with the team.

Some teams do end up putting the Core Values onto their website or their external, market-facing documentation. It can be helpful to advertise your culture and how you work to the outside team. However, it's important to remember when crafting your Core Values that the principal audience you have in mind is not your customers, suppliers, or partners, *it's all about the team.*

Use the language of the 'shopfloor'

Like many of these exercises, it's easy to end up with phrases that sound generic and jargony. The best way to avoid this is simply to pick up on the terminology and language that people use around the place everyday. For example, a popular hot dog chain in Zurich, Dr Dog, have 'Mash is Cash' as one of their Core Values. The intent is to emphasise sustainability and avoid food waste. The actual terminology though comes straight from the kitchen. It's the phrase that the cooks use when they see people wasting food: 'Hey, remember – Mash is cash!'.

At Scale, one phrase we find ourselves using a lot everyday is 'Trust the Process'. It speaks to the fact that we like to have, and follow, clear processes; also that we have a strong process with our members and we have learned over time the benefits of sticking to it. Whenever we face the temptation to do something special, different, or bespoke, we remind ourselves with the words 'Trust the process'. It's like a mantra, and is actually a phrase you hear the team sharing with each other everyday.

6

STRATEGY 2 – COMMERCIAL STRATEGY

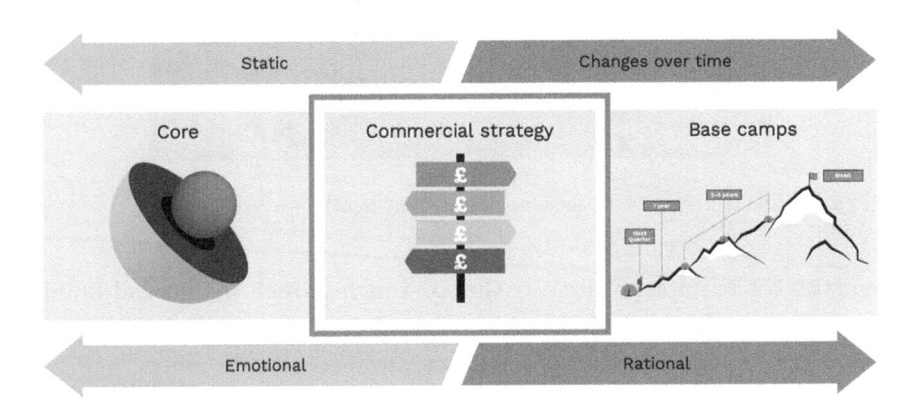

Summary

This is a book about business growth. Many things must align for that to happen, but at heart, there needs to be *insight that delivers on some kind of opportunity*. The Commercial Strategy section lays out the components required to define and go after such an opportunity, such as target customers, and how you will differentiate to appeal to them.

Introduction to commercial strategy

What is strategy?

'**To compete to win, you have to** be competitive'. Reflect on this statement for a moment. To 'be competitive' sounds like an obvious aspiration, but what does it really mean? The key to understanding commercial strategy is that being competitive is not about being better at the same things as others, it's *about doing different things*. Simply 'being better' at similar things to others can get you so far, but will never really drive step change growth.

(From *Tabou windsurf boards* – *my favourite windsurf board brand*)

Take, for example, ThirdWay Group, a high-growth design and build provider for office space in London. When ThirdWay started, the industry had largely operated within two distinct categories: 'Cat A' (empty, undecorated office space) and 'Cat B' (fully decorated office space). They chose not to simply be better at Cat A or Cat B, but to introduce an intermediary category between A and B to the market, which they termed 'Cat A+'.

This has now been adopted across the industry and has propelled Third-Way from newcomer to industry heavyweight. Such a move may seem obvious in hindsight, but at the time, it required insight and vision to define and launch something new like that. It was a gamble on their part. Getting this right — a risky bet on something new, driven by an insight you have in the market — is what leads to the step changes in growth that takes your company through the tiers of growth which involve **order of magnitude** step changes in the business (e.g. number of staff and company sales):

Catagory	# of comapnies	As % Co's w employees	Av employees / Co	Sales / co (millions)	
Micro (1–9)	1,162,155	82.1%	4	£	0.55
Small (10–49)	210,550	14.9%	20	£	3.09
Medium (50–249)	35,620	2.5%	98	£	20.23
Large (>250)	7,655	0.5%	1,390	£	279.47
Total / Average	**1,415,980**		**16**	**£**	**2.93**

You've done it before

If you run a successful company, you will have already done this at some point. Sometime in the past, you had an insight, put in effort and investment to do something new, and are now reaping the benefits of what you built.

Take, for example, The Furniture Practice (TFP) (https://www.thefurniturepractice.com), a London-based furniture procurement consultancy. The founder of the business, Ken Kelly, had the insight over 20 years ago that, when fitting out offices, large companies struggle to deal with the complexity of procuring furniture. Finding the right styles to fit the aesthetic of the design, managing the supply chain, and doing it all within budget is surprisingly tricky in a large project. And because office moves are an occasional event, most businesses don't have a large in-house team to manage it.

So, Ken founded TFP, and, in doing so, launched a new niche, one TFP came to dominate in the U.K. market. The business grew well for many years, continuously becoming better at doing what it does.

Over time, however, growth slowed. The returns of optimising on the existing model started to diminish, especially as competitors emerged doing the same thing.

Ken reached a point where new insight was required, a new leap to do something different again, that could lead to another step change in growth (learn how Ken and the team are progressing in the Unique Selling Promises [USPs] section of this chapter).

Types of commercial strategy

Figuring out a real differentiation strategy for growth is hard, so it can help to look at examples of successful strategies to reflect on which might be relevant to you.

For example, the next step for TFP is an interesting example of a **network effects** strategy. They have discovered that, for every office that they open, it has an uplift to all the other offices, as it allows the other offices to sell projects covering that region. The addition of each node provides an uplift to the whole network.

Flywheel effects

Examples of flywheel effects, where scale can have direct benefits.

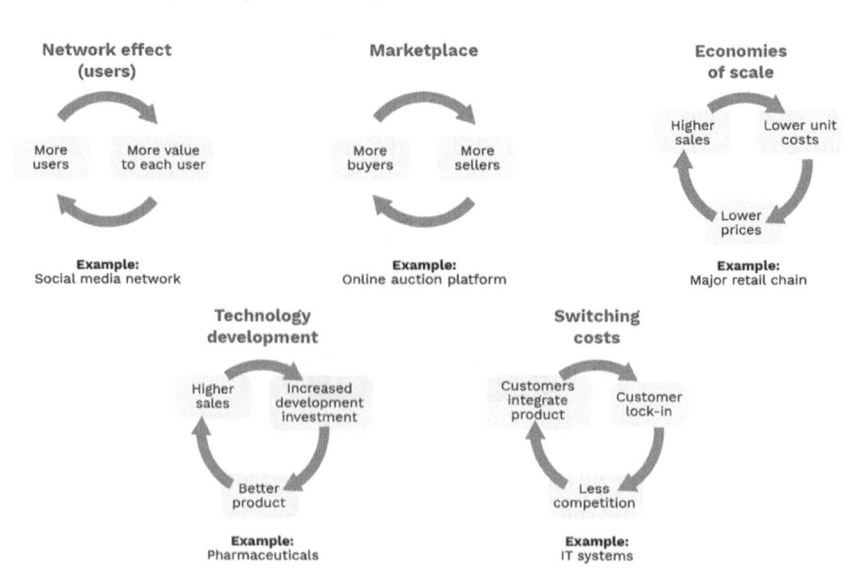

Network effect (users)
More users → More value to each user
Example: Social media network

Marketplace
More buyers → More sellers
Example: Online auction platform

Economies of scale
Higher sales → Lower unit costs → Lower prices
Example: Major retail chain

Technology development
Higher sales → Increased development investment → Better product
Example: Pharmaceuticals

Switching costs
Customers integrate product → Customer lock-in → Less competition
Example: IT systems

Seven such key strategies were defined and described by Hamilton W. Helmer in 'The 7 Powers'. Read through each, and consider, which might be relevant for your company and in your market?

Scale economies

The classic flywheel strategy typically involves a positive feedback loop of increasing scale directly leading to another benefit (such as reduced costs) that in turn can be capitalised on to further drive scale. For example, Walmart and Amazon both used increased sales and reduced customer prices in a positive, scale-driven feedback loop, to drive growth.

Network economies

The addition of a new client or node to the network increases the value to all and tends to have a winner-takes-it-all outcome within that niche, such as social media networks like LinkedIn or Facebook. The key dynamic here is that the addition of one more 'node' (e.g. a new customer or point of sale) brings a benefit to the whole network (beyond the benefit of that single node).

Counter-positioning

A new positioning directly harms or undermines the positioning of the incumbent, making it difficult for the incumbent to adopt the new positioning. Examples include digital cameras undermining camera film, or Netflix undermining DVD rental business. Typically, incumbents do not like to jeopardise existing profitable positionings *even if they know that they have a limited lifespan*, providing opportunities for competitors to do so.

Switching costs

This strategy is often summarised in Blackberry's famous strategy of 'easy in, impossible out'. Examples include software systems such as an ERP or CRM, or a banking relationship where there is a considerable effort and cost required to change a provider. The key element of this strategy is that there is high cost of exiting the relationship and switching to an alternative, for example having to reset all of your emails if you try and change your email provider.

Branding

Sometimes, a company has a brand that is so iconic, or intrinsically tied-in with an industry sector that it is either viewed as the 'originator' brand of that category (such as Hoover, Zoom, or Kleenex) or as the 'gold-standard' brand for an industry (such as Tiffany's, Rolls Royce, or Cunard). This type of brand premium allows for many advantages, such as premium pricing, easy access to PR and marketing, and attraction of talent which can take many years to establish.

Cornered resource

If you can corner a key resource in a market, you control that market. Elon Musk has done this with battery production (also an example of economies of scale) where he identified the constraint in the electric car industry and moved to control the upstream segment through building battery 'giga-factories'. Another example is Pixar, where they were able to corner the market for the combined, nascent skillset of digital animation, story-telling and direction.

Process power

Sometimes a company is able to develop a process for what they do that is so superior and hard to replicate that the process itself becomes a strategic advantage. For example, Toyota developed lean production methodologies and an entire lean culture that sat behind it that competitors found so hard to emulate that it gave them a defensible strategy in the market.

From the examples above, you can see that strong strategy often **self-reinforces**, leading to a cycle of self-perpetuating growth, that is, each step leads to growth in the next step, which then feeds into greater growth on the original input. For example, when review sites such as TripAdvisor emerged, the number and quality of reviews would attract more users to the platform, who would then add to the quality and quantity of reviews.

As you consider your strategy, ask yourself – how might a step in one direction lead to a follow-on beneficial step that could create a constant virtuous circle of growth?

Building out your commercial strategy

This section takes you through the relevant exercises to build out a complete Commercial Strategy. Work through each in order, or go to the relevant section if you are confident, based on the descriptions below, that you have others in place already.

A commercial strategy changes over time, as the business and the market you are in evolve. We observe that companies typically go through 2–3-year cycles of conception to delivery, then re-working their commercial strategy. It often takes that long to deliver something of impact in a market, or successfully launch in a new niche.

This section introduces the key components required to complete a full commercial strategy:

Exercise	Description
Core Customer	Detailed description of the one or few customer types you will target
Market Positioning	Clearly understand where you will position yourself in the marketplace, with respect to the competition
X-Factor	Market insight as to an industry bottleneck, the solving of which will lead to 10× growth
Unique Selling Promises	What few key promises can you make to the marketplace that will appeal to your core customer, differentiate from the competition, and lead to growth
One-Minute Strategy	A simple, 1-minute summary of your commercial strategy, for everyone in the organisation to understand

Core customer

Summary

This is where all strategy must start – who is the customer, and what do they want? As well as being the heart of strategy, a clear picture of core customer profiles is also very important for sales and marketing teams in their work, so the core customer is both a key element of strategy, and a practical tool for use day-to-day in these functional departments.

Concept

ThirdWay Group have appeared in this book numerous times, as a commercially savvy, successful high-growth company. One reason for their success is that they've always have a very clear understanding of who their customer is, and what their needs are.

This is such a part of their culture that it is one of their Core Values, described in the phrase 'Make them Dancers'. This refers to their customer relationships – unless you've danced on the table at their offices at a party, you're probably not one of their customers (yet). It says a lot about the kind of culture they have.

One influence of this Core Value is how they talk about their Core Customers, which are described as different types of 'Dancers', listed here.

7 types of dancer

You must know how to partner with your dancers

1. The Ballet Dancer
2. The Urban street Dancer
3. The Burlesque Dancer

4. The Break Dancer
5. The Tango Dancer
6. The Robot Dancer

7. The Freestyler

These different dancer types refer to different kinds of landlords and tenants that buy their office design and build services. For example, 'Robot Dancers' are large corporations ('machine of a client') that are hard to land, as you have to jump through a lot of hoops, but offer significant opportunities if you can get there.

By analysing and comparing these customer groups, they realised that their key target client is the 'Tango Dancer'. All the relevant teams have detailed descriptions of this customer type trained and understood.

The insight of chasing certain Dancers, and 'Tango Dancers' in particular, has had a transformational effect on their business. They have re-structured the whole business around cross-functional teams, with each team focused on a certain customer type (this organisational change is described in more detail in the section 'Team Structure'). The CEO credits this change alone with a more than 30% increase in the size of the business, whilst reducing costs.

Clarity on customer types can be a huge catalyst for business strategy, leading to growth. Let's look at how to define them.

The exercise

The objective of the exercise here is to create a detailed picture (often called an 'avatar' or 'persona') of the individual who buys from you. This is useful for:

- **Development of strategy.** Everything that follows in the development of strategy hinges upon the leadership team agreeing on who the target customer is.
- **Sales Team.** When training or developing scripts and best practices, having clear customer avatars helps salespeople to more quickly identify whether they are talking to a target customer. They can then filter out prospects that aren't a fit, and focus on those that are, improving conversions and shortening cycle times. (This is covered in more detail in the section Sales Playbook in Chapter 18).
- **Marketing initiatives.** When considering which channels to market through, or creating marketing campaigns, it's important to do so with specific core customer avatars in mind. (This is covered in more detail in the section Marketing Channels in Chapter 18).
- **Decision-making.** I enjoy the story of a company that targets a particular young, female demographic. They have an avatar assembled, called 'Janet' describing her preferences, such as where she likes to shop, what she reads, and her lifestyle choices. As well as introducing all new staff members to Janet, they have a mannequin of Janet sitting at the table in their boardroom. Every time they have an important decision to make, they turn to Janet and ask themselves 'What would Janet have us do?'

When creating a core customer, these are the key guidelines:

- **Not too many**. Spreading yourself too thinly across different customer groups is a poor strategy, as you will struggle to have a strong positioning to them all. Growth comes through targeting narrow niches (counter-intuitive as that may sound). For this exercise, we suggest no more than three to four.
- **Focus on the individual.** It's important to define the details of the company that a core customer works for, but the focus must be on describing the person themselves, even in a B2B sales context. This covers things like their characteristics and personality, and their individual needs. Decision-making happens at two levels. It must meet the needs of the organisation, and of the key individual(s) concerned.
- **Stack rank.** This is a key part of the exercise. Which are your favoured customer groups? It is not an exercise in creating as many target customers as possible, quite the reverse. Rank them (#1, #2, #3) in order of priority.
- **Use real examples**. The Core Customers described need to be examples (or composites) of actual people. They must be the customers that are a keen fans of yours – easy to sell to, refer you to others, pay well, and there are enough similar ones out there to make them worth building the business around. You may have one target customer group (at most) that is aspirational, if you are working towards entering a new target niche.

Halo effects. Plastered T-shirts are one of China's most popular T-shirt brands, originally based out of a courtyard store in the heart of an old city centre district. The founder of the brand, Dominic Johnson-Hill knows his market well. People come from all over China (and the world) to buy his T-shirts, but they're not his 'core customer'.

He's always understood that he needs to make his brand, designs, and look and feel of the business relevant to a certain alternative youth scene within Beijing. It's edgy, rock-infused, and favours a very particular aesthetic that mashes up traditional and contemporary, always at the edge of mainstream.

So, the business is focused on one target customer type, but they do not account for the majority of revenue. This is called a 'halo effect' and is an important component of brand positioning for many companies. When stack-ranking your core customer types, be sure to lead with any 'hero categories' like this that are going to have a significant impact on the rest of the market.

Worksheet

Who is your core customer?

SCALE | Business growth made easy

Name: _____ Company: _____ Date: _____

What is a core customer?

- Focus on real, actual customers. Pick an individual that represents a group.
- They must meet the following criteria:
  - Love your business and actually buy.
  - Fit with your core foundation.
  - Recommend you to others.
  - You and your team like to serve / work with.
  - Enough of them to scale your business.
- Include a memorable name and a picture, to create a persona / avatar.

Map your core customer

Name				
Personality / Personal characteristics				
Demographics & lifestyle				
Role and company				
Needs. Either pains we solve or gains we can help realise				
Potential personas				
Stack rank				

Stack rank your core customers

If you've created multiple core customers, now stack rank them. In what order would you build the strategy of the business around them? It doesn't mean ignoring others, it means investing to build a business differentiated to the particular needs of one key group.

Exercise

Session Basics	
Name	Core Customer
How to communicate	'Agreeing on our Core Customers will allow us to clarify our strategy, and provide sales and marketing teams with clear personas to go after'
Time	60–90 minutes
Format	Workshop session
Attendees	Senior leadership and key people from sales and marketing

Preparation	
Objective and outcome	Define and stack rank key Core Customers
Materials	• Worksheets and pens • Whiteboard/flipchart, and markers

Exercise	
Confirm agenda and objective	Discuss and agree on the objectives and agenda of the session
Concept	Discuss, share, and clarify ideas, concepts, and examples of what is meant by 'Core Customer'
Create drafts	Each person fills out the worksheet, describing each element of the core customer types they have identified
Collate	Invite team members to present their Core Customers. After each presentation, ask if others created a similar persona. Give each core customer type a name, and continue to compile these until you have a complete shortlist
Stack rank	Go through all the core customer profiles you've created, and narrow them down to the maximum top 4, and stack rank them in order of priority
Build out	For the top ones chosen, build out a detailed picture, covering at least the elements described in the worksheet
Next steps	Add the outputs to your Strategic Plan, and agree on the next steps and actions based on the insights from the workshop. This should include appointing a team (probably from sales or marketing) to complete the core customer avatars and present them to the wider team

Market positioning

Summary

To define a commercial strategy, you cannot just look within, you must also establish where you sit, and how your positioning will change, with respect to the competition. This requires defining your niche, and the respective positionings within it.

Key concepts

Owning a niche in a given market, based on a clear understanding of customer needs (see the section on Core Customer in this chapter), is a guarantee of success in business.

Take, for example, The Hamlet, a luxury long-stay accommodation provider in Geneva, Switzerland. They have identified and owned a very specific segment within their market and made it their own. This gives them advantages in pricing, sales, and in promoting themselves to landlords for further expansion.

It started for The Hamlet by working out where they sit vs. other client options within the market. This can be easily visually represented.

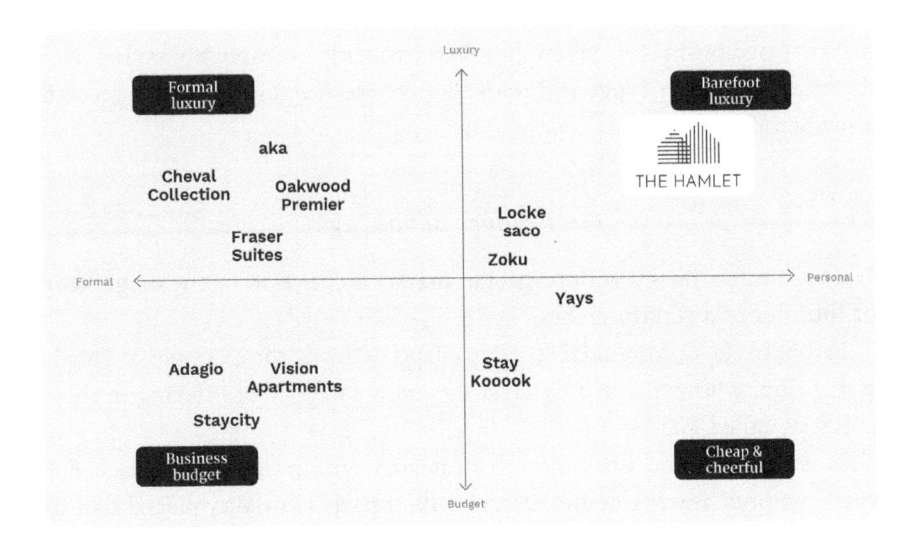

	Luxury	
Formal luxury		**Barefoot luxury**
aka		
Cheval Collection	Oakwood Premier	THE HAMLET
	Fraser Suites	Locke saco
		Zoku
Formal ←		→ Personal
	Yays	
Adagio	Vision Apartments	Stay Kooook
Staycity		
Business budget		**Cheap & cheerful**
	Budget	

Geneva long-term stay market niches

They started by identifying the 'axes' upon which competitors in the market are compared. In their case, the two axes are 'price/luxury' and 'formality'. You can see how this creates four distinct niches that different brands occupy. Their strategy then easily flows from this insight: dominate the 'barefoot luxury' segment in as many target markets as possible.

This process is about getting clarity on your **niche,** that is, what is your **specific market**? A niche can be described as a sub-category, within a sub-category, within a sub-category.

Some companies have very specific, limited niches, and others are generalist. In the animal kingdom, for example, the remora fish lives on the skin of large fish like sharks, in tropical waters, and feeds on their scrap prey, faeces, and skin parasites. The common pigeon, on the other hand, is able to thrive in a wide range of human and natural habitats. In business, I have worked with specialist suppliers to the astro-turf industry, whereas Amazon is a generalist company that sells to a wide range of customers and markets around the world.

Small companies looking to grow generally have to start with small, specialist niches first, before they are established enough to grow and spread to further niches. This leads to the counter-intuitive situation where small companies often need to **narrow down to grow**, that is, offer less, to fewer client types, in order to get bigger. A key inflection point in the growth and maturity of a business is when they start explicitly or implicitly saying 'No' to certain customer types and markets (in order to pursue greater growth elsewhere).

First mover advantage

The optimum strategy with respect to market niches is to be the **originator or founder** of a certain niche.

Earlier in the Commercial Strategy chapter we saw the example of Thirdway group, who expanded by creating a new category of offering in their industry, called 'CatA+'.

This move created a new niche or category within that marketplace. For years, without any marketing effort on their part, ThirdWay placed first in

Google searches for CatA+ and were viewed as the original providers of this service, by virtue of being the company associated with its creation.

This idea of category creation is very powerful. If you can own or be associated with a new category of product or service, that will provide you with a long-standing legacy brand value. I love the example below by gifting entrepreneur John Ruhlin.

The category would traditionally be called 'corporate gifting', the design and production of the ideal gift for business customers. John and his team have called it 'Giftology'. It's a deliberate attempt to name a category they want to own. Furthermore, they also define the type of company they are within this niche: 'Relationship Agency'. Here is how John and their team define a Relationship Agency (as distinct from a 'marketing agency'):

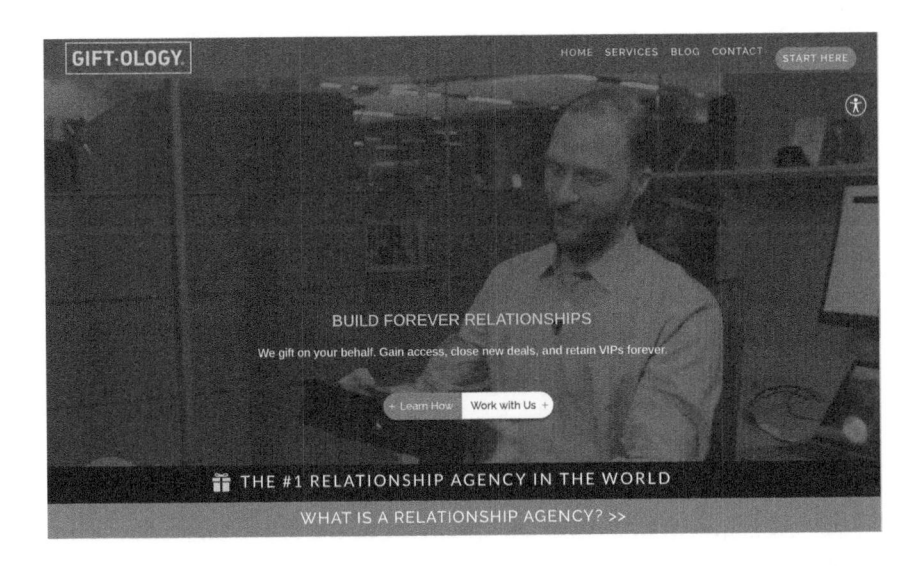

Relationship agency

- What we are NOT = a marketing agency
- MOST agencies sell advertising and promotion. We sell relationships and intimacy
- This stems from our CORE BELIEF: 'relationships can take you places that traditional marketing can't'

- Relationships are FAR MORE VALUABLE than traditional interruption techniques.

It works well for them for several reasons:

- As most people are coming across the term for the first time, it creates curiosity for the customer
- They can claim leadership '#1 in the world' in a blue ocean of their own creation
- They can invent the terminology of the category, such as 'Forever relationships' 'surprise and delight'.

It doesn't need to be the whole company that is positioned in this way. Sometimes, a product or service line is enough. For example, many people refer to any kind of tablet as an 'iPad' even if it isn't of that brand (which is a sub-brand of Apple's).

The main challenges with category naming are:

- You have to move early. If you don't give it a name, someone else will
- It cannot be too obviously a 'product' name. The ideal is to be viewed as the founder of a category name that everyone, including the competition, end up using
- You need influence. It helps to seed conversations with influencers and customers with the terminology you desire.

The exercise

To solve this question, answer the questions in the following order, using the worksheet as you go.

Define your niche

Start by agreeing on a high-level description of what your overall market niche is. These are some of the key criteria that need to be specified in order to define your niche, such as:

- Geography (e.g. Oxfordshire)
- Product type (e.g. web design services)
- Customer type (e.g. female yoga practitioners, 20–35)
- Distribution channel (e.g. buying on Amazon)

For example, a company mentioned several times in this book is Metasphere. Their niche is: 'telemetry monitoring solutions to water and wastewater utilities, predominantly in the United Kingdom and Australia'.

The competition

Once you have defined your niche, you need to understand who else occupies this, or similar, niches. This requires you to describe your nearest competitors.

Axes of positioning

Once you're clear on niche and competition, you can think about positioning – where do you sit relative to one another? A challenging, but very insightful, way to do this is to work out the key 'axes of differentiation' in your marketplace and plot out where everyone sits.

These 'axes' are scales along which players compete in the market, the key things that customers care about and consider in their purchase. An easy example is price. Different client sub-groups have different price expectations, so is a common axis for competitors to adopt a positioning on.

Choosing the right axes

You may find that you can plot your positioning across different axes. Here is an example from our evolving coaching industry, where new technologies are causing new niches to emerge. The industry can be divided by comparing the axes 'Human/AI' and 'Internal/external resources':

STRATEGY

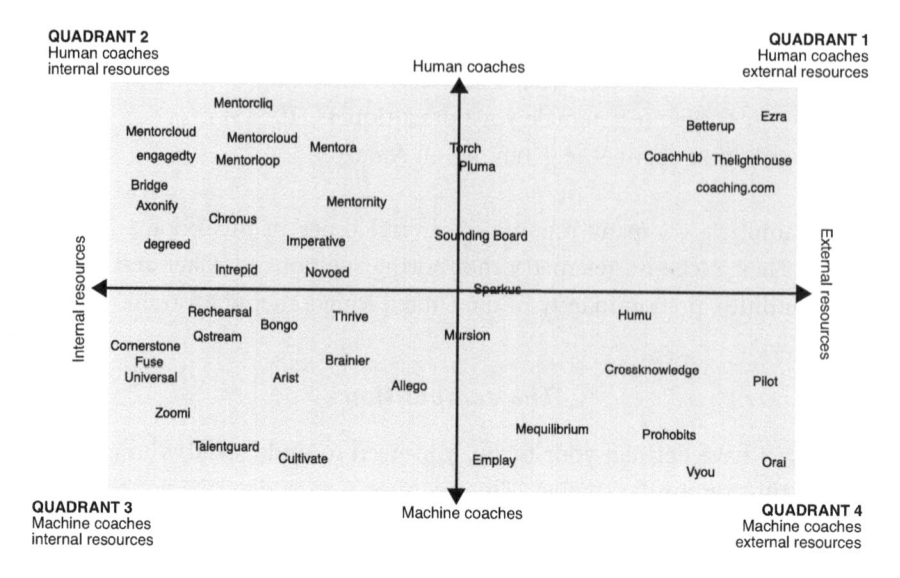

```
QUADRANT 2                                              QUADRANT 1
Human coaches                  Human coaches            Human coaches
internal resources                                      external resources

                    Mentorcliq
      Mentorcloud                                                    Ezra
                   Mentorcloud                              Betterup
      engagedty               Mentora         Torch
                   Mentorloop                 Pluma     Coachhub Thelighthouse
      Bridge                                                     coaching.com
      Axonify              Mentornity
                Chronus
                           Imperative       Sounding Board
         degreed
Internal                                                                 External
resources            Intrepid   Novoed                                   resources
←─────────────────────────────────────Sparkus───────────────────────────→
              Rechearsal    Thrive
                       Bongo                            Humu
            Cornerstone Qstream              Mursion
               Fuse         Brainier                Crossknowledge
             Universal   Arist                                         Pilot
                                  Allego
                Zoomi
                                                  Mequilibrium
                                                              Prohobits
                     Talentguard                                         Orai
                              Cultivate           Emplay    Vyou

QUADRANT 3                     Machine coaches          QUADRANT 4
Machine coaches                                         Machine coaches
internal resources                                      external resources
```

The coaching tech landscape | Source: RedThread Research, 2021

There are, however, other ways of slicing and dicing this new market. For example, by comparing 'Human/AI' with 'Hard/soft skills'. Which is the 'right' one to use? The answer depends on your assessment of who your core customer is and what factors are key in their decision-making. Usually, you will get the right 'feel' for it once you've found the one that fits the best for you.

Direction of travel. Once you have clarified where you sit on this map, reflect on whether you see it changing or moving over time. Is there a direction in which you want to move further?

STRATEGY 2 – COMMERCIAL STRATEGY   103

Worksheet

Market positioning
SCALE | Business growth made easy

Name: _____ Company: _____ Date: _____

Define your niche/market

Ideas to include
- Geography (e.g. Oxfordshire).
- Product type (e.g. web design services).
- Customer type (e.g. Female yoga practitioners, 20-35).
- Distribution channel (e.g. buying on Amazon).

List 3-5 key trends in your market

List 3-5 most direct competitors

1. What axes do you compete on?

2. Who sits where?

3. What is your direction of travel?

From this, can you define a category you own?

Feb23 - © Clarity Strategy Ltd DBA Scale 2023   www.scalecoach.co.uk

Exercise

Session Basics	
Name	Market Positioning
How to communicate?	'To create an effective growth strategy, we need to agree on where we want to position ourselves in the market, with respect to the competition'
Time	60–90 minutes
Format	Workshop session
Attendees	Senior leadership, especially those with an understanding of the market, and a keen eye for strategy

Preparation	
Objective and outcome	Fill out the chart showing where we are positioned relative to the competition
Learning and reading	
Materials	• Worksheets and pens • Whiteboard/flipchart, and markers

Exercise	
Confirm agenda and objective	Discuss and agree on the objectives and agenda of the session
Niche/market	Have each person write out their own definition of the niche the business occupies. Share the ideas and create one agreed statement, covering key definitions of the niche
Trends	Each person records the top 3–4 trends affecting that niche. These could be written in the form of opportunities or threats. Share them amongst the group, and agree on a final list of 3–5
Competitors	Agree as a group who are the three to five most direct competitors to the business
Positioning chart	Share examples of axes of competition/market positioning charts, so that everyone is clear on the concept. Have each person consider and present what they think the key axes of competition for the business are, and where the company and the key competitors sit. Agree one chart as a group
Category	Share examples of categories, and present and agree on ideas for a particular category that the business can/should lead in
Next steps	Add the outputs to your Strategic Plan, and agree on next steps and actions based on the insights from the workshop

Guidelines, pitfalls, and FAQs

Can we have more than two axes?

It is possible to map multiple attributes and add dimensions to the model, though this does add to the complexity, and it is easy to get stuck on creating usable models with clear insights in this way. The most we have seen is 3D models, that is, with three axes, though they are considerably harder to construct and present visually.

Is it a dot or a line?

Looking at The Hamlet's map of brands for an extended stay in Geneva, one recognisable brand that appears there is Airbnb. Airbnb is a large company with a wide range of available property, so strictly speaking, they should occupy a range of positions on the chart (a line) rather than just one point (a dot).

One way to simplify this question is to approach it from the point of brand perception. If we were to ask a consumer to compare the brand Airbnb with one of the other brands on the chart, would they place it at more/less luxury and/or personalised? Generally, you will find that even though a brand may offer a range of products and services, the brand itself will occupy a fairly definite positioning in consumers' minds, which is why it would be difficult for McDonald's to launch premium products, and why Toyota entered the luxury space under a separate brand (Lexus).

There are too many brands in my niche

If you share a niche with others, then replicate the exercise by drawing further axes within your niche. How does it further break down? This will force you to think about how you will position your company and brand to differentiate from competitors.

X-factor

Summary

What is the key to unlocking 7–10× growth? This sounds so ambitious, surely there can't be a way to achieve it? A small number of companies do manage to reach this kind of growth levels, and what they have in common is that they've worked out how to solve an *industry bottleneck* (not just a company one). We call this your 'X-Factor'.

(NB. This section was developed with the support of Barrett Ersek, originator of this term).

Key concepts

Barrett Ersek, from Pennsylvania, United States, started Happy Lawn as a 'lawn boy', that is, he and his team mowed people's lawns. The business resembled many other lawncare companies at that time. Their sales process consisted of knocking on doors, looking for customers that required lawncare. If someone was interested, they would send a team member to the property to measure the lawn, and then send through a quote, to then follow up on. Barrett worked out that the total cost of customer acquisition by this method was over US$250 per customer.

Bothered by this high cost that affected the whole industry, Barrett set about looking for a solution to this bottleneck. In the early 2000s, as the Internet was spreading, satellite mapping started to become mainstream. He worked with a technology company to develop a service that took satellite photos of people's homes, worked out their approximate lawn size, and sent them an automated quote through the post.

As soon as he switched on this new tool, it created a barrage of demand. His cost of customer acquisition plummeted to about US$25, and challenges quickly moved to finding enough staff to cut lawns. The business grew rapidly to cover the whole of the northeastern United States, and was acquired by a large, national group.

Finding your X-factor

This is an example of an 'X-Factor', a transformation that led to a 7–10× improvement in the business. The way to identify potential X-Factor opportunities is to think about **industry bottlenecks**. An industry bottleneck is a significant challenge or cost that you face, and *so do all your major competitors*. Barrett suggests that there are five common types:

Bottleneck	What to ask
An outdated customer experience	• Has the customer experience in your industry remained unchanged for a long time? • Are new technologies challenging it? • Are there repeated steps that could be eliminated?
Superfluous expense categories	• What large categories of expense are common in your industry? • Is it possible to reduce or eliminate any?
Customer-borne risk	• Does buying your product require customers to assume significant risk? • If your company were to assume that risk, would it change customers' purchase decisions?
Disengaged employees	• Do you have a high employee turnover rate? • Do you strive to understand your employees' desires and constraints as well as you do your customers'?
Negative externalities	• Does your product cause adverse side effects that people care about? • Will customers pay a premium to reduce them?

Source: Barrett Ersek, Eileen Weisenback Keller, and John Mullins © HBR.ORG **From:** 'Break your industry's bottlenecks', July–August 2015.

Solving the bottleneck

Solving an X-Factor bottleneck is of course more challenging than identifying one. The key is to focus yourself and the team around an **'essential question'**. In Barrett's case, it was 'How can we reduce customer acquisition costs from $250 to $25?'.

Happy Lawns is a neat-sounding story, but it took Barrett several years of experimentation to come up with his solution. Over the years, he has come up with over a dozen essential questions in his business career, but only ever solved three of them. This aspect of strategic planning covers blue-sky thinking and potential moon-shot solutions: ideas to work on at the same time as developing the core business.

Often, however, the solutions to X-Factor challenges come not from one 'lightning' solution, but the **cumulative effect** of many smaller changes. Having a team coming back regularly to such an essential question can have a powerful effect on the product and service development of the business, and lead to X-Factor outcomes over time.

For example, Real Deal Milk (https://www.realdealmilk.com), run by Zoltan Toth-Czifra in Barcelona, develop milk proteins, using genetically engineered yeast, so as to produce 'real' (i.e. identical to) milk, but without the need for cows. The main challenge in this business is the cost of production, which is one order of magnitude higher than cow-produced milk.

How do you reduce the cost of production for a new product line by 10×? The answer is: through lots of small changes. The fermentation process, the bio-reactors, the organisms themselves. When each provides a 5–10% improvement, these quickly compound to the kind of changes that make industry-changing differences.

REAL DEAL MILK

X-factor exercise

We have worked with Barrett to reduce his excellent presentation and workshop to a one-page worksheet and 90-minute exercise.

Frustration

This is not an easy exercise, and it can take years to get a workable answer. Sometimes, the value of the first few iterations is simply to focus collective minds on the question, to 'prime' our consciousnesses to go out and look for potential answers.

The key is to come up with an 'essential question' and to review it regularly (for example at QPDs), so that you and the team are always focused on coming up with insights and solutions.

Confidentiality

There are few exercises in this book where the outcome is not to be widely communicated. This is one that we do see some teams keep close to their

STRATEGY 2 – COMMERCIAL STRATEGY   109

chest. If you do come up with strong ideas for achieving an X-Factor, this may be commercially highly valuable, so worth making explicitly confidential within the team.

Worksheet

X Factor — SCALE | Business growth made easy

Name: Company: Date:

An unfair, 7-10x advantage over the competition.

First read: https://hbr.org/2015/07/break-your-industrys-bottlenecks

The key is to identify and solve bottlenecks that apply not just to your company (we have this bottleneck), but to the industry (our 3 major competitors also have this bottleneck). Consider across these 5 categories:

Bottle neck	What to ask
An outdated customer experience	• Has the customer experience in your industry remained unchanged for a long time? • Are new technologies challenging it? • Are there repeated steps that could be eliminated?
Superfluous expense categories	• What large categories of expense are common in your industry? • Is it possible to reduce or eliminate any?
Customer-borne risk	• Does buying your product require customers to assume significant risk? • If your company were to assume that risk, would it change customers' purchase decisions?
Disengaged employees	• Do you have a high employee turnover rate? • Do you strive to understand your employees' desires and constraints as well as you do your customers'?
Negative externalities	• Does your product cause adverse side effects that people care about? • Will customers pay a premium to reduce them?

Source: Barrett Ersek, Eileen Weisenback Keller, and John Mullins
From: "Break your industry's bottlenecks." July-August 2015   © HBR.ORG

What is the one bottleneck that, if you could eliminate, change or solve, would give you a 7-10x advantage over your competition? (Continue asking yourself 'Why?' 5 times until you have it)

What metrically-driven essential question can we keep asking (typically of the form 'How can we..') that would deliver 7-10x improvement?

Exercise

Session Basics	
Name	X-Factor
How to communicate	'We're going to work out what industry bottleneck we could solve that could deliver 7–10× growth to the organisation'
Time	60–90 minutes
Format	Workshop session
Attendees	Senior leadership, especially those with an understanding of the market and a keen eye for strategy

Preparation	
Objective and outcome	Define an 'essential question' defining how we can, over time, solve an industry bottleneck, to deliver 7–10× growth'
Learning and reading	HBR article 'X-Factor' (https://hbr.org/2015/07/break-your-industrys-bottlenecks)
Materials	• Worksheets and pens • Whiteboard/flipchart and markers

Exercise	
Confirm agenda and objective	Each person share/write down the objective of the session: work out a strategy for 7–10× growth, based upon overcoming an industry bottleneck
The Concept	Discuss the difference between a company bottleneck and an industry one (company bottleneck = only you have; industry one = your top 2–3 competitors also face)
Brainstorm	Discuss through the common types of bottleneck listed on the worksheet, and brainstorm which occur in your industry
Bottleneck	Each person writes down which industry bottleneck would be best to go after overcoming. Share the ideas as a group, asking 'Why?', until you narrow down to the one you want to work on

Essential question	Agree on the definition of the X-Factor essential question (for example 'how can we reduce cost of customer acquisition from current industry standard of $250, to $25?'). Each person writes down essential question, discuss, share, and agree as a group.
Brainstorm	Discuss and share ideas for actions for the next Q in order to work on reaching the answer to the essential question?
Next steps	Agree to: • Regularly (weekly) review progress on action items agreed today • Review the essential question at each upcoming QPD • Set times/schedules for both

USPs

Summary

Once your market and niche are clear, and you understand your core customer and their needs, you must work out a market offering that differentiates you. This requires defining specific promises to make to your customers that the business is built around delivering. For example, The Body Shop grew rapidly in the 80's on the back of one simple promise: no animal testing on their products.

Concepts

USPs

> What's a USP?
> We know, we know. USP normally stands for 'Unique Selling Proposition (or Point)'. We use the word 'Promise' because it stands for something more – a clear commitment to repeatedly deliver something valuable to your customers.

The Furniture Practice (TFP) are a rarity amongst British SMEs – they're going global. The London-based furniture sourcing consultancy founded this niche in the United Kingdom, which led to fast growth in their early years. But as competitors entered the market, growth started to level off, and they knew they needed a new positioning in order to make the next step change in growth.

For TFP, this next phase means growing from being a £40 million business to one of £0.5 billion. They are already well on their way, having just passed 50 team members (which means they're now a 'medium' SME, no longer a 'small' one). So how are they doing it?

Take a look at TFP's website (early 2022). It makes just one simple statement: *'We are an international furniture specialist. We deliver complex projects anywhere in the world'*.

We are an international furniture specialist.
We deliver complex projects anywhere in the world.

This is a great example of a **USP**. It's a clear promise to a specific customer group. This promise sits at the tip of a whole strategy for the business. The opportunity they are realising is to be the only truly international service provider in their industry with the ability to offer solutions to global clients anywhere in the world. They are the first movers into this niche, which is opening up significant markets to them – large global corporations who have the challenge of delivering offices around the world that meet the combined needs of their local and global teams.

Differentiated activity

It's important to emphasise that achieving this positioning is **hard**. Delivering the service that they already provide requires careful recruitment and training of a highly specialist team. Having to now do this across teams worldwide, dealing with complex local supply changes globally, and having to deal with myriad local tax and compliance regulations, gets really difficult.

These are not problems on which its competitors are currently working. TFP could have chosen to focus on doing what it already does for their existing market, but better (indeed there was much discussion of it). But that would not have been a strategy for growth. TFP have chosen to do different things from the competition. We call these '**Differentiated Activities**'.

One way to think of it is like a duck on a pond. The USPs provide something that is clear, beneficial, and makes things easy for a customer. But the delivery of that USP typically is something that is tough to deliver.

An oft-quoted example of a USP is from FedEx in the 1980s, when they were first to market with a next-day delivery of packages across the United States. A very clear promise for customers, and a challenging problem for FedEx to solve, as it required the development of a complete, end-to-end logistics system across an entire continent.

Within the 'Run it – Improve it – Transform it' model, this type of change is more than an improvement of what they already do. They must build new capabilities, such as building global supply chains, recruiting and training internationally, and managing a new tier of client. It's not a total overhaul of the business model, more a challenging evolution than a complete revolution.

```
Run      Improve   Transform
it         it         it
```

USP guarantee

If you really believe in your ability to deliver a USP to every customer experience, then a powerful tool for emphasising this to the market – and ensuring consistency of delivery from the organisation – is a USP Guarantee. This puts in place a penalty for you, or a benefit to the customer, if you fail to deliver on your USPs. For example, if low price is a promise of yours, then a guarantee would be to offer compensation if a customer can find a cheaper alternative.

The challenge here is to find a guarantee that doesn't feel weak, such as vague 'satisfaction guarantees'.

Guarantees that seem challenging or original are much stronger. For example, this is from a book (on the topic of writing books) where the author genuinely offers a refund if the reader reflects that it's not the book for them.

> book that is better suited for you (if this story has nothing to do with you, yet you've already paid for it, then email me directly and I will give you your money back: ▆▆▆@▆▆▆.com. I'm totally serious).

Jim Collins referred to these as **'catalytic mechanisms'**. What he means by this is that the prospect, or occurrence of such a penalty on the business changes behaviour to the point whereby you work on improving the USP so much that you avoid the penalty. For example, we include the following terms in all of our Agreements:

Short Pay Guarantee
If you ever receive an invoice and feel you did not receive at least the value of the fee, please contact us directly and we will adjust your invoice accordingly to an amount you deem fair for the services we provided. *We will not be offended*. We always want members to feel that they have received the value of the fee.

It's uncomfortable, because if ever we have any kind of disagreement with our members about fees, they can invoke it. For example, we also have a 1-month termination clause in case a member chooses to leave, but the short pay can supersede it. So, it puts us on the back foot, and the only way to avoid having it invoked is to *give great value*.

STRATEGY

Worksheet

Unique Selling Promise (USP)

SCALE | Business growth made easy

Name: | Company: | Date:

What few promises are you going to make to your core customers?

USPs are the few key things your customers trust you to deliver, which:
- Meet a core customer need (either a pain or a gain).
- Differentiate you - i.e. be different to your competition.
- Are measurable somehow.

Your USPs may be implicit (what you deliver), or explicit (you also market it).

What are the top 3 needs (reducing pain or enhancing gain) of your core customer?

1.
2.
3.

Why do customers choose you rather than the competition (actual, real reasons)?

Lead USP	USP KPIs

2nd USP	USP KPIs

3rd USP	USP KPIs

Differentiated activities

The few key competencies, attributes, or capabilities the organisation must have to deliver these USPs.

Is there an explicit USP guarantee that you could make?

Feb23 - © Clarity Strategy Ltd DBA Scale 2023

www.scalecoach.co.uk

Exercise

Session Basics	
Name	Unique Selling Promises (USPs)
How to Communicate	'We must be clear and aligned as a team on what the few key points of differentiation are that we want to lead in the market with'
Time	60–90 minutes (though you may find it takes numerous discussions to nail it)
Format	Workshop session
Attendees	Senior leadership and key leaders from sales and marketing

Preparation	
Objective and outcome	One to three statements of what we deliver to the market, driven by doing something different, that allows us to successfully compete for customers.
Learning and reading	Michael Porter 'What is Strategy?' HBR article. (https://hbr.org/1996/11/what-is-strategy)
Materials	Worksheet, post-its/flipcharts

Exercise	
Confirm agenda and objective	As a team, share/write down the objective of the session
The concept	Share examples of USPs and Differentiated Activities, and discuss and clarify the concepts so that the team are clear and aligned
Customer needs	Each participant fills out what they believe the top 3 needs of the company's core customers are. Share answers and create one, agreed list (use Post-Its/flipchart)
Reasons for customer choice	Each participant fills out what they believe why customers choose our brand. Share answers and create one, agreed list, stack ranked in order of importance
USPs	Based on the insights from the first two exercises, have each participant fill out what they think the Company USPs should be (max one to three per persons). Discuss and agree what the company ones should be

Differentiated Activities	What are the key capabilities or attributes of the company that allow for the delivery of these USPs. These may already be in place, or require construction
Unique Selling Promise Guarantee	Is there an explicit, customer-facing guarantee that you want to attach to a USP, that includes a penalty for you or benefit to the customer if you fail to deliver on your USP?
Next steps	Confirm the wordings of the statements you have agreed and add them to your Strategic Plan. Then agree on the next steps in the implementation of these strategies – who will do what, by when?

Tips, pitfalls, and FAQs

Strategy vs statement

When discussing USPs, teams often have a tendency to come up with 'slogans', that is, customer-facing catchy catch-phrases that might fit in an advert. This is not the intent with USPs at this stage. They are predominantly statements of *strategy*. For example, one of the core USP strategies of McDonalds is about *consistency of experience*. No matter where you go in the world, you can expect the same level of cleanliness in toilet facilities, the same level of speed of courier delivery, and the same essence of taste offered by food services. Yet, you will not see this concept highlighted in adverts for McDonalds; it is **implicit** in the experience you enjoy. It is a cornerstone of strategy, however, and something the company has invested, and continues to invest huge amounts of effort to achieve and maintain.

Some USPs will clearly form the core of your external marketing messaging. This is explored and developed more in Chapter 18. Work with your marketing team or external branding consultants on how you take your Strategic USPs, and turn them into the tools you need to communicate with the market.

Do USPs change over time?

Markets evolve. Competitors catch up, and customer preferences change over time so, USPs do sometimes need updating. What often happens is that yesterday's USP becomes today's 'green fees', that is, a basic requirement to compete in the marketplace.

For example, FedEx's promise of next-day delivery across the United States might have been news in the 1980s, but it is a basic expectation of a service provider in that space today. So, brands in the marketplace have to move on (in this case, to 'trackability').

Take the example of TFP above. Their USP evolved from what they originally established the market for – simplification of the management of complex furniture sourcing projects – to doing so *globally*.

Having said that, there are many brands who maintain a consistent positioning for many years without significant change. IKEA, Tiffany's, and McDonalds still compete on broadly the same lines they have done for decades, for example.

It's important to emphasise though that even to maintain the same USPs in the market, the Differentiated Activities may certainly have to change over time.

For example, Toyota have had a consistent promise to their customer to provide economic vehicles. For decades, this meant improvements to their combustion engines. But since the 90s that has meant mastering and pioneering hybrid and battery technologies. The promise remains the same, and has driven them to develop new competencies, to completely reinvent parts of their business.

That serene-looking duck needs to keep paddling hard just to maintain its place in the currents of the market.

Brand Promises

Differentiated activities

The 1-minute strategy

Summary

The ultimate test of any strategy is whether it can be succinctly and clearly described. If it's too complex to be explained to an intelligent lay-person in under a minute, then it's probably either over-complex, or not fully thought through.

You can use this exercise in two ways – either as a summation of all the deep strategy work you have done, or as a lazy shortcut to come up with a strategy if you don't want to go through the work of doing all the other exercises on Commercial Strategy.

Concept and examples

Most of the millions of decisions being made in your business day-to-day are invisible to you. They're being taken by team members across a whole range of activities. It is impossible and futile to attempt to be involved in them all. The best you can do is ensure that the whole team is fully aware and bought into one clear and common strategy, and that that informs their decision-making.

Your 1-minute strategy is the tip of the iceberg, the distillation of all the complex strategy work that you have done. It is the difficult task of making something complex simple.

It's what you will say when:

- You're explaining to a candidate considering working for you why you're a company that will thrive
- You have to impress a potential investor as to why they should put money in your company rather than somewhere else
- You're in front of the whole team, and have to remind them of where you're going, and why it's going to be successful.

Here are some well-known examples:

- *Wheels up.* (Southwest Airlines). The more time their planes are in the air, the more profit they make
- *It's not about the servers, it's about the support.* (Rackspace). One of the first mega server farms realised their service provides more differentiation than their technology.

The 1-minute strategy exercise

This exercise is a summary of many of the key components of Commercial Strategy covered. It requires the team to make simple that which is complex. It's common to simplify the strategy into a few easy-to-remember words, particularly if it's connected with an initiative at the time (such as 'Going Mobile' for Facebook in the early 2010s, or 'Metaverse' in the early 2020s). The ideal is to then agree on a few short sentences so that anyone could explain it in the time one journeys in a lift.

STRATEGY

Worksheet

One minute strategy
SCALE — Business growth made easy

Name: _____ Company: _____ Date: _____

What is the difficult thing you are going to build that will lead to a step change in growth?

Key market insight
For example: new technology, new regulation, unmet customer need, industry bottleneck

Differentiating Activity
The difficult thing to be built (that will deliver differentiation)

Why it gives us an advantage
For example: customer benefit, exclusive market access, key differentiation from competition

The size of the prize
What scale could this allow us to achieve?

1 min

One minute strategy

Suggested reading: 'What is Strategy?' By Porter, M. (1996). HBR 74(6) 61-78.

Feb23 - © Clarity Strategy Ltd DBA Scale 2023   www.scalecoach.co.uk

Exercise

Session Basics	
Name	The 1-Minute Strategy
How to communicate	'I want each member of the team to be able to understand a describe the core of our strategy in a clear and concise way. If we're all agreed and aligned on this, for sure we can win in the market'
Time	30–60 minutes
Format	Workshop session
Attendees	Senior leadership and key line managers

Exercise	
Confirm agenda and objective	As a team, share/write down the objective of the session
The Concept	Share some examples of clear 1-Minute Strategies. Explain that it typically comprises four parts: • Driven by an insight • Requires us to do something hard that is different from the competition • That differentiation brings a clear customer/market benefit • Will bring a big 'prize' (typically 7–10× growth) • Much of this is clear in our detailed strategies; we are now bringing it together into one succinct description
Brainstorm	Each participant fills out the worksheet, then transcribes their proposed 1-minute strategy onto a Post-It note
Collate	From the presentations made, create at least one preferred 1-minute strategy. It might be verbatim the best one presented, or it could take elements from different ones
Next steps	You now need to craft a short (max 15 word) statement that represents the concept in a way that is memorable, unique, and compelling

Preparation	
Objective and outcome	Create a short, memorable sentence to describe the core and essence of the company's commercial strategy.
Materials	Bring all existing key elements of the completed strategy. Flipcharts or Post-Its for recording drafts and ideas

7

STRATEGY 3 – BASE CAMPS

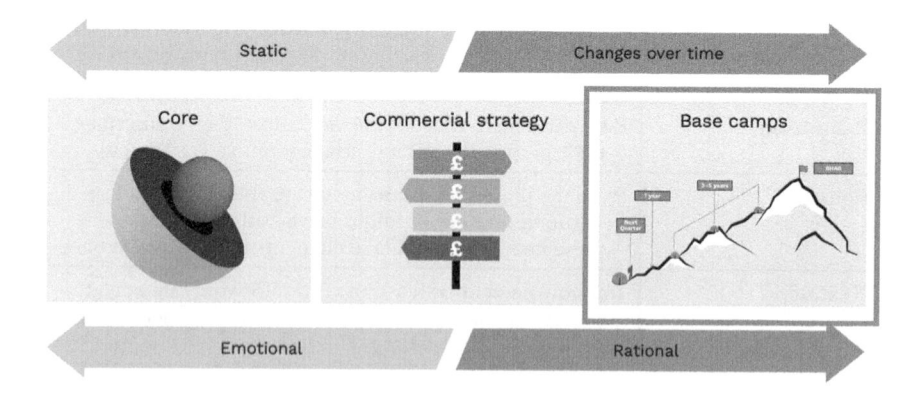

Summary

Strategy and visioning are of limited use unless we turn them into plans. 'Base Camps' is where strategy merges into planning, where you describe in more detail how to get from 'here' to 'there'.

What do we mean by 'base camps'?

Once your strategy is clear, you have to work out how to turn it into reality, how to get from where you are now, to where you want to be. This journey can be thought of as climbing a mountain, with each key period being a 'base camp' on the way towards that goal.

If the whole team has a clear 'line of sight' of this journey, then the members will accelerate progress to the goal, as they're clear on where you need to get to.

Planning is about having a clear line of sight across the team - where you're going, and how to get there.

- BHAG
- 3–5 years
- 1 year
- Next Quarter

This requires dealing with uncertainty; future projections will always be inexact. The key is to define goals that are clear enough to provide a consistent sense of direction, and a planning process flexible enough to account for the inevitable changes required along the way.

This section covers two key 'base camps' on the way up the mountain:

- A Clear Picture of 3–5 Years. Create a clear picture of what the business will look like in several years, and what capabilities need to be developed to get there.
- Annual initiatives. Focus the team on a few key initiatives to complete in the upcoming year.

A clear picture of 3–5 years

Summary

It's exciting when a clear, detailed picture of what the business will look like in 3–5 years emerges. It provides a clear objective to shoot for, and is incredibly motivating to describe and share. The 3–5-year Clear Picture is a key milestone on the way to achieving your BHAG®.

Whereas a BHAG® is one clear goal a long way in the future, the Clear Picture exercise is more about building out the details of what the business will look like in 3–5 years.

Concept

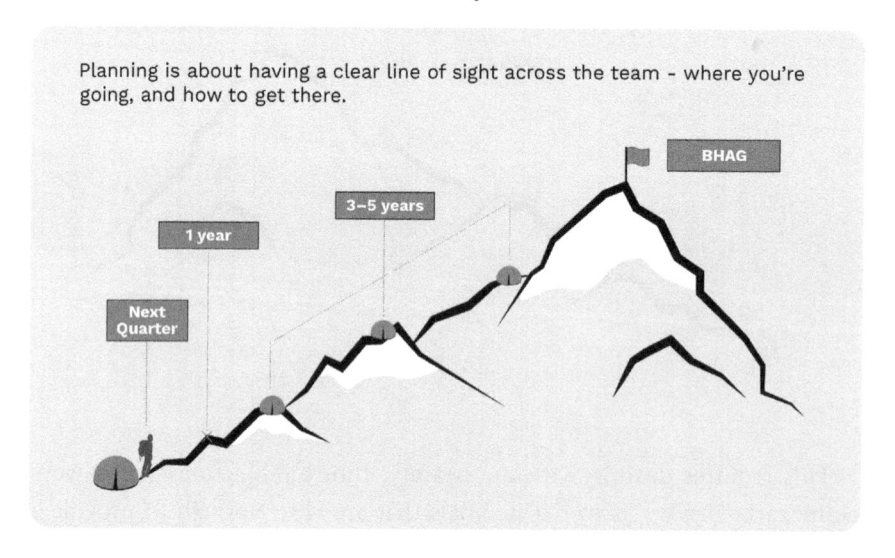

Planning is about having a clear line of sight across the team - where you're going, and how to get there.

One team we worked with had a BHAG® of going global and becoming a billion-pound company. These goals seemed abstract and unachievable when presented to the team.

So the team did the 3–5-year Clear Picture exercise to create a common understanding of what the business would look like in 3–5 years. What emerged was an image that was detailed enough for people to be able to see and believe it. It felt challenging yet achievable, and when they looked at it together, they suddenly realised that their BHAG® was attainable as well; it was just a question of breaking down the milestones on the way.

This 3–5-year Clear Picture has guided all their key actions since, so far including one acquisition, and two new offices. They are well on their way to achieving both their Clear Picture and the BHAG®.

For them, and all the other teams we work with, the exercise had several key benefits:

- Irons out areas of misalignment. The team must reach a common vision of what the business will look like. Everyone must go in one direction.
- Breaks long-term BHAG® into something more immediate and tangible. Creates something the team feels it can realistically shoot for.
- Clearly explainable to the team, and directly affects short-term planning.

Whereas a BHAG® is one clear goal a long way in the future, the Clear Picture exercise is about building out the details of what the business will look like in 3–5 years.

One CEO we work with describes it as: 'Seeing the village on the hill, and the house in the village, and the front door of the house, and describing what the front room looks like'.

Exercise

When considering your 3–5-year Clear Picture, have the other parts of your strategic plan to hand, such as your Vision/BHAG®, and your commercial strategy. This exercise will help you to think in what order the key elements of your plan will be implemented, and the progress you will have made at this key milestone.

Start by setting metrics of the business. It can be challenging for teams to conceive a reality where they are achieving numbers significantly greater than at the moment. For example, if you currently have a team of a few dozen people, envisioning several hundred is hard to absorb. This process forces teams to think about what capabilities will need to be developed in order to achieve and sustain such scale and to plan accordingly.

Then consider how other key elements of the business, such as positioning and infrastructure, will have changed. Compiling these provides you with your Clear Picture. Pull out the key points to create a summary.

Finally, think about what key initiatives or projects you will have to execute in order to deliver on the Clear Picture.

Once you have the Clear Picture conceived, add the key components to your strategic plan document (see Chapter 4). This will be an important reference point when doing your quarterly planning (see Chapter 11).

Worksheet

3-5 year clear picture

SCALE — Business growth made easy

Name: | Company: | Date:

Reflect on your BHAG and review your Strategic Plan. Set a date in the future, and picture what each of these elements of the business will look like then

Date

Targets

Annual Revenue	Annual profit
# team members	# Offices / production or sales sites
# active customers	# leads generated per month

Descriptions (changes in...)

Service / product offering	Customers types
Positioning	**Key competencies**
Markets	**Infrastructure**

Initiatives

Key Initiatives (how to get there)

1.
2.
3.

Exercise

Session basics	
Name	A 3–5-year Clear Picture
How to communicate	'To achieve our long-term vision, and guide our short-term planning, we need to agree on what the business looks like in 3–5 years'
Time:	60–90 minutes
Format	Workshop session
Attendees	Senior leadership and key line managers

Preparation	
Objective and outcome	Create and memorise sub-1 minute description of the core of our commercial strategy
Learning and reading	3HAG Way by Shannon Suzko, Watch 'Vivid Vision' video by Cameron Herald
Materials	Have the 'Core' and 'Commercial Strategy' elements of your strategic plan to hand. Printed worksheets and pens + Flipchart to record outcomes

Exercise	
Confirm agenda and objective	As a team, share/write down the objective of the session
Period	Confirm the period you're working on – is it 3 years, or 5, or some other period, and write down the date you are describing (e.g. 1 Jan 2025)
Targets	Individually fill out, then share, discuss, and agree on the key metric targets listed (or relevant equivalents for your business)
Descriptions	Individually fill out, then discuss and agree for these six key areas, anywhere the business will be different by the target date
Initiatives	Discuss and agree on what key initiatives the business would have to pursue in order to realise the clear picture. These may be key competencies, investments, or projects that the business must fulfil in order to make the picture become real
Sharing the picture	Invite someone to share the picture in one short description. Refine it until there is an agreed 'script' for the picture. Record this, and add to your strategic plan

Annual initiatives

Summary

Before the end of every year, it's vital to spend at least half a day defining the few key initiatives that will guide planning through the following year. This creates a blueprint for planning throughout the year.

Concepts

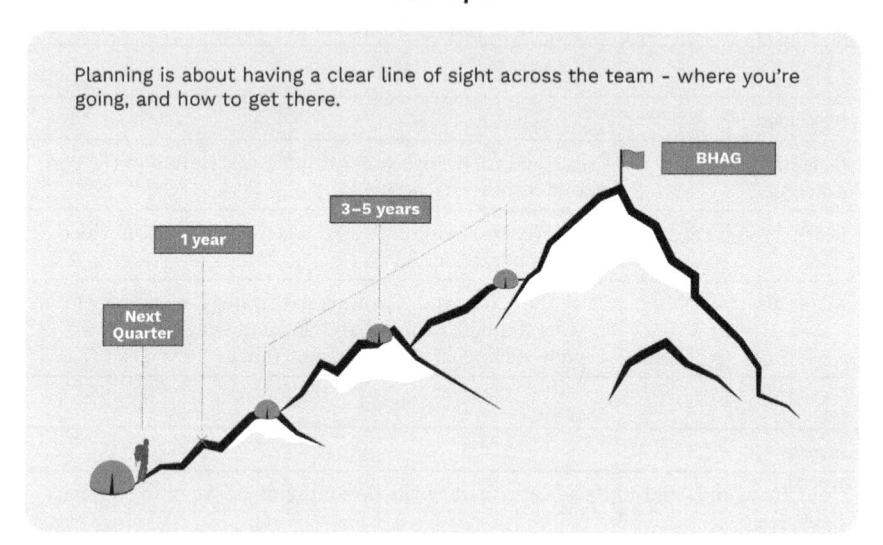

Planning is about having a clear line of sight across the team - where you're going, and how to get there.

- Next Quarter
- 1 year
- 3–5 years
- BHAG

Annual initiatives are the most immediate and clearly definable of the base camps on our mountain. As such, they are vital, and it is an important habit each year to set annual initiatives for the upcoming year (usually in the final planning session of the year). These are key reference points for quarterly planning sessions, setting the direction for Quarterly Sprint projects throughout the year.

When setting annual initiatives, two key inputs are valuable:

- **Targets and Metrics**. What are the key performance metrics for the year that must be achieved? These may be in the form of an annual budget, or a scorecard for the year's detailed key performance targets.
- **SWOT Analysis**. Described below.

Here is an example – a set of clear targets for the year, along with key initiatives to be implemented throughout the course of the year.

Targets (1 year) (Where)				Key initiatives (This Year)
Catagory	**Projected**	**Actuals**		
Staff appraisals / reviews / 1 to 1's	80%			1. Net New Business Drive
HR Qrtly Appraisals	100%			2. Cash Collection
Training	3hrs per month			3. Culture of engaged, happy, supported and aligned team
eNPS	> 0			4. Process automation, ticketing system
A-players	80%			5. Maximise share of wallet from satisfied existing clients
Customer NPS	> 0			6. Defined roles & responsibilities, fully supported by secure A-players
Monthly Recurring Rev	90,000			
Annual Turnover	1,800,000			
Gross margin	35%			
MQLs – monthly	20			
SQLs – monthly	60			
Monthly Appointments	6			

This team chose to put more of the details of their annual initiatives into a PowerPoint slide, so the headline initiatives look a little vague to someone outside of the team. The more specific they can get, the better.

SWOT analysis

A SWOT analysis is a commonly used tool for determining short- to midterm strategy and focus. It invites the team to assess and define key items in four categories: Strengths, Weaknesses, opportunities, and threats.

There are multiple schools of thought on the definitions of these four items:

- **Internal vs. External**. Treats strengths and weaknesses as being internal to the organisation, and opportunities and threats as external influences, such as market forces and competitor activity. The advantage of this method is that it forces you to look at the market as well as what is happening in the company.

- **Present vs. Future**. This treats the strengths and weaknesses as currently extant, and threats and opportunities as future or 'potential'. This temporal distinction encourages thinking about current and future effects.

Both of these approaches have merit. Our approach is to collect team input in advance, through the following survey content:

INTRODUCTION TO SWOT

Strategy is like a game of chess. To win the game, you need at all times to have an honest appraisal of the pieces you actually have on the board, your opponents' pieces, and what options you have in terms of available moves. SWOT analysis is a simple tool to make this appraisal in your business and work out what moves to make next.

The key to the successful use of a SWOT analysis is frank honesty. For example, if your market segment is under threat, like Kodak's was by digital cameras in the 90s, then it pays to cast a clear spotlight on it. SWOT is not a tool designed for team motivation or feel-good factor, but allows the team to take necessary strategic steps to ensure the continued growth of the business. To use the tool successfully:

- **Be specific**. Don't talk in general terms. If a particular department or process is the cause of an issue, then say so. Think in terms of 'root causes', not just 'surface symptoms'.
- **Think relative to the market**. The question is not asking what you think you do well or poorly, but how well you do compared to the competition.
- **Focus**. The process is designed to encourage open thinking at first, then strict focus on a few key points.

SWOT consists of four components:

- **Strengths**

    The strengths of the business are advantages that exist internally at the current time. These strengths give you a competitive advantage and are worth protecting or building on further.

When writing strengths, it's important to think relative to the market. For example, people often write things like 'Leading brand' as a strength, but is it really? Is that why you're chosen or recognised in the market? Try and think critically about what actually distinguishes you or makes you unique in some way.

- **Weaknesses**

    Weaknesses are current, actual flaws, shortcomings, or problems within the business that significantly hold you back. These are key issues in the business that must be resolved in order for it to continue to grow, or to succeed in the market.

    Be specific, not general. For example, people sometimes write general terms like 'Communication' as a weakness. What specific communication is failing? Is there a particular process holding the company back from growth?

    Also, think from a Company perspective, not just your own functional unit. This is not a list of gripes and complaints. Remember, all healthy businesses have issues, the key is to pick the few ones to fix.

- **Opportunities**

    What is happening externally – in the market – that is, or will have, a significant positive impact on the business? Identify external opportunities that we can capitalise on either now, or over the next 12 months. Don't spend too much time considering whether it is an opportunity or a threat; they are often two sides of the same coin, just put it into whichever feels the best fit. Again, be specific, for example if you see 'New Markets' as an opportunity, explain which ones, why, and for which products and services.

- **Threats**

    Threats are negative external factors that may impact us now or over the next 12 months. We cannot eliminate threats, but we will be able to devise ways to mitigate their impact on us. When writing threats, be specific. For example, people often write 'Competition', or 'Competitors entering the market' under threats. If that's the case, then specify what particular competitive activities are a threat, for example, new competing products, or particular market segments under threat.

Once answers from the team are compiled, the key is then to narrow down each of the three categories to just the **top 3**, that is, top 3 strengths, top 3 Weaknesses, and so on. Once narrowed down in this way, it will give you a clear view on what the initiatives for the year need to be.

Creating annual initiatives

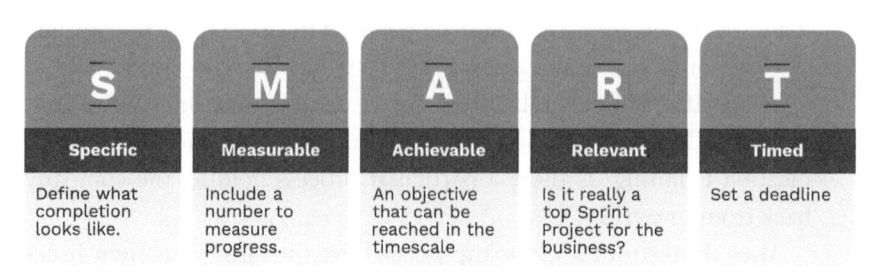

S	M	A	R	T
Specific	**Measurable**	**Achievable**	**Relevant**	**Timed**
Define what completion looks like.	Include a number to measure progress.	An objective that can be reached in the timescale	Is it really a top Sprint Project for the business?	Set a deadline

Pulling together your views on the targets for the year and the refined SWOT analysis, now set the key initiatives for the upcoming year.

These initiatives need to be stated as SMART goals, that is, a detailed description of what success or completion looks like:

It can be helpful to think of the statement in terms of its constituent elements. There should be a:

- **Subject**. This is usually the person accountable for the Objective. E.g. '*Ryan*'.
- **Verb**. Describes the action that shall be complete. Conjugate in the past form, that is, implying completion, for example, '*reached*'.
- **Object**. This is being worked on. Ideally, this is where the metric comes in. For example, '*100 sign ups for new partner event*'.
- **Period**. Include the completion date. For example, '*by 1st Sept*'.

Worksheet

SWOT

| Name: | Company: | Date: |

Understanding SWOT

- Set your period. From now until when?
- Write your ideas in notes, then select the top 3 from each category.
- For each item, include the consequences. For example, if you have the Strength of '*Strong cash reserves...*', might lead to '*...which allows us to invest in new products / people / equipment.*'
- Think relative to others. You may think 'great team' is a strength, but is it really great, compared to your competitors?
- Strengths & Weaknesses may be internal or current; Opportunities & Threats may be external, or potential.

SWOT analysis

Strengths
What does the organisation do well?
(Must give a comparative advantage)

Identify your top 3
1.
2.
3.

Weaknesses
Where and how is the organisation under-performing, have problems, or is failing?
(Must give a comparative disadvantage)

Identify your top 3
1.
2.
3.

Opportunities
What should we capitalise on?
(Accelerate growth / achieve our goals)

Identify your top 3
1.
2.
3.

Threats
Where is the potential for harm?
(Could significantly derail us)

Identify your top 3
1.
2.
3.

Exercise

Session Basics	
Name	'SWOT' and 'Annual Initiatives'
How to communicate	'We need to set key objectives for the upcoming year that will guide our Priority setting at Quarterly planning'
Time	60–90 minutes
Format	Workshop session, generally held towards the end of the year to plan the following year
Attendees	Senior leadership, and key line managers
Objective and outcome	Use the SWOT analysis to create clear objectives for the upcoming year
Materials	• Send out and collect answers to the SWOT as a survey in advance (see link here). This will save a lot of time in a day. • Prepare numeric targets and metrics for the year in advance

Exercise	
Confirm agenda and objective	As a team, share/write down the objective and agenda of the session
Share the survey	Assuming the SWOT has been filled out as a survey in advance, then share a collated SWOT include the team answers. If not, then ask the team to fill out the SWOT analysis, explaining the difference between the four elements
Top 3	Go through each of the four elements of the SWOT and discuss and agree which are the top 3 for each. You may find that some naturally merge or cluster. The output at each stage is three clear statements describing the top 3 for each of the SWOT elements
Idea sharing	Review the 12 statements together as a team. A clear picture should emerge of what the key initiatives for the year should be. Discuss and agree – what changes must be made in the organisation in the next 12 months? At this stage, reference the targets and metrics for the year. If you have set a budget or clear targets for sales or profit, for example. Make sure that all initiatives agreed will lead to those outcomes.
Defining objectives	For each of the key changes or initiatives, state them now as clear objectives. This means describing them as the end state, that is, what completion looks like. SMART is a helpful tool (see explanation and example below) to check your objectives against

Guidelines, pitfalls, and FAQs

Rigorous honesty

When teams are asked to state their strengths and weaknesses, interesting biases appear. When asked to list strengths, the same answers come up: 'People', 'Team', or 'Culture' are often included. Under weaknesses, common answers include 'Communication', 'Processes', and 'IT Systems'.

Firstly, one-word answers are a problem. They are not specific enough to be of any help, and must be challenged for more detail.

The deeper issue with these answers though is that they are merely statements of what people see in front of them, the positives and negatives in their day-to-day lives. They reflect the basic realities of working life, things like 'we like the people we work with' and 'there are often processes that go wrong'. There is not much of strategic insight in such comments.

The question that helps to refine thinking is 'is it a strength/weakness *compared to the competition?*' The words 'strength' and 'weakness' are comparators. They exist and have meaning only in comparison with other reference points. You may have great people in your team, but if the competition has too, then 'great' loses its meaning.

It doesn't matter what box an item is in

There is no benefit to debating whether something is an opportunity or a threat (or a strength or a weakness). Most things that happen are both. This easily descends into a glass half full/half empty debate that has no value. Just ascribe the item to one of the boxes and move on. The objective of the exercise is not to get things in the right box, it is to have an accurate overview of the state of the business, so that decisions can be made on what needs to change going forward.

Reaching clarity

If you involve a group in a SWOT analysis, inevitably you hear a range of views on where the business should focus. This has a tendency to create an outcome that is diffuse, which is why it is so important to maintain the discipline of narrowing each down to just the top 3.

How many initiatives?

Sometimes, there is just one key thing that needs to get done. For example, the team at The Hamlet needs to have a second property agreed upon and signed within 2022. That's it. Everything else counts as business as usual.

More often though, a team can, and must, progress on multiple fronts in order to achieve their objectives. There is no hard and fast rule, but there does seem to be a Sweetspot of around five annual initiatives: the fewer, the better. This is focused and memorable, with a hit list broad enough to progress the business on multiple fronts.

Part III

CHECKLISTS – DIAGNOSING BOTTLENECKS

8
SMC 2 – MEETING EFFECTIVENESS

Checklist item

Issue

Our **Meetings** are not effective enough

Manifestation

- Time in meetings is not used well
- Meetings not delivering changes and results we need.

Summary

Meetings are great. At least, they can be great. They can make you more efficient, improve team relationships, and accelerate decision-making to progress on key projects. Or, they can be a huge drain on performance, productivity, and morale. If you have low scores for this item, you must look at how you run your meetings.

The good news is that it's not complicated to fix. In fact, most people know in theory what good meeting habits look and feel like. It can just be difficult to maintain the discipline to stick to best practice. Let's show you how. There are three components:

- Setting a meeting rhythm and meeting best practices
- A weekly management meeting that gets things done and doesn't waste time
- Daily Huddle to ensure everyone is clear on their #1 thing, every day.

Concepts

The case for meetings

Face-to-face communication (in person or virtual) trumps alternatives such as email and messages in several ways:

- **Richness of information.** Humans are designed to see one another when they communicate. Much of what we infer from someone's message comes from physical cues, including tone of voice and body language.
- **Avoidance of miscommunication.** The extension of the point above is that constant written communication leads to miscommunication. This ranges from dropped balls and errors, to damaged relationships and conflict.
- **Batching of issues and solutions.** If every separate item requires an email or message string, this quickly becomes highly inefficient. A regular cycle of meetings allows for issues to be batched. Rather than an email for each item, it simply gets added to the meeting agenda for resolution.
- **Discussion and decision-making.** People generally make better decisions as a result of discussion with other people. Brainstorming, discussion, and decision-making for complex issues demand group discussion.

- **Group bonding and relationships**. A company is at heart a group of people; it's our community, the people with whom we choose to share our lives. Bringing them together in positive, fun, and constructive ways is a part of what being in a community is all about.

Common meeting problems

So, if meetings are so good, where do things go wrong? A lot of teams hate their meetings. These are common bugbears:

- **Not starting on time**. If start time is hijacked by late-comers, or too much chit-chat, it eats into everyone's time. That sense of time wasted is intensely frustrating and feels disrespectful to people and their time.
- **Not finishing on time**. This is one of the greatest frustrations of any team. It makes people feel like they have no control over their time and diary. They have already planned out how to use the time after the meeting, so if it doesn't end on time, it throws out the rest of the day.
- **Spectating**. Few things are more frustrating than being in a meeting where you're not needed. It may be a client meeting where you're only needed for 5 minutes, but feel obliged to sit through it all, or inter-departmental meeting where others from your team can represent just fine.
- **Repetition**. People hate to cover the same points in multiple meetings. If a report is presented in one meeting, then it frustrates people to have to hear it again.
- **Discussion with no conclusion**. The purpose of discussion is to make a decision and move on. No one likes bad decisions, but people get at least as frustrated if they feel analysis paralysis and a decision isn't made so they can move on to the next issue.
- **No follow-up**. If a meeting doesn't conclude with clear actions, or there is no follow-up to actions agreed, then people lose confidence that their time is well-spent in meetings.
- **Listening to reports**. Meetings are at their most dispiriting when they are simply people reporting back the things they've done. Such information can be shared in reports, the purpose of meetings is to discuss and decide what comes next.

- **Listening to a minority**. Some people have a tendency to dominate meetings. By virtue of personality or position, they take up the majority of the speaking time. If a meeting is not participative and people feel stuck listening to the same voice, they quickly disengage.
- **Spending meetings/planning meetings**. The curse of comparing diaries to find common availability in order to book the next meeting. The digital equivalent such as a Doodle can be a little less painful, but the back and forth is nonetheless time-consuming.

Solving your meeting problems

What to do about it, how to take the good and avoid the bad? Follow these guidelines to ensure great meetings in your organisation. We cover three key areas:

- Set your meeting rhythm
- Establish and stick to sets of **meeting best practices**
- Plan **two key meetings** in more detail: Daily Huddle and Weekly Meeting

Have a meeting rhythm

There are two types of meetings:

- **Regular**. Repeated at a set time.
- **Ad hoc**. One-off, arranged in response to issues arising.

What is the ideal balance of these two types? The answer is that you will improve productivity and spend less time on meetings overall if you can move more meetings from the latter to the former.

For example, rather than dealing with finance issues as and when they come up, have a weekly finance meeting to review accounting or receivables, or weekly project check-in calls for key priorities. These are predictable and controllable, and happen at a fixed time. A key point to emphasise is that *you don't have to use the full time allocated* if it's not needed.

Another reason this method is effective comes down to human psychology. People are motivated by accountability to their peers. This translates into the behaviour that they get work done in response to deadlines where they have to present progress to peers. Therefore, if you are delivering a project, the best way to ensure it gets done is to bring the project team members together according to a set rhythm. The faster you control this pulse, the quicker things will get done.

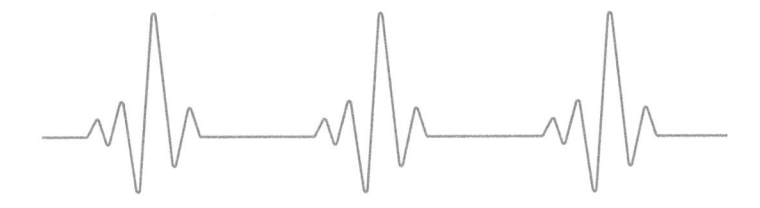

Interestingly, this principle also applies to communications with clients. If you are in a service business then, rather than a lot of back-and-forth email communication and ad hoc meetings, put a weekly account check-in call in the diary every week (or fortnight, or month, or whatever makes sense based on your level of engagement). This will do wonders not just for efficiency, but also for your client relationships.

It also works for suppliers. If you're not happy with the service from your accountant, require them to get on a call with you once a week / fortnight / month, no excuses, and to use that call to raise and solve all issues on your account.

Set your rhythm

With this concept of 'rhythm' or 'pulse' in mind, it's important to think about what the particular rhythm of your organisation is, and how it relates to the execution of strategy. The updating and delivery of strategy and planning have to happen to a certain rhythm. It is helpful to chunk this down into component units, as follows:

Period	Key Focus
5–30 years	• Update Vision/BHAG
3–5 years	• Update Clear Picture
Every year	• Annual Planning Day. Update Annual Initiatives
Quarter	• Quarterly Planning Day. Set key Sprint Projects for the Q
Month	• Monthly Management Meeting: Detailed check-ins and discussion/resolution of roadblocks
Week	• Tactical operational meetings • Weekly management meeting • Status updates on Sprint Projects
Day	• Key Priority for today

Above is a template example of certain key rhythms and habits associated with strategy and planning. Now take some time to work on the rhythm in your organisation.

SMC 2 – MEETING EFFECTIVENESS   147

Worksheet

Meeting rhythm
SCALE | Business growth made easy

Name: Company: Date:

"Those who pulse faster, grow faster" – Verne Harnish

Period	Meeting	Key focus / agenda	Who? Meeting owner	When? How long?
Day	Daily huddle.	Key priority for today.		
	Tactical operational meetings.	Day-to-day issue resolution for that function.		
Week	Weekly management meeting.	Status updates on sprint projects.		
Month	Monthly management meeting.	Detailed check-ins and discussion/ resolution of roadblocks.		
Quarter	Quarterly planning day.	Set key sprint projects for the quarter.		
Year	Annual planning day.	Update annual initiatives.		

Feb23 · © Clarity Strategy Ltd DBA Scale 2023   www.scalecoach.co.uk

Exercise

Preparation	
Objective and outcome	Improve efficiency and accelerate execution by having a predictable rhythm of meetings
Attendees	Management team and team leaders
Learning and reading	• *Scaling Up*, by Verne Harnish
Materials	• Bring Calendars

Exercise	
Confirm agenda and objective	As a team, share/write down the objective and agenda of the session
Review worksheet	Explain the objective of the worksheet
Fill out 1.	Go through the worksheet as a team, recording the template of meetings required in the business. Agree who will be accountable for each one
Fill out 2.	Request the owner of each meeting to confirm the time, duration, and key agenda items of each meeting
Follow-up	Agree next steps. Ensure that this includes getting these meetings as repeated invites into diaries there and then

Meeting best practices

Have a set of rules

Bad meeting hygiene is less about knowing what to do, and more about the discipline of actually applying best practices to yourself. Having said that, it is worth being clear on good practices. So, here are the **golden rules of meetings**:

- **Agenda in advance.** If you're going to take people's time for a meeting, respect that time by having a clear list of topics for discussion and resolution in the meeting.
- **Set objectives and agenda** at the start. State clearly what the outcomes of the meeting need to be at the outset.

- Have a **start time and an end time** and stick to them. No running over, no exceptions (though it's fine to finish early if you get things done).
- Have and stick to a **rhythm**. For example, Marketing meeting 2–2.30 on a Monday afternoon. It's so much easier to plan life around, rather than ad hoc meetings.

The list above represents the bare meeting of good meeting practice. You may have your own particular expectations and best practices for meetings. **Set your own charter or constitution for meetings**.

Stick to them

The key now is: **how to stick to it**? For this, you have to apply some hacks in order to actually change behaviour.

- **Meeting rules are prominently displayed**. If you have a physical meeting room, display them clearly on the wall or the desk. This could be a poster on the wall, laminates on the desk, or a sign on the door as you come in. If you meet virtually, it's central to whatever screen or platform you use for the meeting, it could be in the form of an automated pop-up.
- **Start all meetings with the charter**. Whoever is leading the meeting, take the 1–2 minutes at the outset to review the meeting charter, and follow the actions therein. The leader of the organisation will have to model this, and this new habit will require some chasing in the early days, but it quickly becomes second nature.
- **Rotate** who chairs the meetings. You'd be amazed how this simple tweak can improve engagement, as each person has a chance to make their mark on a meeting. Rotate alphabetically, or by hair length, or whatever fun method you like. If there is a charter for the meeting, then chairing it becomes easy.
- **Score meetings**. At the end of every meeting, request a score. A good question is: 'On a score of 1–10, how would you rate the use of your time in this meeting?' Even if you only score for a few weeks, you will quickly learn which meetings to keep, and which to dump. More often though, the score reflects not the necessity of the meeting, but how effectively the meeting was managed. So, you may well need a weekly

finance review meeting, for example, but if it gets a low score, it may make sense first to look at how the meeting is being run before canning it.
- **Reduce the time** of all meetings by 25–50% (e.g. all 60-minute meetings default changed to 30 or 45 minutes). This is a common and effective hack recommended by productivity gurus, which taps into **Parkinson's Law**:

> **Parkinson's Law** The demand upon a resource tends to expand to match the supply of the resource, if the price of the resource is zero. (The reverse is not true.) For example:

- The amount spent by a department will rise to meet the budget allocated to them
- The amount of time spent discussing an item in a meeting will expand to match the time allocated for that meeting.

As an example, below is our Weekly Huddle Constitution at Scale. It's not a great work of literature, but it does the job and is referenced **every week**, that is, whoever is chairing the huddle that week explicitly brings up (screenshare) and reads the relevant parts of the Constitution.

Scale Huddle Constitution

Advice process:
- Decision /Advice requests to be written up in advance.
- Max 2 per weekly huddle. Otherwise, get escalated to the monthly Deep Dive, or to Scale School.

Agenda items and agenda review:
- Agenda items must be added to the Huddle Agenda by previous Friday (no additions on the day please)
- Team mates expected to review agenda items on Friday / ask clarifying questions
- After ice-breaker, start huddle by reviewing and ordering agenda items ("Do we need to cover this?", "Do we need to cover this today?", "Can this be taken care of on a 1:1?", "Should this be moved to the monthly Deep Dive?", "What order should be discuss these issues in?")
- Apologies for next week's huddle
- Confirm next week's chair

Ice-Breakers.
Start with ice-breaker every time, according to following schedule each month:
- Week 1: Intense moments. Share a story of an intense moment you've had with someone over the past month. Could be from coaching, Member sessions, or with a team mate. An example where you went deep, touched on something profound, or had a great breakthrough.
- Week 2: Lessons learned. One key learning from something that went wrong in the past month, that would be of value to the rest of the team to learn from.
- Week 3. Celebrating Core Values. Share a story from the past month that is a great example of someone in our team living one of our core values. State which core value its an example of, and what they did.
- Week 4. Great resources. Share a 'resource' (e.g. book, tool, soft ware, article, podcast, show..) that would significantly benefit the rest of the team.

Chairing the huddle
- Chair rotates each week (in alphabetic order)
- Chair ensures agenda items confirmed at start of huddle, then all items agreed get covered.

Other ground rules:
- Bell / call out work for double speak / using the word 'but'
- Attendance is expected from everyone. This is our key heartbeat of the organisation. If you miss it, you will miss key information relevant to your work.

Our Constitution is in the notes section at the top of the monday.com board that we use for our Weekly Huddle, so it's always at the top of the page of the core board we use for that meeting. It couldn't be closer to hand (NB. See section below regarding task management software).

Action-focused meetings – task management software

Meetings go hand-in-hand with task management software. You cannot have effective meetings if the team is not using one common platform to manage tasks and projects.

At a simple level, this can be shared using Excel or Google sheets. At Scale, and amongst our members, we are huge fans of task management software, particularly at monday.com. Monday has made life so much easier for us and all the companies with whom we work, as you can easily collaborate on meeting agendas in advance, set and follow up on task lists easily, and get quick updates on project plans.

Declare meeting bankruptcy

If the team is really frustrated with the extent of meetings, an extreme approach is to essentially hit Control-Alt-Delete on your meetings, and cancel all meetings effective immediately. Any meetings that are then really necessary will naturally start to reappear.

Two key meetings

Given how important meetings are, it's surprising how little time and attention teams put into their design and management. In the next section, we highlight two meetings of particular importance, and provide exercises and worksheets for you to significantly improve the effectiveness of these two key meetings:

- Weekly Management Meeting
- Daily Huddle.

Weekly management meeting

Summary

How is your weekly management meeting working for you? Many teams we meet have drifted into formats that are dull and make poor use of time. The worst are where it cycles through each team member reporting on what they've done that week. Yawn.

Revitalising your weekly management meeting will not only make better use of the time, but will also give the team a renewed sense of vigour and purpose that they will take to each of their respective parts of the business.

Key concepts

> Your meetings should be passionate, intense, exhausting, and never boring.
>
> Patrick Lencioni

The #1 focus for a weekly management meeting should be **resolving two to three key issues** that the business is stuck on. These discussions should be intense, focused, and typically involve people working through differences of opinion. The art is in picking the few right issues to resolve, and guiding the discussion so that it teases out the issue, without hurting relationships.

Taking this approach to meetings takes a little courage – a willingness to air dirty laundry and 'go there' with difficult topics. It is rewarded many-fold.

Issue resolution may happen in the format of discussion: brainstorming or problem-solving. The outcome needs to be a few clear decisions and actions to take the issue forward. And remember: the meeting must start on time and end on time (if you can't get it all fixed, arrange a follow-up rather than extending the time).

Scale weekly management meeting

Below is a format and agenda for weekly meetings that will ensure progress and engagement. Every team that has adopted this process has reported huge improvements in productivity and engagement from their meetings. 'Hit refresh', stop what you're currently doing, and simply adopt this format.

Weekly management meeting — SCALE | Business growth made easy

Name: _____ Company: _____ Date: _____

"Your meetings should be passionate, intense, exhausting, and never boring" – Patrick Lencioni

Agenda

1. Staff & customer **headlines** (5 mins)
2. Scale **scorecard** review (5 mins)
3. Scale **priority** review (5 mins)
4. **To do list** review (5 mins)
5. **Issue solving** (60 mins)
6. **Recap** (5 mins)

1-4 This week's potential issues

Staff & customer headlines (5 mins)	Scale scorecard review (5 mins)	Scale priority review (5 mins)	To do list review (5 mins)

5 Key issues for resolution

Determine top 2-3 issues – what is the real issue?	Diagnose. Everyone share solutions.	Decide. Stated and agreed decision.

6 Agreed actions and outcomes

Actions	Owner	Deadline

Feb23 - © Clarity Strategy Ltd DBA Scale 2023 — www.scalecoach.co.uk

The objective of the Scale Weekly Management Meeting is to:

- Understand and resolve current key issues facing the business, and
- Solve any issues faced in the Quarterly Sprint Projects.

The first phase (agenda items 1–4) is short (15–20 mins), to identify potential issues for resolution, which are added to the issue list, which is then prioritised. **The majority of the time is assigned to issue-solving**. This forms the bulk of the meeting (60 minutes), and any actions are put on the to-do list. The recap is then a review of the agreed-upon actions (who needs to do what, by when).

Here is a breakdown of each section:

1. Staff and customer headlines

The key here is 'headlines'. A member of staff has resigned. A customer relationship is in jeopardy. The time for this is intentionally brief. If this were a newspaper, what is on the front page? Headline only, not the full story and not something that doesn't belong on the front page. If it presents an issue (i.e. it's not already being handled), then add it to the issue list. If you have 10 people in your meeting, that's 30 seconds per person, so keep it brief.

2. Scorecard review

Refer to your Scorecard (for guidance on how to establish this, go to Chapter 9, Intro) to review status on the key metrics for a past period. This needs to be a shortlist of key numbers with each expressed as: 'On track', 'Target reached', 'Above target', or 'Below target'. If you're using Monday.com, add a column for 'Last Updated' so you can easily see if the person accountable has updated their numbers.

This is not a full spreadsheet of weekly numbers or trends but a summary that can be used to manage goal performance. Naturally, owners of these goals will have a supporting data set but for the purpose of this meeting, we want to know if goals are on track or not. If anything is off-track and of concern, it gets added to the issues list.

Examples: revenue, gross margin, average time to close a service request, debtor days, £ value of overdue accounts, £ value added to pipeline.

3. Quarterly sprint priority review

The priority review is to track the Sprint Projects set at Quarterly Planning. The relevant project plan must be updated with accurate progress on the status of each item before the weekly meeting, and displayed during the meeting (this is an important detail – don't just let people give a verbal update – get the plan up on the screen). Each Priority owner gives a short update, emphasising anywhere they are off-track, or stuck, to be added to the issues list.

4. To-do list review

Review the outstanding to-do list to see if there are actions or items where team members are stuck or off-track. This ensures follow-through on agreed actions, and picks up anything that isn't getting resolved. Completed items should have been moved to a separate section so that you can only see outstanding items (easily done via an automation on monday.com). Also, using the creation log feature on Monday.com makes it easy to see how long items have been on the list.

Add any 'Stucks' to the issues list. Most items on the list from the previous week should be anticipated to have been completed. However, be aware that issues do re-surface (make sure people feel it's okay for the same stuck to be re-reported if it's still an issue). Noticing this is important to identify root causes or deeper issues at play.

5. Issue-solving

Issue-solving is where you allocate the majority of your time during the Scale Weekly Management Meeting. The list should have a clear description of the issue, a record of who recorded the issue and when. You should also record the date an issue is solved and a way to separate solved issues.

The first task is to prioritise your list. If you have more than four issues, focus on prioritising your top three to save time. If you solve all three, you can return to prioritising. Once you have your top three, follow the DDD process.

DDD: determine, diagnose, decide

The purpose of the DDD process is to improve the discussion and resolution of issues:

Determine: The stated problem is rarely the real issue. Therefore, the first step is to dig down and find the real issue or root cause. Don't move forward until you have clarified, stated, and agreed upon the real issue. Sometimes you will uncover multiple issues. That's fine, but exercise the discipline to prioritise which one to solve first so that your process and thinking remain clear.

Diagnose: Everyone must share their thoughts, ideas, and concerns openly and honestly for discussion and debate. With everything on the table, the solution is usually simple but sometimes not easy.

Decide: It's more important that you decide, rather than what you decide. The decision must be stated and agreed upon. Once agreed, the action steps must be owned by someone and put on the to-do list.

About 80% of the time, everyone will agree with the decision but the rest of the time, they won't, and the person owning the decision will have to make the final decision. As long as everyone has been heard and the team is healthy, they can usually live with the decision and must support it. There must be a united front moving forward.

6. Recap

There are three points to cover in your recap: to-do list, communications, and meeting review.

- Recap the to-do list and make sure every item has an owner accountable. It should include a description of the task, a person accountable, the date the item was generated, a completion date, and a status, for example, working on it, stuck, done.
- As a result of any decisions made, are there any messages that should be communicated with others in the company? If so, add these to the to-do list to ensure completion.
- Meeting review: ask what could have been done better? Record this for continual improvement of the meeting and to avoid the meeting from atrophying: a common theme with company meetings.

Exercise

Session basics	
Name	'Weekly Management Meeting'
How to Communicate	'We have to make our weekly meeting effective, so that we can save time, make quality decisions, and accelerate the pace of progress'
Time	30 minutes
Format	Discussion meeting
Attendees	Leadership team

Daily huddle

Summary

The morning is a vital part of each day. We know we must start the day with a clear sense of focus. Imagine if every person in the team did so, and that each person knew what the others were focused on too. Imagine how much time and how many errors would be saved during the day. This is what the Daily Huddle can do for you.

Key concepts

The daily huddle

One of my first jobs was at B&Q, the DIY retailer, as a trainee in-store. Every morning, all the store staff on shift that day would get together for a 'morning huddle'. We would stand together for 10–15 minutes, and communicate key information for the day, such as incoming shipments, key promotions, projects, or communications from HQ. It was short, effective, and created a real sense of being part of a team. It got the tone just right between having fun together as a group of young people, and the seriousness of getting a job done.

Toyota is famous for such stand-up 'daily huddle' meetings, doing something similar on the manufacturing line 'shopfloor'. In fact, in many blue-collar environments, these kinds of morning huddles are common practice. Yet, when you move to the office environment, and particularly when people work remotely, this great practice often doesn't happen.

This is a shame, as a Daily Huddle is a fantastic focus point for a team. It helps to:

- **Batch communications**. About 10–15 minutes of team communication at the start of the day significantly reduces time spent on emails and ad hoc communications throughout the rest of the day.
- **Give each person focus**. Having each person describe their key action for the day to the rest of the team, forces them to think it through beforehand. This encourages the positive daily habit for each person of setting priorities for the day.
- **Spot issues**. It's amazing how many issues are caught in Daily Huddle before they escalate and become problems later in the day. Duplicated meetings, missed client issues, or logistics slip-ups are all common examples of what gets nipped in the bud at Daily Huddle.
- **Team spirit**. Knowing what's going on around you within a team has a powerful effect of bonding, as each person understands what the others are contributing, as well as what's going on in their lives. Daily Huddle really does provide a strong connection between teammates.

Establishing daily huddles

To set up Daily Huddles across the business, each team needs to decide how they want to run their own huddle. It's best to provide a set of best practices (see worksheet below), and let each team decide for themselves how they want their huddle to run. Even within a huddle, it's a great practice to rotate who manages the huddle, so that each person can stamp their own personality on the huddle. People have to feel ownership over their huddle, in order to make it work.

If you have multiple teams in the business, you will need to work out how huddles cascade. Members of the leadership team, for example, will need to attend the leadership team huddle, and the huddle of whatever team they manage. Some teams prefer for 'senior' huddles to happen first, so that information can be communicated down as necessary. What is more common though is for the senior huddle to happen last, as collecting insights from huddles across the business is a powerful way of keeping your finger on the pulse of what's going on around the company.

SMC 2 – MEETING EFFECTIVENESS   159

Getting the most out of your daily huddles

Ceramic Designs's post

Ceramic Designs
42 m

'The Power of the Huddle'

Everyday, at 9:30 a.m, our team gathers for the 'huddle'. Cases are discussed between departments of the lab as well as future plans, creative ideas and problem solving.

This simple daily meeting gives everyone the opportunity to engage and air views and opinions constructively which is a positive and powerful team-building exercise.

Do you do daily meetings or huddles in your team?

👍 Like   💬 Comment   ↪ Share

👍 Like   💬 Comment   ↪ Share

Start time

Pick an unusual start time. Ours is at 7.44. Due to whatever quirk of human psychology, unusual (i.e. not 00, 15, 30, or 45 minutes past the hour) start times cause people to turn up exactly on time.

Never go over time

Even if you have to leave issues unresolved or a discussion incomplete, it's more important that you finish Daily Huddle on time (i.e. never longer than 15 minutes). If you allow Daily Huddle to become a discussion and talking shop, you will quickly fall out of the habit.

The power of hand-offs

Issues often come up in huddle that are tempting to solve there and then. If it's something that can be clarified in one sentence, then do so. If not, take it off-line for follow-up. 'Hand-offs' here are important. Have an agreed terminology for shutting down discussion and debate, such as 'Let's take that off-line' or 'Let's let xxx come back with some thoughts', or 'Please could you follow this up that xxx meeting?' Don't let Huddle get hijacked by debate and problem-solving (as tempting as that may be).

Personalise

The internet is full of quirky videos of how teams have added their own unique personalities into Daily Huddles, from throwing round the office toy as a hand-off, to full-blown costume huddles. Do it your own way, make it an expression of the team personality and culture. Some teams make it meditative and personal, some serious and target-oriented, others emphasise fun and goofing around. A great way to accelerate personalisation is to rotate the chairing of a huddle, and allow each person to find new ways of improving or personalising Huddle.

Worksheet

Daily huddle

Name: _____ Company: _____ Date: _____

Huddle constitution

Huddle leader (or rotation function)		**Timekeeper**	
Huddle time & place		**Attendees**	

Set your ground rules from these daily huddle best practices

Item	✓	Item	✓
ALWAYS end within 10-15mins.		Rotate huddle leader.	
No more than 2-3 agenda items.		EVERYBODY shares.	
Same items each day.		Be specific.	
Same time each day.		Best done standing up.	
Set unusual start time (eg. 08:44).			

Daily huddle agenda item options (pick max 2-3)

Item	✓	Item	✓
What's your number 1 thing today?		Quarter priority progress.	
Where are you stuck?		What does the team need to know? / good news story.	
Progress to KPI's.		What's your daily number?	

Set your specific timings

Agenda item	Seconds per person

Huddle cascade

Are there multiple huddles throughout the organisation to plan?

Exercise

Session Basics	
Name	Daily Huddles
How to communicate:	'In order to reduce ad hoc communications during the day, and foster collaboration within each team, we're going to explore how to set up Daily Huddles in each team'
Time	30–60 minutes
Format	Discussion meeting to establish new habits
Attendees:	Start with the leadership team, then cascade to all teams (starting with team leaders)

Preparation	
Objective and outcome	Agree on rhythm, agendas, timing, and attendees for Daily Huddles in each team
Learning and reading	Watch some of the many YouTube videos on Daily Huddle examples and best practices, such as: https://www.youtube.com/watch?v=WSOFHniInxQ&t=19s
Materials	Use the worksheet as a guide to the meeting

Exercise	
Objective	Review and agree on the objective and agenda of the session
Key concept	Discuss and agree why you want to start Daily Huddles. What are the potential benefits, and the pitfalls to avoid. Share stories, examples, and knowledge about Daily Huddles.
Huddle Constitution	Agree on the fundamentals of the Huddle, including timing, attendees, and how you will rotate the leading of the huddle
Ground rules	Confirm your ground rules, for example, how you will manage timing to ensure that everyone shares
Huddle Cascade	If you have multiple teams in a business, then you will need multiple huddles (see explanation below). Agree on the structure of your huddle cascade
Action list	Agree any further follow-up actions to get Daily Huddles started, such as getting them in the diary, setting up con call settings, or preparing a physical space

9

SMC 3 – ACCOUNTABILITY AND TEAM STRUCTURE

Checklist item

Issue

Accountability and Team structure. We're not fully clear on who's accountable for what, or our team structure is creating silos.

Manifestation

- Confusion and dropped balls due to a lack of accountability and who's measured on what
- Silos hindering teamwork and customer service
- Turf-building or politics creeping in

Summary

As the leader of the organisation, the happy fact is that you don't have to solve anything. The only question you need to answer is 'Who?' i.e. 'Who needs to be accountable for solving the key issues we face?' Be warned though, the CEO may be clear in their own mind who is accountable for what, but that doesn't mean that the team is. It's vital to clarify who's accountable for what functions, how they're measured, how the organisation is structured, and that everyone is held accountable for their commitments.

Tools and exercises

The exercises in this section focus on improving clarity on who does what, how they're measured, and how that performance is held accountable, which includes:

- **Accountability**. The Accountability Scorecard exercise clarifies which individual is accountable for each key function in the business, and how the performance of that function is measured. It is the precursor to creating a full set of **Key Performance Indicators (KPIs) and scorecard/dashboard** for the organisation, which can then be made engaging through **gamification and theming**.
- As organisations grow, the traditional functional department model becomes a hindrance, impacting customer service, the ability to drive change in the business and internal cooperation. This requires understanding and developing **flexible organisation structures**.
- The key skill of **holding people to account**, includes best practices, and an opportunity to score where the team is doing this well and less well.

Accountability

Summary

'Is everyone clear on who's accountable for what?' It sounds like such an easy question. I've asked it of many CEOs, and often received the confident reply 'Of course!'. Then, when we've sat down with the leadership team and asked them to write down who is accountable for what, we **always** find areas where:

- No one is accountable
- Multiple people are accountable
- Different people think different people are accountable
- One person is accountable for a large number of areas

As CEOs, we almost always overestimate how clear accountability is within the team. To compensate for this bias, it's important to go through the process of clarifying accountability. Furthermore, naming accountability ('the perception of accountability') is not enough, it requires ongoing tracking and holding to account to actually have an effect.

Concepts

Accountable for outcomes

What does 'accountable' really mean? Well, the clue is in the name – it contains the word 'count'. True accountability is not so much to actions, but to **outcomes**. And the best way to measure outcomes is through **numbers**. Therefore, a core part of assigning accountability is through clarifying targets and metrics.

Intrinsic in this definition is that the person *accountable* for outcomes is not necessarily the one *responsible* for all the tasks associated with it. At the level of a leadership team, 'accountable' means the individual who:

- Reports back on the key number(s) associated with that accountability
- Lets the team know if things are stuck or off-track
- Brings together the relevant people to find solutions
- Coordinates and drives the planning of related initiatives.

One important ground rule to get right with respect to accountability is that it needs to **sit with one person**. Avoid the temptation to allow multiple people to own initiatives or targets, it's a recipe for muddle and confusion.

I worked with a team once where two people ran a business unit together. Everything had always been the purview of both of them. One of the most valuable sessions they ever had was working through each of the key functions of the business and deciding which one of the two would be accountable for it. It was as if a weight had been lifted from their shoulders, as they were finally clear on what they could rely on the other one for and let go of themselves.

This underscores a key thing to understand about accountability which is that *good teams want and expect it*. Good people welcome the challenge of being put in charge of something and expect to deliver on it.

Dashboards and games

Developing metrics (or KPIs) is a vital component of accountability. Please do not think that this process is just about top-down enforcement of targets and expectations though. Good people want to be held accountable, to take on, and beat targets. For most of us, numeric targets are a source of joy in our lives, such as in sports and computer games. So, there is tremendous scope to gamify and make them enjoyable.

Never underestimate the power of human beings chasing numbers and targets. In Jack Stack's 'The Great Game of Business', he shares a story of when he had acquired an underperforming factory. His first action was to turn up at the end of the day shift, take a piece of chalk, and write the KPI metric for that shift on the factory floor. The following morning, when he came in, night shift had beaten the number. So, he rubbed it out, and replaced it with the night shift's performance. Each team continued to out-compete the other until they solved the underperformance of the factory. Total investment: one piece of chalk.

One of my favourite examples of this was a team at one of our Member companies had a key project to complete that had 12 components to it. They used a 3D printer to create a 12-piece jigsaw puzzle, and added one piece each time they passed the relevant milestone. At the end of the period, they had proudly assembled the full jigsaw, and hit their target.

The solution to these issues is a simple workshop exercise called the 'Accountability Scorecard'.

SMC 3 – ACCOUNTABILITY AND TEAM STRUCTURE

Worksheet

Accountability Scorecard

SCALE | Business growth made easy

Name: _____ Company: _____ Date: _____

"If everyone is accountable, then no one is"

Instructions
1. Add any functional areas specific to you (e.g. 'Design').
2. Assign 1 person accountable for each area.
3. Fill in key activities, how they're measured, and the specific period targets.

Check
- Is there more than 1 person in a seat?
- Are there empty seats?
- Is one person in too many seats?
- Do we have the wrong person in a seat?

Area	Person	2-3 key activities	What are they measured on?	Next period target
Example	John Doe	• New customer sales. • Managing the sales team. • Updating sales best practices.	• Sales £ to target. • Conversion rate %. • Av. lead closing time.	For 2023 • £2.56m • 27.6% • 27 days
Head of Company				
Marketing				
Sales				
Operations				
Finance				
R&D / Innovation				
Internal IT				
HR				
Customer satisfaction				

Feb23 · © Clarity Strategy Ltd DBA Scale 2023

www.scalecoach.co.uk

Exercise

Session basics	
Name	'Accountability Scorecard'
How to Communicate	'Everyone in the team needs to be clear on who's accountable for what, and how we're going to track and measure their progress and performance'
Time	This exercise usually takes several sessions to complete. The initial accountability can be set in one 30–60 minute session. But building up a good scorecard of metrics can take several months of work and repeated sessions.
Format	Workshop, with worksheet
Attendees	Leadership/management team.

Preparation	
Objective and outcome	Clarity on who is accountable for which function, and how performance will be measured
Learning and reading	
Materials	Use the worksheet as a guide to the meeting

Exercise	
Objective	Review and agree on the objective and agenda of the session
Functions	Review the list of functions in the business, and add any that are relevant to your organisation (for example 'design').
Accountable person	Request each person in the team to separately fill out who they think is the accountable person for each function. Then review each function as a team and compare answers. Look out for empty boxes, multiple people, or one person in too many boxes. Agree on one name for each box.
Key responsibilities	Have the accountable person for each function list out the two to three key responsibilities of that function
KPIs and targets	Discuss and agree what the measurable outcomes for each function are
Targets	Agree on specific targets for the upcoming period
Action list	Agree any further follow-up actions to get the scorecard together, and how you will hold functional leaders to account

Creating a scorecard

The worksheet here is intended as a starter to the process of creating a scorecard. It will take the team time to come up with a complete set of KPIs with specific targets, and longer still to get in place the processes to regularly and accurately report on them. This is time well spent, as it will help you enormously in being able to understand the performance of the business. In the same way that a doctor would not think to prescribe medicine or surgery for a patient without a thorough review of their vital statistics and test results, so you cannot hope to accurately run the business, hold people accountable, and set focus without clear metrics.

The approach to take to this project on is **agile** which means:

- **Define a Minimum Viable Product**. What is the smallest set of KPIs with which you could 'launch' the scorecard? Don't make the mistake of setting out to record everything, as you will get stuck, and end up with nothing.
- **Use it regularly**. The more regularly you meet to look at the scorecard, and use it in management meetings for decision-making, the quicker it will progress and improve.
- **Iterate**. Once you have a working version, then figure out changes, to improve accuracy, timeliness, and 'complete-ness' of reported data.

Guide and pitfalls

'Accountability' may not mean 'Department'

The benefit of this exercise is clarity on who's accountable for what. It's incredibly helpful. However, there is a risk with it. It's easy to jump from the thinking 'xxx is accountable for this part of the business, therefore xxx needs to manage a department doing that'. In some cases, this may be the case, for example, if John is accountable for Marketing, it may be that John runs a department called 'Marketing'.

However, if that logic is pursued across all departments, then you end up with an organisational structure that looks like this:

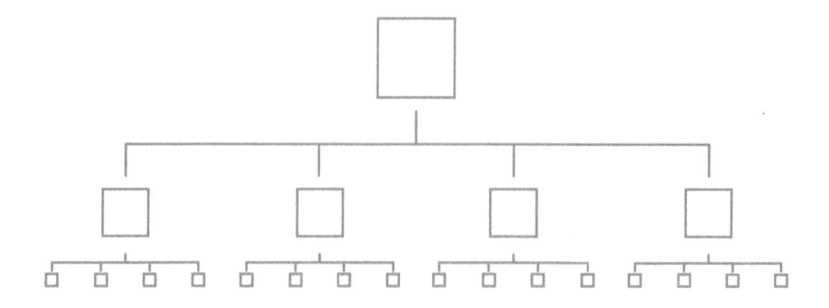

Command
A traditional top-down structure.
The conections that matter are between
workers and their managers

This organisational structure brings problems as an organisation grows, such as silos, inflexibility, and poor customer service. Read on to the next section – Team Structure – to find out more on this topic, and how to avoid this pitfall.

What do I need to let go of next?

As a CEO of a growing company, this exercise almost always leads to the realisation that there are areas of the business which need to be let go. This process sits at the heart of growth in the business – finding someone great who can take away a part of the business that we're probably managing less well than they can. Sometimes, this is an internal promotion, sometimes an external recruitment.

This reflection may happen during the exercise itself, or sometimes it is in the days and weeks afterwards, as we reflect on it, that we realise what we need to do.

KPIs – the eternal project

As teams grow, the need for clear accountability mounts, and therefore for targets and metrics, which drives the need for 'KPI systems'. A KPI system takes the scorecard described above and applies more detailed sets of targets and metrics through to members of teams across the business. Ultimately, these can become an important part of individual performance

SMC 3 – ACCOUNTABILITY AND TEAM STRUCTURE

Accountability Scorecard

SCALE | Business growth made easy

Name: _____ Company: _____ Date: _____

"If everyone is accountable, then no one is"

Instructions
1. Add any functional areas specific to you (e.g. 'Design').
2. Assign 1 person accountable for each area.
3. Fill in key activities, how they're measured, and the specific period targets.

Check
- Is there more than 1 person in a seat?
- Are there empty seats?
- Is one person in too many seats?
- Do we have the wrong person in a seat?

Area	Person	2-3 key activities	What are they measured on?	Next period target
Example	John Doe	• New customer sales. • Managing the sales team. • Updating sales best practices.	• Sales £ to target. • Conversion rate %. • Av. lead closing time.	For 2023 • £2.56m • 27.6% • 27 days

Feb23 - © Clarity Strategy Ltd DBA Scale 2023   www.scalecoach.co.uk

management. This can be a very beneficial tool to develop, especially when combined with core values reviews (as described on page 301 in the section on Talent Assessment) so that you can provide the right support for each person in the organisation.

Once again, though, the approach to take with KPI systems is **agile**. Get a simple working version up-and-running as quickly as possible, then work on iterations and improvements, otherwise this is a project that easily ends up in perpetual development hell.

What if I run a department and not the whole company?

The best practices described in here still apply if you are running part of an organisation, not a whole company, such as having one owner accountable for each area, and using metrics to track performance. However, the functional areas of what you manage will be different from those on the list above. For this reason, we have a blank template of the Accountability Scorecard that you can fill in with whichever functions you manage:

Team structure

Summary

Deliberate design of the organisational structure of the business becomes more important as the size, and hence complexity, of the team grows. Teams commonly start by developing a top-down command structure that creates counter-productive outcomes and then needs to be evolved. Much can be learned from modern organisational structures to create a team model that is efficient and responsive.

Concepts

Complexity

In a small team where everyone is sat in the same room, questions about team structure and how things are organised don't matter too much. When you've 200 people in offices around the world, they matter very much. Getting from one to the other is a difficult process which requires decisions and trade-offs along the way.

It's worse than that though. Not only is it more important to be clear as you get bigger, it's also more difficult, because of the effects of complexity.

Think about the number of connections in the network of people as the number of people increases. It's not a 1:1 increase, the number of connections increases more rapidly (specifically, it increases *quadratically*, which is slower than exponentially, but much faster than linearly).

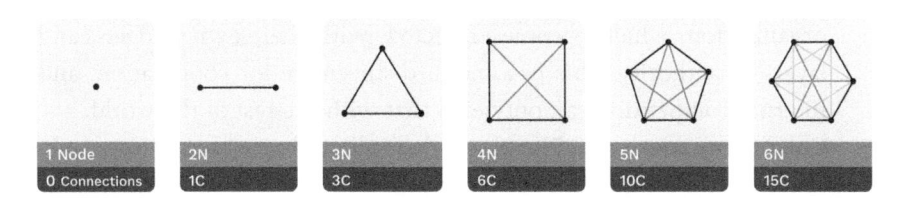

1 Node	2N	3N	4N	5N	6N
0 Connections	1C	3C	6C	10C	15C

The standard answer

The default answer to this problem is to build up what is known as a 'command structure'. The leadership team is accountable for specific functional departments and the buildout of those teams under them. This makes a lot of sense for managing complexity, as it is clear how information and decision-making travel in the organisation – up and down to the respective department heads.

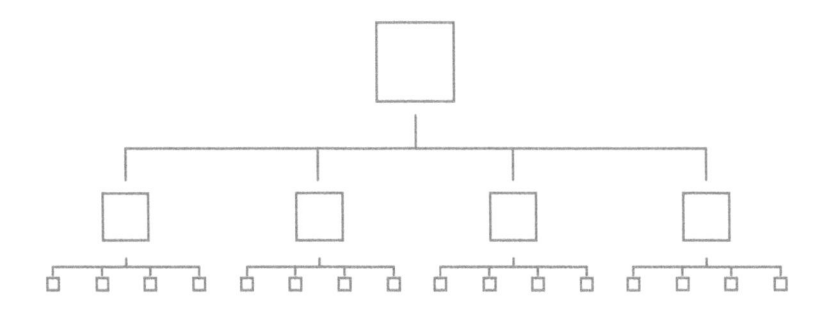

Command
A traditional top-down structure.
The conections that matter are between
workers and their managers

However, this approach has some serious limitations which can end up significantly impeding further growth:

- **Decision-making**. The shape of the structure above indicates how both information flow and decision-making work — they get narrowed to the top. This ends up asking a lot from the people at the top. Ultimately, everything converges at only one point — the CEO. The consequence of this is that each convergence point (i.e. manager) becomes a bottleneck for decision-making.
- **Silos**. Almost inevitably, people build up power structures in such an organisation, which become protected, with their own budgets, and layers of authority. This becomes a disincentive for cooperation, and internal competition can outweigh that with the rest of the world.
- **Customer experience**. The place where these shortcomings ultimately are felt the most is in the customer experience. As consumers, we have all experienced the acute frustration of being passed between different departments, things getting lost in hand-offs, and dealing with people who do not have the authority to make decisions to solve our issues. As long as distinct functional departments exist, these hand-offs are unavoidable.
- **Change**. It becomes difficult to enact change projects in such an organisation structure, because anything that affects the whole customer experience, such as measuring customer satisfaction, or improving response times, has to be managed across multiple teams, increasing complexity, and making innovation more difficult.

How to break free?

The solution to this lies in one simple question: 'Do you remember a time when it all worked easily?' In larger companies, this generally evokes thoughts of a time when there were around 10–20 people and could handle client projects within just one manageable team. It takes you back to a time when you were a **cross-functional team**.

Take the example of Thirdway (www.thirdway.co.uk), a London-based 'design & build' company — they design and build offices across the city (and the country). With a team of around 150 people, they were divided into departments, just like the diagram above. They had departments for, amongst others, sales, design, project management, project delivery, and a whole separate business for furniture. The CEO, Ben, was getting increasingly frustrated at how 'far from the customer' the leadership team felt, and the difficulty of making changes and improvements to the customer experience.

THIRDWAY

So, he broke up the whole organisational structure. He had to let some people go from the leadership team and, thinking back to a time when things had worked well, create a new structure.

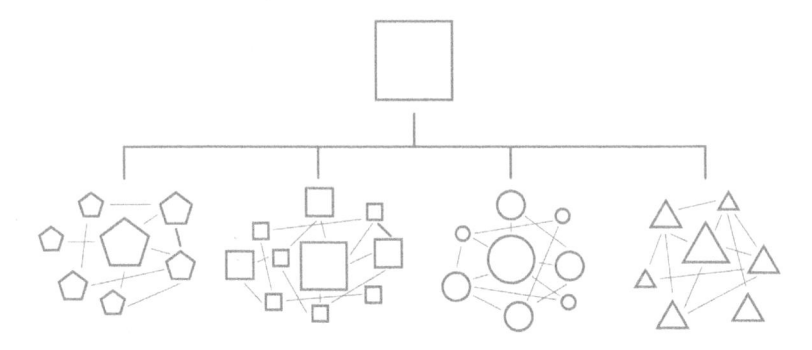

Command of Teams
Small teams operate independently
but still within a more rigid superstructure

They created 'packs'. Each pack is a cross-functional team that has at least one expert from all of the previous departments and are able to autonomously deliver end-to-end customer projects. The benefits this has delivered are astonishing! The business is performing at a higher level now than it ever has before. All the key metrics are up: conversions, closing times, time to site, and margins across the board. They have been able to drive over 30% from their central costs, and the business is more profitable now than it has ever been.

The business also *feels different*. There was a noticeable shift to being closer to the customer when this change occurred, and people seem to really enjoy being in their own packs, being able to see the direct impact on their work to their own customer projects.

What's exciting going forward though, is where the team is taking this next. The new structure has changed how they approach innovation within the company. In the past, projects were large and tortuous, having to work through multiple large departments. Now, it works like this:

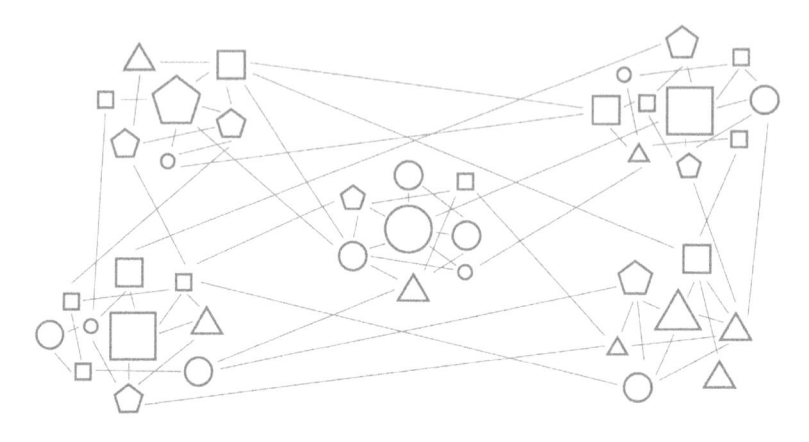

Team of Teams
The relationship amoung teams resembles the closeness among individuals on those teams

Each pack is a crucible for innovation. In any given quarter, they are all working on separate improvements. For example, some are working on new service lines to generate revenue; some are working on process improvements to improve customer service or reduce cycle times; others are experimenting with better ways to collect customer feedback.

When they meet together every month and every quarter, the emphasis is on *experience-sharing between packs*. Good ideas naturally spread; bad ones fall away. All the leadership team needs to do is ensure that a culture of sharing is maintained.

This model is called 'Team of Teams', from the book of the same name by General Stanley McCrystal. He was the General leading the U.S. special forces in the second Iraq war. Despite having better weapons, more soldiers, cutting-edge intelligence gathering, and the full technological prowess of the U.S. military, they were being defeated by the rag-tag terrorists of Al Qaeda in Iraq (AQIR).

The reason was that AQIR had a different **organisational structure**. They operated as decentralised, cross-functional 'cells'. Each cell was autonomous, but they communicated and stayed interconnected. They were nimble and adaptable, and could make decisions on the fly. The U.S. forces, on the other hand, had to coordinate multiple departments, didn't share information well, and it took them time to collate information and assemble unconnected parts of the bureaucracy to work together. So, they were always turning up on the battlefield too late.

His insight was to create nimble, cross-functional teams, and focus all his efforts on seeding relationships, insight, and cooperation between those teams. In effect, he created an eco-system, a network, in which information could spread, and the key factor for success was the speed of cycle times (rather than security of information). The results on the battlefield spoke for themselves, with AQIR leaders one-by-one identified and eliminated, ending up de-fanged and redundant as a fighting force.

CHECKLISTS – DIAGNOSING BOTTLENECKS

Worksheet

Team of Teams

SCALE — Business growth made easy

Name: _____ Company: _____ Date: _____

Draw your current organisation structure (on a separate piece of paper)

What is currently working / not working in your organisational structure?

Working	Not Working

Team of Teams

Command
A traditional top-down structure. The connections that matter are between workers and their managers

Command of Teams
Small teams operate independently but still within a more rigid superstructure

Team of Teams
The relationship among teams resembles the closeness among individuals on those teams

What is an ideal team size in your organisation? Why?	Which teams are/were most effective in your organisation? Why?	Where could there be opportunities to test cross-functional teams?

What actions or changes should you make based on this discussion?

Feb23 · © Clarity Strategy Ltd DBA Scale 2023 | Model taken from 'Team of Teams' by General Stanley McChrystal | www.scalecoach.co.uk

SMC 3 – ACCOUNTABILITY AND TEAM STRUCTURE

If you need a worksheet to draw out your current organisational structure, you can use this one:

Exercise

Session basics	
Name	'Team Structure'
How to Communicate	'Let's create a team structure that allows us to re...'
Time	60–90 minutes. Given the scope of potential changes, this is a process that can take multiple quarters to plan and deliver
Format	Workshop, with worksheet. The initial workshop tends to be the start of a discussion and dialogue process, subsequently required multiple follow-ups and planning sessions
Attendees	Leadership/management team

Preparation	
Objective and outcome	Figure out where the business might benefit from cross-functional teams, to improve cooperation, autonomy, and customer service
Learning and reading	This is a topic where pre-reading and knowledge around the topic is highly beneficial, or bringing in an expert with knowledge and experience of *Team of Teams*, by Stanley McCrystal, *Reinventing Organisations*, by Frederic Laloux
Materials	Use the worksheet as a guide to the meeting

Exercise	
Objective	Review and agree on the objective and agenda of the session
Working/not working	Ask each person to reflect and fill out on what is currently working/not working with the organisation's current structure. Share ideas as a team, and agree on the top 3 of each
Team of Teams model	Review and share knowledge and experiences of the Team of Teams model
Ideal team size, effective teams, and cross-functional teams	Have each person consider and record their own answers, then share answers and discuss, on each of the three questions posed. Based on these questions, discuss and decide which areas of the business would benefit from such a transition of team structure
Action list	Agree follow-up actions to test or transition to new team structures or cross-functional teams

10

SMC 4 – WE'RE TOO BUSY!

Checklist item

Issue

- **'Busy-ness**. Everyone is too busy, caught up with low-value tasks'.

Manifestation

- We don't have enough time to focus on key projects
- Team is overworked and stressed out

Summary

Let's start with the bad news. You are wasting time. So are your team. Lots of time. The good news is that it can be fixed. Here we introduce a simple, easy-to-understand exercise that often brings >100× ROI on the time spent on it. It allows you to work out where each team member needs to focus their time and reduce or eliminate time spent on other things.

Key concepts

Why are you overworked?

Working in a high-growth company always brings a certain level of stress and hard work; however, 'Busy-ness' can become such an issue that the team is no longer able to focus on key change projects, effectively stalling the company's ability to scale. Ironically, this can often happen during or after periods of particularly high growth.

'Busy-ness' can get out of hand and tip over into serious over-work and burn out, which can then self-compound if it causes people to leave. So, it's vital to deal with the causes of over-work.

'Busy-ness' is a factor of two components:

- **Productivity**. How efficiently time is being used.
- **Capacity**. The number of people/working hours available.

$$\text{Capacity} \times \text{productivity} = \text{output}$$

If output does not meet the requirements of the business, then you have a problem, and it can be hard to diagnose whether to resolve it by recruiting or focusing on productivity improvements. An overworked team will typically clamour for more recruitment, and it is often necessary. However, digging into root causes often shows that a lot of 'busy-ness' comes from unproductive use of time, such as unnecessary or poorly run meetings (see Chapter 8 SMC 2 – Meeting Effectiveness), inefficient or outdated systems and processes (see Chapter 16 SMC 10 – Systems & Processes), or waste due to a lack of accountability or team structure (see Chapter 9 SMC 3 – Accountability & Team Structure).

In this chapter, we introduce a tool that will uncover poor use of time, and make people think about what activities they are actually spending their time on. The exercise – called 'Sweetspot' – allows team members to free up huge amounts of the time, and focus on what they're best at, making them up to 100× more productive.

The second reason for overwork – lack of capacity – can be diagnosed through reviewing labour cost ratios. In the exercise 'Power of One' page 258, you can work out your labour ratio, and compare it over time, to find the right ratio for the business.

Sweetspot

This is Gika, Marketing Manager at Cambridge Mask Co (https://cambridgemask.com), one of the world's top mask brands for filtering out pollution and pathogens. '3,727' is the number of hours she and her team identified as savings for their team of 18 people, per month, based on doing a Sweetspot workshop. That's >200 hours per person per month, not bad for a workshop they organised themselves, and took them 1.45 hours to complete. That's a ROI of >100× per person, an outcome we commonly see with Sweetspot workshops.

How does it work? Sweetspot is a simple concept at heart, based on this model:

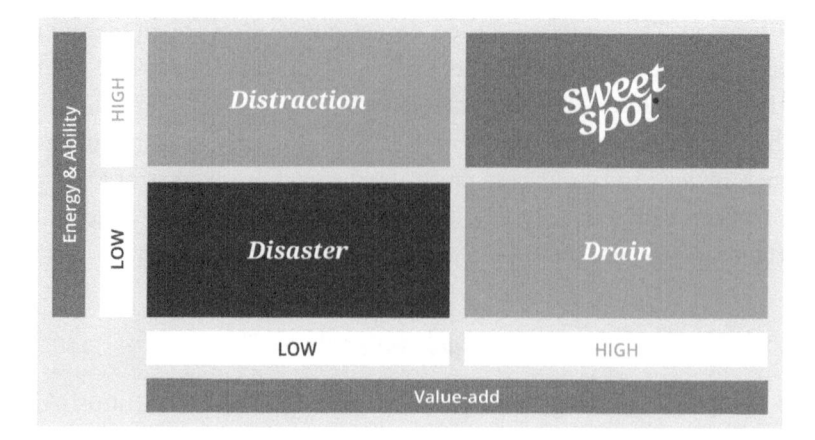

		Value-add	
Energy & Ability	HIGH	Distraction (LOW)	sweet spot (HIGH)
	LOW	Disaster (LOW)	Drain (HIGH)

Think about how you're spending your time, what activities you're actually spending it on, and consider those activities across two axes:

- **Value**. Is it relatively high or low value add to your life, career, or business?
- **Energy and ability**. Is it something you're good at and enjoy, or are weak at and dislike?

This way you can put all of your activities into four categories – Sweetspot, and the '3Ds':

- **Sweetspot**. Things you love doing, are good at, and add real value. The more time you can spend in your Sweetspot, the better results you will get, the more you will achieve enjoyment and fulfilment. *My example*: I'm a patterns-spotter. I love to pull together experiences and learnings into models and concepts, so my Sweetspot includes time spent writing, sharing and training our concepts, tools, and ideas.
- **Distraction**. Things that you are good at, and maybe still enjoy doing, but have outlived their value and usefulness. *My example*: I enjoy and am good at spreadsheets. I get a secret pleasure from putting together our monthly finance reports. It's not a good use of my time though, and I should delegate it.

- **Drain**. Important things that must get done, but don't fit with your skillset, so are either not getting done well or causing you disproportionate effort and energy to complete. *My example*: I strongly dislike networking and going out to meet new people, but it's important for what we do. If this work is left to me, our marketing and lead generation suffer, so I always have to have people to help me with this work.
- **Disaster**. You hate doing it, and it adds low value.
  My example. I've been pretty good at getting rid of disasters. Sometimes, if we have a changeover of members of the team, I end up doing things like materials management (sending out books and swag), which frustrates me and is a really bad use of my time.

How can you spend more time in your Sweetspot? The answer is to reduce and eliminate time spent on the 3Ds. How to do that? Use the simple SODA model:

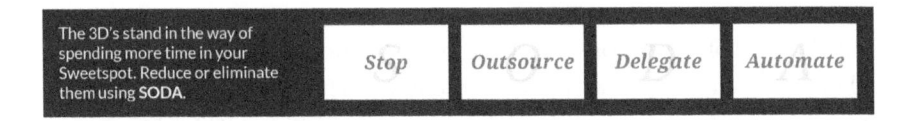

The 3D's stand in the way of spending more time in your Sweetspot. Reduce or eliminate them using **SODA**.	*Stop*	*Outsource*	*Delegate*	*Automate*

There are four ways to eliminate time spent in your 3Ds:

- **Stop**. Many activities in life can just be stopped. It's often about good boundary-setting and finding effective ways of saying 'No'. It's easy to over-commit and may require an awkward conversation to go back.

Example: A highly successful entrepreneur, also a celebrity in his field, was often being asked to 'just have a coffee and meet with' all sorts of followers from his community. After doing the Sweetspot exercise, he saved 1 week per month by working with his assistant to clear all these invites from his diary, and instead offer monthly clinics where people could come and meet him together.

- **Outsource**. There are so many activities that can be handed over to people and providers outside of the organisation.

Example. An entrepreneur in Switzerland who, after doing the Sweetspot exercise, sold his car and decided to outsource the job of driving to others. He now takes taxis, Ubers, and trains only and uses that time to get work done.

- **Delegate**. The time ROI of delegation is crazy. However, it takes some time investment at the outset, and this is what often gets people stuck. It takes effort (and trust) to identify the right person, get agreement from them, and teach them the task.

Example. The head of operations of a mid-size U.K. industrial company, one of the highest paid people on the team, blurted out half-way through the exercise 'I still buy the milk for the office!'

- **Automate**. There are so many repetitive tasks that can now be handled by software. With a small investment in time to set these up, huge rewards can be reaped.

Example. Head of Operations for a major U.K. Membership organisation spent 5 hours to set up Zapier to automate the movement of candidate references from one application to another, and now saves his team 500 mins – more than a full working day – every week.

Sweetspot and motivation

What is the #1 way to motivate people? Initiatives such as giving people autonomy, inspiring them to a great vision, or providing a culture that fits their values will all make big contributions. However, according to great business author Jim Collins, the #1 way to motivate people is actually to *remove the things that de-motivate them.*

This sits at the heart of Sweetspot. One way to think about productivity is like a closet, or a garage. When you move into a new house, it starts out empty, or at least tidy and organised. Then, after a few months, no matter how carefully you have tried to manage it, it always ends up cluttered. So, you have to maintain a rhythm of, once every few months, applying energy to tidying it out.

Work is just the same. It comes down to a universal law called **entropy**. Left to their own devices, systems naturally tend towards randomness and disorder. *Order requires the application of energy;* it does not happen by itself. Ordered systems operate more efficiently, therefore regular bursts of energy are required in order to be constantly maintaining and improving efficiency. In this case, it means regularly repeating the Sweetspot exercise, in order to continually maintain your focus and productivity.

This concept is beautifully brought to life by Stephen Covey in this story from 'The 7 Habits of Highly Effective People':

> Imagine you are going for a walk in the forest when you come upon a man sawing down a tree.
> "What are you doing?" you ask. "I'm sawing down a tree," he says.
> "How long have you been at it?" You ask.
> "Two or three hours so far," he says, sweat dripping from his chin.
> "Your saw looks dull," you say. "Why don't you take a break and sharpen it?"
> "I can't. I'm too busy sawing," is his reply.

A habit, not an exercise

Teams have found that the best rhythm for doing the Sweetspot exercise is once every 3 months. Some of the teams we work with actually include Sweetspot as part of their staff annual review.

What happens, if you maintain the routine in this way, is that it fundamentally changes how people think about their time and the activities with which they fill them. Imbued with a Sweetspot mindset, teams are less likely to take on non-Sweetspot activities in the first place. They become more proactive about ensuring that they, and everyone in their team, is only taking on activities that sit in their Sweetspot.

Exercise → **Habit** → *Mindset*

Worksheets

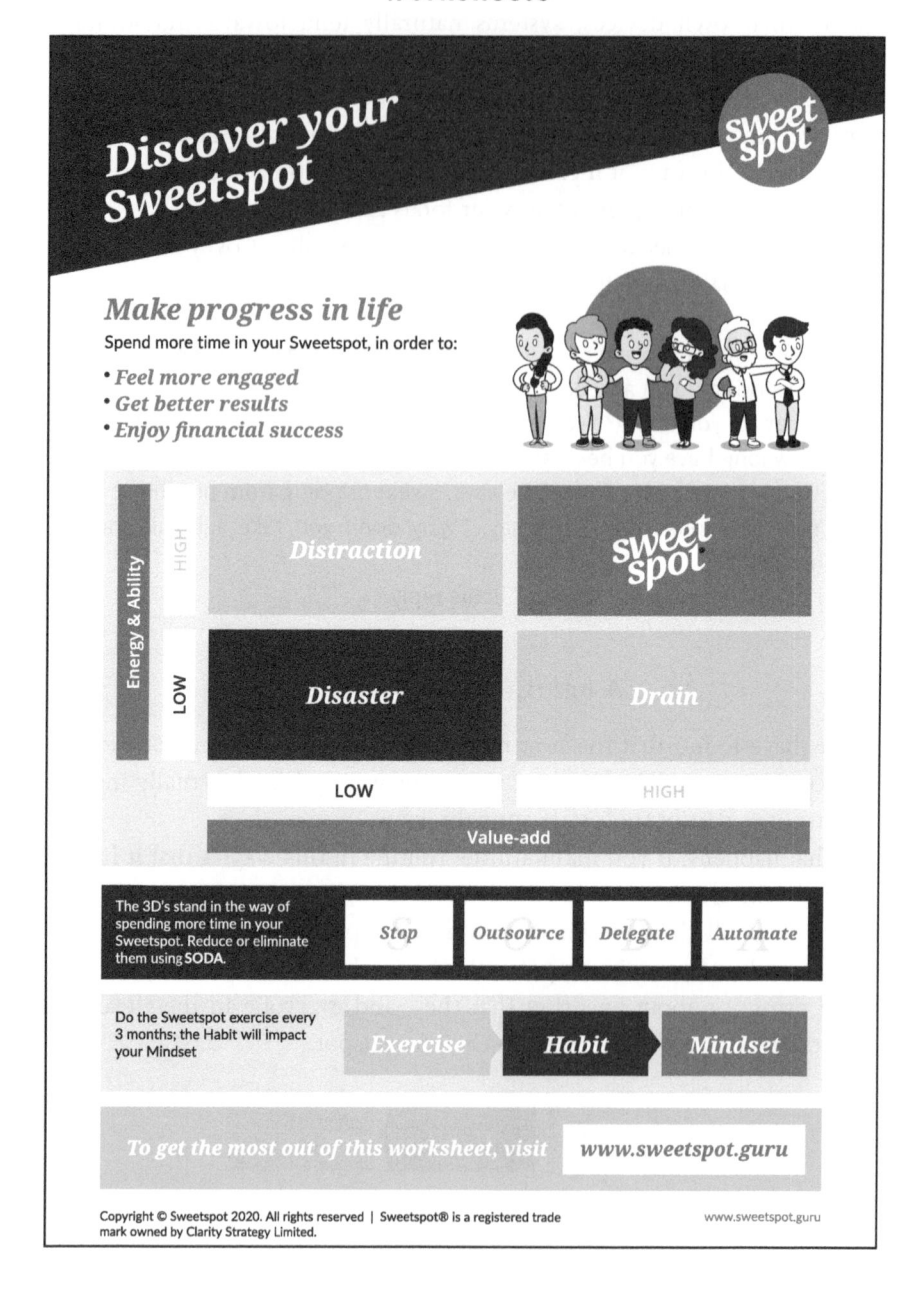

Discover your Sweetspot

Make progress in life

Spend more time in your Sweetspot, in order to:

- Feel more engaged
- Get better results
- Enjoy financial success

	Value-add LOW	Value-add HIGH
Energy & Ability HIGH	Distraction	sweet spot
Energy & Ability LOW	Disaster	Drain

The 3D's stand in the way of spending more time in your Sweetspot. Reduce or eliminate them using **SODA**.

Stop | Outsource | Delegate | Automate

Do the Sweetspot exercise every 3 months; the Habit will impact your Mindset

Exercise → Habit → Mindset

To get the most out of this worksheet, visit www.sweetspot.guru

Copyright © Sweetspot 2020. All rights reserved | Sweetspot® is a registered trade mark owned by Clarity Strategy Limited.

www.sweetspot.guru

Discover your Sweetspot

Brainstorm and make notes

- Distraction
- Sweetspot
- Drain
- Disaster

Select the most important answers from your notes

1. Identify your sweetspot

My Sweetspot abilities & activities:

2. Eliminate or reduce 3D activities

3D Activities to Reduce or Eliminate:	Specific Actions to accomplish that:	Time saved

3. Take action towards your Sweetspot

Actions:

Copyright © Sweetspot 2020. All rights reserved | Sweetspot® is a registered trade mark owned by Clarity Strategy Limited.

www.sweetspot.guru

Exercise

Session basics	
Name	'Sweetspot'
How to Communicate	'For us to enjoy our work, get great results, and not waste time, it's important to get rid of low value or low ability tasks. We're going to get together to understand what's in each other's Sweetspot, and what we can do to eliminate activities that are getting in the way of spending more time there'
Time	90 minutes
Format	Workshop session
Attendees	Best done in teams that work together including the leader/line manager of that team

Preparation	
Objective and outcome	Each person identifies specific changes they can make to identify time savings, so they can spend that time in their Sweetspot
Learning and reading	*Sweetspot*, by Andy Clayton. Go to www.sweetspot.guru
Materials	Printed worksheets and pens

Exercise	
Objective	Share and discuss the objective of the session, be specific that we're looking to identify the actions people will take for change, and the hours of time saving they can achieve
Key concept 1	Review the Sweetspot model. Discuss what is meant by 'Value' and 'Energy & Ability' and take examples of Sweetspots and 3Ds from the team
Worksheet exercise 1	Each participant writes their Sweetspot. Either share in pairs first, or directly with the rest of the team
Worksheet exercise 2	Each participant fills out the 3D activities they're spending the most time on. Go through recent calendars, email inbox, and to-do lists to find data for where time is being spent
Key concept 2	Discuss the SODA model, and take examples for each of the 4 elements of SODA

Complete exercise 2	Individually, then in pairs, brainstorm ideas for how to reduce and eliminate time spent on 3D activities, using the SODA model. Fill out anticipated time saving for each one
Presentation and 'Sweetswaps'	Each member of the team presents their 3Ds and how they will reduce/eliminate time spent, and how much time they will save. Encourage solution brainstorming for items where team members face common challenges and solutions. Tasks may be swapped between team members ('Sweetswaps' – 'I'll take this from you, you take this from me')
Worksheet exercise 3	Each participant fills out and shares the actions they will take, once they've achieved their time saving to actually spend the saved time in their Sweetspot
Next steps	Agree on key actions, and a rhythm for check-ins or coaching calls/meetings, to keep everyone on track with the changes they've planned

Guide, Pitfalls, and FAQs

Will anyone want to take away my 3Ds?

I love how Sweetspot coach Antony Enright deals with this question. He stops the workshop and asks, 'Who here likes doing the ironing?' There is always at least one person who puts their hand up (to the astonishment of others). The question can be asked for ironing, filling out spreadsheets, doing admin, or even filling out your taxes. Different strokes for different folks.

This is the most important mindset shift – realising that your 3Ds are other people's Sweetspots. This is how teams (and societies) work – people have different skills and interests that complement each other. For all the tasks that get you down, there are other people that would love to pick them up.

Does my Sweetspot change over time?

Absolutely; it can. The Sweetspot exercise was devised in my former China business, for a team member called Tianna. The company was still small, and she found herself wearing many hats, including finance, HR, and supply chain. She was struggling as she was operating in areas outside her Sweetspot. Once she did the exercise, we made a plan to allow her to focus only on her Sweetspot (which was finance). It took 2 years of recruitment, delegation, and outsourcing (which required growth in the business to achieve), until it was achieved, and she was just operating in her Sweetspot. At that point, we did the Sweetspot exercise again, and we found that within Finance, there were now sub-divisions of work that sat within and outside of her Sweetspot. So, a second round of focus began.

This story shows that your Sweetspot can evolve over time. You may gain interest in new areas, get deeper into topics, or discover skills to develop.

Should I share my Sweetspot with my team?

100%, yes. Leaders often feel a need to be 'in the trenches taking grenades' with their team which means getting involved in the work the team is doing, to avoid a sense of privilege in the team. For example, one CEO I work with feels like he's 'not being fair to the team' if he doesn't personally get involved with client work.

The fact is that the team wants you operating in your Sweetspot. You probably bring something amazing to the business. Maybe you lead research, or make inspirational speeches, or have an incredible network. Whatever it is, everyone wants you doing more of it, and they want to be left alone to do what they do best.

How often should I do the Sweetspot exercise?

Once every 3 months. It's like a cupboard (or a garage) when you move house, it's clean and tidy. Yet, no matter what you do, 3 months later it's somehow gotten messy. And so it is with how we spend our time; we let clutter accumulate, and that needs to be cleaned out.

Should I include only work activities or personal too?

This is a common question, and the answer really is that it depends. Most teams that are working together professionally prefer to focus on work activities. However, the boundary between the two is often blurred. For example, time spent commuting is lost and wasted either way. Is it personal or work time? The distinction is often not clear. For people working at home, it's even harder to distinguish. So, personal and work productivity often overlap.

When doing the exercise with entrepreneurs, I almost always suggest to include both, because I see a high degree of interoperability between 'work' and 'personal' time for entrepreneurs, in that savings in one affects the other.

How to make it stick?

It's easy to identify changes for better use of your time at a workshop. The challenge comes in actually executing those changes, and this is where the follow-up to a Sweetspot workshop is crucial. Never end a Sweetspot workshop without agreeing and getting in the diary a rhythm of follow-up sessions in order to review progress, hold one another to account, and brainstorm/solve the inevitable problems you will have on the way with execution.

Follow-up sessions do not need to be with line managers; team-mates can support one another and hold each other accountable. In fact, the best relationships for such follow-ups are to do them with a coach. Anyone in the team can be a good coach (read the next section to find out how to do this effectively), or you can lean on external coaching resource to help the team with this.

11

SMC 5 – EXECUTING STRATEGY – QUARTERLY PLANNING

Checklist item

Issue

Executing Strategy. We're not delivering on our agreed strategic plans.

Manifestation

- Our strategic plans are gathering dust on the shelf
- Not seeing plans through to actual change

Summary

The only thing worse than not having a strategy is spending time developing one that's then not used. Creating strategies is the easy bit, the true measure of success comes from the discipline to execute them. The good news is that it's not onerous; it just requires the establishment of certain rhythms.

Let's make sure that none of your carefully crafted strategic plans end up gathering dust on a shelf.

Key concepts – the 'QPD' (Quarterly Planning Day)

ANZ UK is a worldwide placement company for teachers, started in 2004, with offices in the United Kingdom, Australia, New Zealand, Canada, and the United States. They find capable teachers from around the world and place them in schools where they're needed.

anzuk.education

They have a great method for ensuring that their strategy gets delivered across the business and delivers actual change. They start by thinking about their three circles – Run it, Improve it, Transform it.

```
   Day to day              Deal with              Create and
   operation              bottlenecks           deliver growth
                          to growth                strategy

    RUN IT                IMPROVE IT            TRANSFORM IT
```

They know that most people on most days are working on Run it and Improve it activities, which is as it should be. But several times a year, they focus on 'Transform it' – key projects that will deliver their Strategic Plan and ensure long-term growth. To do this, they pull together their 'Transform Team', a small group of people who are in a position to work on the thinking and planning of key projects over the next quarter.

This habit introduces a rhythm into their year, breaking it up into a series of 'sprints'. ANZUK do 3 × 4-month sprints, to align with the annual termly calendar, but most teams we work with do it on a quarterly basis, so 4 × 3-month sprints a year.

This habit fits into a structure they maintain through each planning period:

- **Planning day**. At least one full day, offsite, including a set agenda and preparation work, to set key Sprint Projects for the period.
- Regular **check-ins** throughout the period, typically on a weekly basis, to review progress and unblock stucks on the Sprint Projects.
- **Recording and tracking**, using effective software to plan and record progress.

If you establish those practices now, I promise you that within months you will start to see your strategy flourish around you.

Let me show you how it works.

What is a QPD? And why are they important?

Once you've defined a strategy for the business, it's time for 'the rubber to hit the road', and to turn this vision into specific clear projects that can be executed.

In many organisations, strategic plans get recorded into a document somewhere, and the following day business as usual takes over again. We are always astonished at the number of organisations with whom we work where leadership teams pull out old versions of strategies that have simply never been implemented.

The answer to this is regular Quarterly Planning Days ('QPDs'). QPDs resolve this problem by bringing the team together to review both the Strategic Plan of the business, as well as the current situation that the business faces, and turns them into detailed, actionable change projects.

Lean (or scrum) theory introduces two key concepts:

- **Minimum Viable Product (MVP)**. Rather than plan for an outcome that include every feature and benefit you are looking for, plan to launch a working version with the minimum outcome required to start.
- **Sprints**. Break down the development of the MVP into short, plannable bursts of work, called 'Sprints', and have regular progress reviews and check-ins along the way.

When to do QPDs?

The best time for your first QPD is on the day immediately after your Kick-Off – your day of strategic planning (see Chapter 4 for more on using a Kick-Off to develop a Strategic Plan) – strike while the iron is hot. This will maintain and capture all the energy from your strategic planning and allow you to turn ideas into plans while they are still fresh on your mind. Plan to repeat the QPD process every quarter after that (in fact, it's best to get those dates in the diary at your first session – always have QPDs in the diary 9–12 months in advance).

A quarter is an important period of time because it is long enough to achieve significant milestones to drive changes, and short enough to be able to accurately plan for specific outcomes, that is, it's perfect for sprints. If a team sets three to four Sprint projects for a quarter, it is reasonable to expect that most of them will be completed as envisioned (but rarely all of them, if you find that regularly happening, you're probably not being ambitious enough). A Quarter is a 13-week sprint.

Why a quarter?

Three months is long enough to achieve significant milestones and short enough to meaningfully plan.

However, if you are in a period of high growth or want to accelerate faster, consider shorter bursts – 2, or even 1, month per planning day.

The actual timing of QPDs is an important detail to get right. Here are a few tips:

- **Book the full year.** Get all four dates in the diary now. Avoid using each QPD to organise timing for the next one.
- **Anticipate periods to avoid.** What does a typical year for the business look like? Is there a key event that keeps everyone busy at a certain time, like a big industry conference? Are you seasonal, for example a big Christmas rush? Do people take the summer off? Schedule accordingly.
- **Financial year vs. calendar year.** It's important to have good financial data at QPDs, so it can be helpful to time sessions shortly after numbers come in.

Where to have QPDs?

As with KOs, the best location is offsite. This may be in a rented office or meeting room, or maybe somewhere large and comfortable enough at home.

Workshops virtual vs. in-person

A very real issue these days for Kick-Off and QPD meetings is whether to hold them in the real or virtual world. Running sessions entirely virtually is viable, but in-person is preferable. Virtual sessions require a virtual white-board (we use www.miro.com), to replicate what you might use the walls and post-its or flipcharts for in an in-person setting.

Who should attend QPDs?

By and large, a QPD is a game of two halves, a more strategic 'thinking' first half, where decisions are made on what to focus, and a more practical 'execution' second half, where Projects are planned out in more detail.

Smaller teams tend to have the same leadership team present for both parts. As companies get larger though, they often start to include more people in the second half, for two reasons:

- Starts the process of communicating key projects, and their reasons for being chosen, across the wider team
- Includes individuals key to the execution of those projects into the planning process

Partly for this reason, some teams prefer to divide these two halves into two separate half-day sessions, especially planning sessions that are done virtually, so as to minimise impact on day-to-day work.

Cascading QPDs

Once teams get beyond about 50 people, covering the whole organisation with one QPD starts to become more difficult, because the organisation has started to break into more groups or tiers than can be effectively covered by one management team.

In this situation, it becomes necessary to start cascade planning. This means arranging parallel planning processes where the Leadership team and teams across the business have to set and communicate their areas of focus for the upcoming period with each other.

QPD agenda

Key concepts

What to cover in a QPD? The first thing to be clear on is the key outcome from any QPD, which must be: detailed plans for a few (no more than five) key **Sprint Projects** for the upcoming quarter. Whatever else you choose to use the time for, this outcome is non-negotiable.

So how do you get there?

Driving growth in the business requires pulling off the trick of dealing with current or upcoming bottlenecks, and delivering on a strategy for growth (all whilst ensuring day-to-day operations carry on smoothly). So, your Sprint Projects must be informed by both the Tactical (dealing with bottlenecks) and the Strategic (driving your Strategic Plan forward). We use two key tools to achieve this:

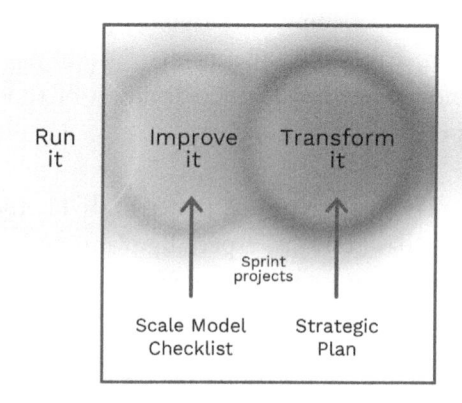

```
   Run      Improve      Transform
   it          it            it
                ↑            ↑
                    Sprint
                   projects

            Scale Model     Strategic
            Checklist         Plan
```

- The Scale Model Checklist. Every QPD, run the Scale Model Checklist process, in order to identify which part of the business requires improvement in the upcoming quarter.
- Review the Strategic Plan (Chapter 4 – Scale Strategic Plan), to decide what steps to take next in its realisation.

The process of planning itself breaks down into four parts:

Four stages of planning

The process of planning can be divided into four stages:

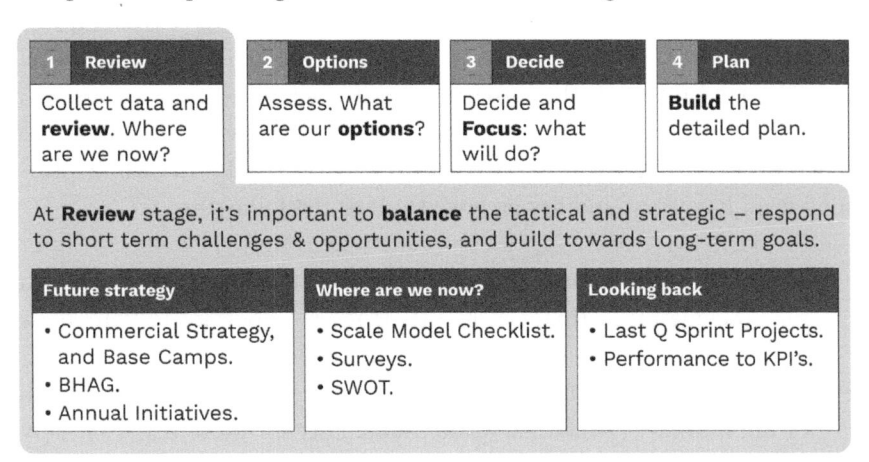

1 Review	2 Options	3 Decide	4 Plan
Collect data and **review**. Where are we now?	Assess. What are our **options**?	Decide and **Focus**: what will do?	**Build** the detailed plan.

At **Review** stage, it's important to **balance** the tactical and strategic – respond to short term challenges & opportunities, and build towards long-term goals.

Future strategy	Where are we now?	Looking back
• Commercial Strategy, and Base Camps. • BHAG. • Annual Initiatives.	• Scale Model Checklist. • Surveys. • SWOT.	• Last Q Sprint Projects. • Performance to KPI's.

1. **Review**. Get everyone on the same page about your situation. Sharing data and perspectives on how you're doing. At each stage, draw up ideas for areas to focus on in the quarter.
2. **Options**. Pull those ideas together into a few options for review, and define those options clearly.
3. **Decide**. The essential step. To which of those options will you apply focus and resource?
4. **Plan**. Build out detailed execution plans for the chosen options, and get those plans recorded in task management software.

Scale has a full QPD workbook which we use for all of our Quarterly Planning sessions. It has been refined and improved over the years and thousands of planning sessions. You are welcome to download the QPD workbook from the Scale website here: https://scalecoach.co.uk/worksheets/, in printable version for in-person sessions, or PDF version if you're meeting remotely. Many of the key pages from the workbook are contained in this section.

Now let's run through a practical breakdown of how to organise a QPD.

The QPD process

Data sharing

Preparation for a QPD starts well in advance of the QPD itself. 'Intelligent people, presented with the same data, will reach the same conclusions'. Make life easy for yourself. If everyone sees the same issues, it makes it so much easier to diagnose and fix what's wrong. Make sure the whole planning team has access and has reviewed at least the following:

- **Financial performance**. Typically, P&L and cashflow analysis, though may include other financial reports that are important to your business, such as balance sheet or debtor/creditor reports.
- **KPIs/Scorecard**. Whatever dashboard you use to measure the health of the business (go to chapter Accountability for more detail on how to create this).
- **Customer and staff feedback**. Ensure that reporting of these data matches the quarterly planning cycle, so that they can be prepared for review.
- **Targets**. Ensure everyone is clear on what the targets or budgets for the business for the period are.

Homework

Ouch, a nasty word. You will have much better use of time of the day if you invest a little time in advance to collect thoughts and ideas. Key ones include:

- **The Scale Model Checklist**. Have the team think about and write their top 3 in advance of the QPD (you will find a form here to fill out to create a unique survey for your team).
- **Planning survey**. Have the team think about the state of the business, and where they think focus needs to be applied (you can find the questions here: planning survey).
- **SWOT analysis**. Particularly if you are planning for a more strategic session, such as Annual Planning, have the team think about the state of the business and the market (there is a chapter on this here: Annual Initiatives).

Preparing tools

Based on the outcome of your Scale Model Checklist scores, navigate to the relevant chapter (they're listed in order here: Checklist Chapters, page 35). For example, if the team has chosen 'Busy-ness' as its top item to resolve, then read SMC 4 – We're too busy! about the Sweetspot exercise. Think about how you would go about resolving the issue, using that tool, during the quarter. Expect to have to present to the team at the planning day an outline plan built around the relevant tool. Also, print copies of the printed QPD workbook for participants (see the download link on page 201).

Pre-call

Once the data sharing and homework are complete, in the week prior to QPD, have a 20–30-minute pre-call to review:

- **Agenda**. Review and agree the agenda for the day.
- **Logistics**. Is everyone clear on where and when? Who is dealing with practicalities such as AV, food, and preparation of materials, such as printed worksheets, post-It notes, and stationary?

On the day

Set the scene

Start the day positively. Set yourself up for success by following these steps:

- **CEO intro**. Start with a few words from the CEO, a short 'state of the nation', outlining their view on the company's situation, feel of the team, and the opportunities and challenges.
- **Ground rules and agenda**. See 'Ground rules' section below.
- **Ice-breaker**. Get the team sharing with each other, or working on something fun and energising. We have a list at the link here you are welcome to dip into.

Ground rules

QPDs are highly valuable time. At one level, taking the whole leadership team away from front line work is a considerable investment. More importantly though, there is the opportunity to use this time to achieve great things. This cannot be wasted through sloppy discipline and poor use of time. It's important to establish ground rules for the sessions, so everyone is operating from the same expectations. These are the ones that we use:

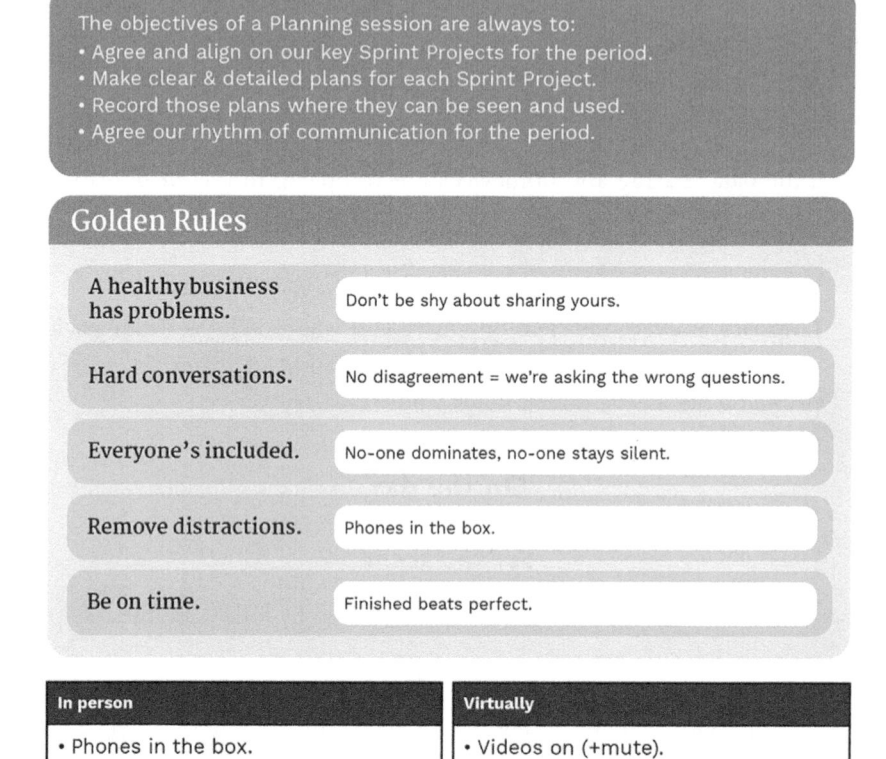

> The objectives of a Planning session are always to:
> - Agree and align on our key Sprint Projects for the period.
> - Make clear & detailed plans for each Sprint Project.
> - Record those plans where they can be seen and used.
> - Agree our rhythm of communication for the period.

Golden Rules

A healthy business has problems.	Don't be shy about sharing yours.
Hard conversations.	No disagreement = we're asking the wrong questions.
Everyone's included.	No-one dominates, no-one stays silent.
Remove distractions.	Phones in the box.
Be on time.	Finished beats perfect.

In person	Virtually
• Phones in the box. • Back from breaks on-time. • Pre-book meals.	• Videos on (+mute). • Distractions off. • Understand how breakout functions work.

Feel free to use these, or develop your own. Pay special notice to 'phones in the box' item. To be clear, this means requiring everyone to put their mobile phone in a box or basket which is put to one side, only to be retrieved during breaks (or better still, at the end of the day).

This may feel drastic. Bear in mind the effect that phones have on us. Numerous studies in education and work environments have shown that access to mobile phones reduces performance, such as test scores. One study at schools in Germany found that even the presence of phones in students' bags had a significant impact on performance, simply because their presence occupies mind-space. Students are sitting there anticipating what they will see on their phones.

Our experience has always been that people have thanked us for removing this distraction, so that they can get the most out of their time and achieve quality focus on big questions and decisions.

Review

Follow these exercises in order to build out ideas and options for priorities for the quarter. As the team works through each one, have them write out their answers and ideas to each of the questions (NB: the Scale QPD workbook is an excellent tool to use)

- Review progress on last **Quarter Sprint Projects**. This is both a key point of accountability (people will get projects complete if they know they will be required to present progress to the team), and a source of potential priorities for the next Quarter, as there may be significant unfinished business that still requires focus. *Key Question: 'Based on last Q Projects, is there significant unfinished business that requires focus in the next Q?'*
- Review **The Scale Model Checklist** scores. The teams' scores generally cluster around a few key points. Discuss, based on the scores and, which issue you want to resolve in the upcoming quarter. *Key Question: 'Based on the SMC, what's one thing we should focus on in the next Q?'*
- Survey answers. If you've run a team survey in advance, then review and discuss the team's answers. *Key Question: 'Based on our survey answers, what's one thing we need to focus on in the next Q?'*

Strategic Plan review, include the following parts:

- **Core**: For each of the Core Values, Purpose, and Vision, go through the exercise of scoring how you think the company is doing and where the

opportunities for improvement are. *Key Question: 'What's one thing we need to focus on to improve the delivery of our Core Foundation this Quarter?'*
- **Commercial Strategy.** Review your USPs and X-Factor essential question. *Key Question: 'Based on our USPs and X-Factor essential question, what's one thing we need to focus on this Quarter?'*
- **Base Camps.** Review your 3–5 year Clear Picture, and Annual Initiatives. *Key Question: 'Based on our Base Camps, what's one thing we need to focus on this Quarter?'*

Options

By this point, each person has built up a list of ideas for Sprint Projects for the period. The focus now is for each person to decide on their final shortlist to share.

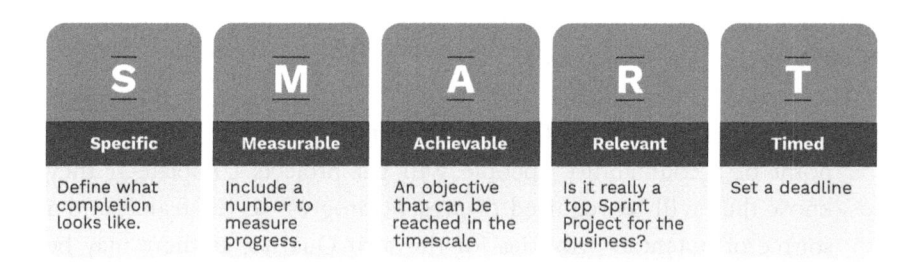

S	M	A	R	T
Specific	**Measurable**	**Achievable**	**Relevant**	**Timed**
Define what completion looks like.	Include a number to measure progress.	An objective that can be reached in the timescale	Is it really a top Sprint Project for the business?	Set a deadline

It's important at this stage that ideas are prepared in the form of objectives that must meet the SMART criteria. This starts by stating them in the format of 'end state' or 'what does completion look like?' Thinking of the structure of the sentence can be helpful with this.

VERB	Recruit & Hire	Launch
# / 100%	2	(100%)
Subject	Sales Reps	iOS Version 2.0
Deadline	by June 30	by June 30
Owner	Jane (HRD)	Bob (CTO)

It can be helpful to have people work in pairs or teams to coach one another on setting these clear objectives. One thing to avoid is what we call 'weak words', common verbs and adjectives that generally do not convey clearly enough a specific objective. Help each other to weed these out.

Refine

Weak words

These often-used words are not specific enough, and make it hard to know if we've hit our objective or not at the end of the period:

• Assist	• Faster	• Improve	• Regular
• Better	• Focus	• Increase	• Streamline
• Consistent	• Help	• More	• Strengthen
• Continue	• Implement	• Optimise	• Try

Less obvious weak words can be common terms like 'hire'. Does 'hire' mean 'offer accepted', or 'candidate onboard', or what?

Courtesy of Petra Coach, USA

It can also be helpful to have specific coaching questions to challenge one another on how well-defined their Sprint Project objectives and ideas are.

Coach

Work with a coaching partner to define your sprint projects well.
Ask coaching q's:

Coaching questions
"How will you measure success? What does success / completion look like?"
"Can you actually get that done, given the time and resources?"
"What are the risks and costs? Consider especially time / hours required."
"Define the scope. What's in / out in terms of deliverables?"
"Does this really have to be done now?"

When choosing their top 3, members of the team have numerous reference points from which to pull their ideas together.

Review your notes from:	
Scale Model Checklist	Next Q critical #'s
Core Foundation	SWOT
Core Values	Surveys
Unique Selling Promises	Last period Sprint Projects
3-5 Year	Last period critical #'s
Annual Initiatives	Parking lot and other notes

Decide

Now comes the key stage, you need force focus, by deciding which of these options you will actually execute.

Once each person has filled out their top 3, have them transcribe them to three separate Post-It notes. You will now start a heat-mapping process in order to see where within the team there is high alignment around priorities for the period.

Have the first person place their first Post-It note on the wall, and invite anyone who has stated a similar point to stick them underneath.

Once the heatmap is complete, the team needs to have a means to decide which of the potential options to choose as Sprint Projects for the quarter. At this stage, it is helpful to review the key outcomes and deliverables of each of the options, and to take a pulse check from the team. Assign one owner to each of the Sprint Projects: this is a vital step. Then, decide. If the answer is clear and obvious, then go for it. If not, then ultimately it is for the Chief Executive to decide what's in and what's not. The key to success is focus: it's as much about deciding what to leave for another day as it is of what you will do.

POST-IT PARADISE

Many of the exercises in this book recommend using 'Post-it' notes. They are a valuable tool for collaboration and brainstorming within a team. Make sure you get large ones (76x127 mm), and follow these guidelines:

- Always write using a Sharpie or marker, not a biro (otherwise it's not visible).
- Write horizontally, in capital letters.
- Write with the sticky strip at the top.

Continue this process until all Post-It notes are on the wall. What emerges should be several 'hot-spots' where there is a clear alignment of areas of focus from the team.

Plan

Once you've decided on your few key Sprint Projects, it's time to plan them out in more detail. Do not scrimp on this step – it is key in deciding whether you actually get the outcome delivered or not. Once people get back to their busy day-to-day lives, they simply do not take the time to actually create these vital plans.

This involves creating clear plans for each Sprint Project. Start with a simple template such as this one here, either as a worksheet or on a flipchart. This is the best way to work out a draft plan with the Project team.

Priority Planning — SCALE

Priority
(State as the key outcome. What specifically will be achieved by the end?)

Owner

Scope / Outcomes
(List what's in and what's out)

Costs and Investment
(People (hours) / costs / equipment / tools)

Risks
(What could derail the Priority?)

Team
(Remember RACI)

Communication Rhythm
(When are the team meetings?)

	Milestone	Owner	Deadline
1			
2			
3			
4			
5			
6			
7			
8			
9			
10			

©2021, Scale

Once that has been agreed, it's time to put together a more detailed plan into task management software.

Task management software

Here is an example of a simple project mapped out on monday.com. You can see the objectives defined at the top, a clear owner, and the project broken down into work streams and milestones.

This is how the status looked at the end of the period – largely a successful completion.

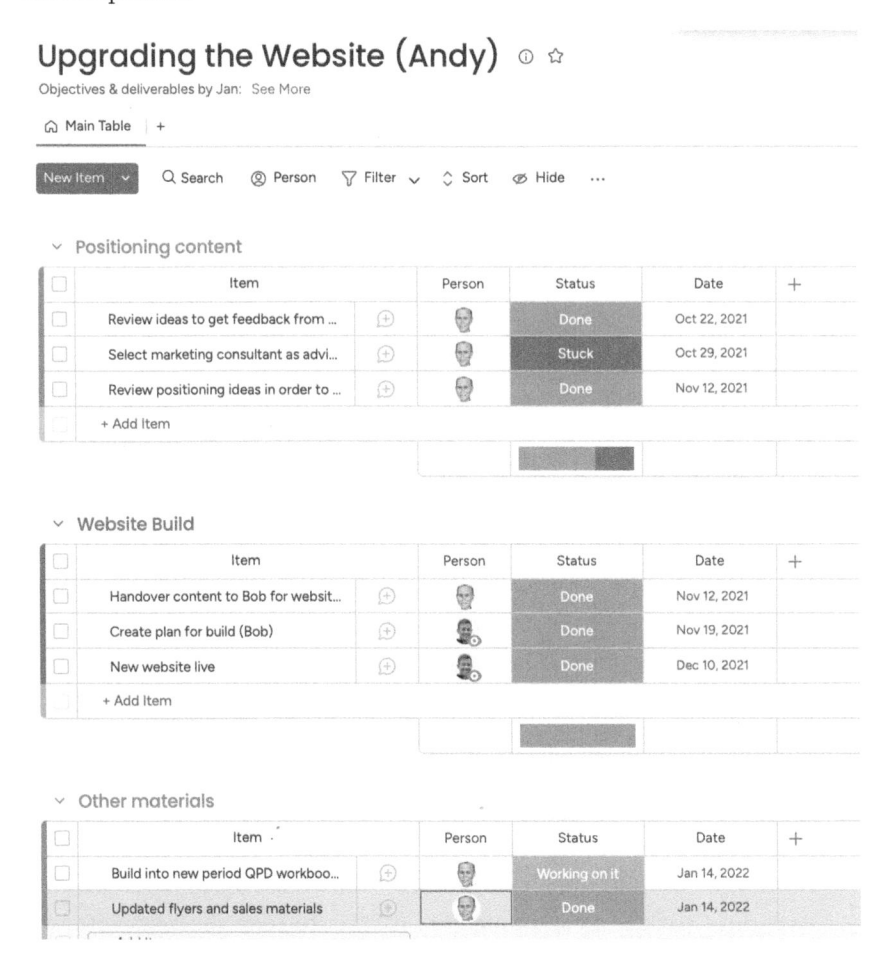

Upgrading the Website (Andy)

Objectives & deliverables by Jan: See More

Positioning content

Item	Person	Status	Date
Review ideas to get feedback from ...		Done	Oct 22, 2021
Select marketing consultant as advi...		Stuck	Oct 29, 2021
Review positioning ideas in order to ...		Done	Nov 12, 2021
+ Add Item			

Website Build

Item	Person	Status	Date
Handover content to Bob for websit...		Done	Nov 12, 2021
Create plan for build (Bob)		Done	Nov 19, 2021
New website live		Done	Dec 10, 2021
+ Add Item			

Other materials

Item	Person	Status	Date
Build into new period QPD workboo...		Working on it	Jan 14, 2022
Updated flyers and sales materials		Done	Jan 14, 2022

Good software like this also allows you to track progress through functions such as dashboards and Gantt charts/timelines.

Leading a Sprint Project

Once a Quarter kicks off, Project owners need to be accountable for ensuring that their Sprint Projects get executed. Here is a short guide to leading a Sprint Project:

- **Understand the difference between Accountability and Responsibility.** You are Accountable for the Priority, meaning you are ultimately answerable for the activities or decisions within the Priority, and bringing the team together to ensure completion. It does not mean you are Responsible for completing all the Tasks within the Priority.
- **Create a plan.** During the QPD, ensure that you agree on crystal-clear outcomes, a deadline, and identified milestones for each section of the Priority, with the Leadership Team (or whoever the 'Client' of your Priority is). It's crucial that everyone agrees on what must be delivered, and by when.
- **Establish the team.** In Special Forces, an effective team brings together experts from each discipline to complete a mission, such as demolition, medic, and engineering. When choosing your team, ensure you have the right people with the right skills to ensure completion of the Priority, and that they can represent and work with all the important groups necessary to ensure success.
- **Set and maintain communication rhythms.** Decide at the outset how regularly you will meet/check-in as a team. Does it need to be every day/every week/some other frequency, and at what time? The single most important thing you can do to ensure successful completion of the Priority is to maintain this rhythm. Own and stick to the agendas of your meetings.
- **Find a Coach.** A Coach is someone you can check in with once every 2–3 weeks who can help you think through where to focus on your Project, or how to unblock anywhere that you're stuck. You can also use your Coach as an accountability partner to keep yourself on track.

- **Set Check-ins.** During the execution of your Priority, set larger 'Check-in' Meetings, where you meet with the Leadership Team (or whoever your 'Client' is), as well as your Coaches. These check-ins will correspond to the Phases within the Priority. Check-ins are to clarify progress, discuss and solve roadblocks, and update prioritization and plans. A key component of Check-ins is to ask, 'How can we do this better?', in order to increase the Velocity of execution.
- **Shout when you're stuck.** If anything is getting in the way of staying on track, you must make sure it's dealt with quickly. This may require support from the Leadership team, so raise it quickly.
- **Maintain accurate data.** Decide where progress is going to be updated and visible to the team. This may be a software platform, or a board on the wall with sticky notes (or both). It's your job to ensure the whole team is keeping progress up to date, including completion of tasks/milestones, and making sure that KPIs and target metric progress are up-to-date.

Manage team dynamics. The success of your Priority depends upon the team. So, if there are members of the team who are not working well together, this will need your attention to solve. Understand what is driving any dysfunction, and coach the team members through their issues.

12

SMC 6 – TEAM LEADERSHIP

Checklist item

Issue

Team leadership. We have problems within our teams, stemming from how they are led.

Manifestations

- Team conflict (overt or implicit)
- Poor retention
- Micromanagement
- Poor team dynamics
- Poor staff engagement

Summary

If team leadership is an issue in the business, there may not be one 'magic bullet' solution to improve performance. It requires leaders within the business to learn and practice a range of behaviours and habits to get better performance from their teams.

The terms 'Leadership' and 'Management' are often used interchangeably. We distinguish leadership from management in that it is principally about the *emotional engagement* with team members (if the more rational skills of management are the issue, spend some time in the section on Accountability), though the two can be hard to separate. The tools and exercises described here are focused on improving the emotional engagement and dynamics of teams. Think about which of the skills in your leadership team would benefit from improvement:

- Common **team dynamic** dysfunctions and how to resolve them.
- Using **personality profiles** to promote understanding of working styles between team members.
- Learn how to use the skills of **Coaching** in order to improve delegation and give team members space and support to solve their own issues.
- A checklist/diagnostic tool allowing leaders to assess themselves against common **leadership characteristics**.
- The skills and best practices on the difficult habit of **giving feedback**.

Concepts

Introduction

Space agencies around the world are figuring out how to send crewed missions to Mars. As well as being a daunting technological challenge, one of the toughest problems mission planners face is getting crews to work well together during multi-year missions. Astronauts are outstanding people, chosen from elite groups, and amongst the most physically and intellectually capable people around. Yet, they have the same struggles working together as teams as elsewhere (only in their case failure may prove terminal).

So, the approach that NASA takes is similar to what high-performing teams do. They:

- Understand the personalities in the crew
- Ensure that a crew has a mix of personalities that will interact well
- Monitor team well-being and look for signs of strain and stress
- Do exercises and activities to develop and improve team dynamics
- Ensure that team leaders are focused on team dynamics.

Defining leadership

Leadership refers to a particular skillset, one that is naturally stronger in some people than others. This skillset can be learned, though it will always be easier for some personality types than others. To understand it, start by reflecting on some of your own personal, internal skills. Look at the two sets of skills below – Intellectual and Emotional, which would you personally rate highest on? Would you say you have a bias to one side or the other?

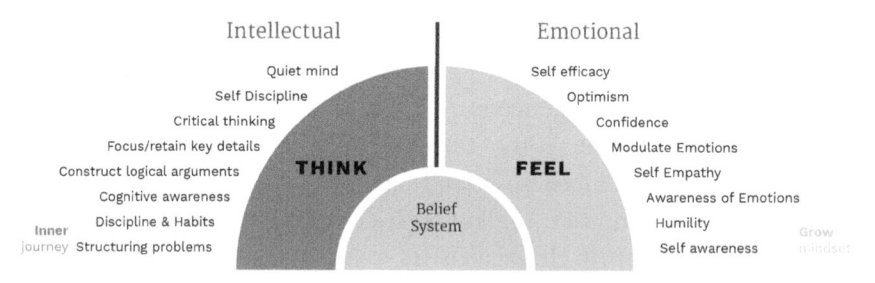

Intellectual	Emotional
Quiet mind	Self efficacy
Self Discipline	Optimism
Critical thinking	Confidence
Focus/retain key details	Modulate Emotions
Construct logical arguments **THINK**	**FEEL** Self Empathy
Cognitive awareness	Awareness of Emotions
Discipline & Habits	Belief System	Humility
Inner journey Structuring problems	Self awareness Grow mindset

(Images available by Creative Commons licence, courtesy of Les Hayes and Scott Offerdahl from work done as part of the Entrepreneur's Organisation Leadership Model)

In general, most people tend to identify with a stronger innate skillset on either the left or right side. Our internal skillsets map to our skillsets regarding how we interact with the outside world, such as with teams that we lead. Let's see how they map….

This model, developed by Les Hayes and Scott Offerdahl, as part of the Entrepreneur's Organisation Leadership Model, outlines the key difference between Management and Leadership:

- **Management**. Principally a *rational* engagement with people, such as helping them prioritise tasks, structure projects, or use data to make good decisions.
- **Leadership**. Principally an *emotional* engagement with people, such as inspiring them to a higher purpose, or making them feel they are part of a team.

SMC 6 – TEAM LEADERSHIP

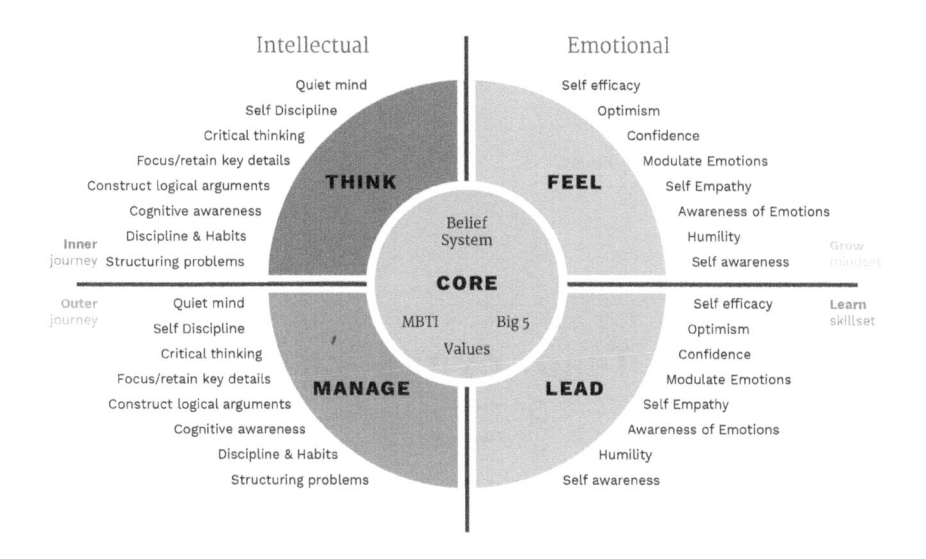

```
                 Intellectual         |         Emotional
                   Quiet mind         |         Self efficacy
                Self Discipline       |           Optimism
               Critical thinking      |          Confidence
             Focus/retain key details |      Modulate Emotions
           Construct logical arguments|         Self Empathy
                              THINK   |  FEEL
            Cognitive awareness       |      Awareness of Emotions
   Inner     Discipline & Habits      Belief      Humility          Grow
  journey   Structuring problems      System    Self awareness      mindset
                                      CORE
   Outer         Quiet mind                       Self efficacy     Learn
  journey      Self Discipline      MBTI   Big 5    Optimism        skillset
               Critical thinking        Values      Confidence
             Focus/retain key details             Modulate Emotions
                              MANAGE   |  LEAD
           Construct logical arguments |       Self Empathy
             Cognitive awareness       |    Awareness of Emotions
               Discipline & Habits     |          Humility
              Structuring problems     |        Self awareness
```

What does the team think?

Another way to look at the same question is from the perspective of the needs of the employee. Research has shown that employees have needs that range from requirements for:

- **Satisfaction** (such as a safe environment and the tools to do their job),
- **Engagement** (being part of a great team, having autonomy, and opportunities to learn), and
- **Inspiration** (finding meaning, and being inspired by leaders)

Inspired employees have been shown to be >2.2× more productive than Satisfied ones. The point here is that you cannot reach the higher levels of Leadership without having the foundations of Management in place. But to get great performance from a team, you need both, and it's the Leadership skills that really make a big difference. (NB: many of the tools of Management, including taking and measuring employee engagement, are covered in the section on Accountability).

Tools

What are some of the practical tools that you can use in order to develop the skills of Leadership?

- Team Dynamics
- Personality Profiles & Myers–Briggs Type Indicator (MBTI)
- Coaching
- Leadership Characteristics
- Giving Feedback.

Team dynamics

Summary

Much has to happen for a team to work well, such as having a common purpose, clear strategy, and agreed culture. A crucial factor in team success, however, is the nature of the relationships and dynamics between team members. A great strategy will not save a team that cannot work together. Fortunately, this is a function that can be worked on for significant improvement. As Pat Lencioni, author of 'The 5 Dysfunctions of a Team' famously says:

> Teamwork is not a virtue, it is a choice – and a strategic one.

Key concepts

Spotting the problem

When we run planning sessions with teams, we send out a survey in advance, including the question: 'How is the feel of the team?'. Sometimes tough answers come back. One team we worked with one time had answers peppered throughout like: 'fed up', 'deflated', 'tense', and 'painful'. And this is from a team that almost doubled their business in the previous year.

When asked about it, the leadership team described a negative team culture, with words like 'fragmented', 'paralysed', and 'trust' (as in 'lack of'). The growth of the business had created stress that was spilling over into problems in relationships within the team, which had in itself become a problem.

These kinds of situations are difficult because they require solving on two levels:

- Solve the underlying resourcing and process problems causing stress
- Fix the relationship and team dynamic problems

In this section we're going to focus on the latter, but remember, you will have to solve any underlying business issue, maybe a faulty process or troublesome team member as well.

Where is the problem?

In the situation above, the team were asked to describe the problem. Listening to the answers, it was like they were talking about another team. Nothing was said directly about themselves or one another, it was all described in a passive tense, for example: 'People keep saying "It's not my job"'. It didn't feel like they were describing their own behaviour. So, the first question to ask in the face of such comments is:

In who's power is it to solve this problem?

We can complain about investors, suppliers and supply chain, staff, or growth – too much of it, not enough of it. But ultimately there is only one group of people that can make or break the culture and team dynamics of the business: **the leadership team**. It all starts and ends there. Acceptance of this basic fact is the taproot from which any resolution must grow.

If there is a problem with team dynamics and culture, you as a leadership team have the sole and unique responsibility and the ability to solve it.

This can take time to really sink in, especially if finger pointing or a sense of hopelessness has set in. It takes reflection to fully grasp that the answer lies just with the people round the table. Only once that is established, can we look at how the team dynamics may be failing, and what to do about it.

So, if you face this problem and are ready to tackle it, you're in the right place:

1. Read through the list of potential causes below and reflect on where you think the issues lie
2. Share the article with the team, and arrange a discussion on identifying and solving the issue

3. Run the exercise at the end of the section to draw up a list of practical solutions.

Common causes of team dynamic breakdown

The problem you face may be one (or several) of the issues below. The list is not exhaustive, but should start you thinking on where your issue(s) lie.

Lack of trust	
Issue	There are many levels of team performance, but the most basic one is that there must be a foundation of trust. Members of a team must feel secure with each other and be willing to open up and be vulnerable. Without this, little else can be developed. If there exists a lack of empathy and understanding of each other, this prevents the establishment of any higher levels of cooperation, and establishing this must be the starting point of any team dynamics work.
Resolutions	The key to solving trust issues is that people must fundamentally understand one another's situation and believe that the other has positive motivations. It's all about **intent**. What does each team member believe the motivation of the others to be? It doesn't mean that everyone has to get on. It's not about establishing friendships (though that helps), it's about believing that other team members have positive, and not threatening motivations.
Example solutions	• Team-building activities outside of work • Safe words to call out undermining behaviours • Role swaps and shadowing • 360 feedback exercises on strengths and weaknesses
Accountability	
Issue	If people aren't clear about who's accountable for what, it can lead to a sense that some people are not delivering, which fosters resentment. Also, if targets or expectations and standards are perceived to be higher in one part of the business to another, this has a similar effect. The worst manifestation is if people have targets or objectives that are in direct conflict with each other: for example, product team raising prices to hit margin objectives that puts them in conflict with sales teams incentivised on sales targets.

Potential resolutions	People are motivated by incentives and objectives, especially if they are financially linked. And they will act to protect any benefits derived. So, conflicting incentives between teams can be hard to call out. Resolving this requires frank conversations, and ultimately some arbitration on what's fair. There may be losers in any change to incentive systems, so they will need a clear understanding of why such changes are being made.
Example solutions	• Discuss and re-design of bonus/targets/incentive system • Clarity on accountability of each team member (the Accountability Scorecard on page [164] will help with this).
Wrong roles	
Issue	Sometimes someone (or several people) is (are) in a role that isn't playing to their strengths, resulting in a team or department that causes problems for everyone.
Potential resolutions	This can be hard to call out because it involves pointing the finger at someone. It takes courage for a team member to call out underperformance in another. Is there someone holding on to a function that they need to let go of, or someone who has outgrown their current role?
Example solutions	• 360-degree reviews • Changing/updating team member roles
Living the culture	
Issue	Sometimes, when a team is busy, it can become easy to forget to do the things that made the team a good place to work in. Celebrations and rewards, taking time together in a social setting to reinforce relationships, and finding ways to acknowledge successes.
Potential resolutions	The obvious place to start is to think about a time when it wasn't a problem. What things worked well when people did feel acknowledged and recognised. Especially if you've had a period of growth, it can be easy to have let slip previous good practices. If it was never a strength, then drawing ideas and inspiration from the team or the wider world on what works to recognise people and success. Communication is also a common one here – is the team sharing information and coming together regularly so that each understands the situation of the other, their focus, priorities, and challenges?
Example solutions	• Recognition time at meetings • Recognition award schemes • Celebration events • Review of meeting rhythms (see page [26] for more on this)

\textit{Weak links}	
Issue	It can take just one person to undermine a whole team. The Talent Assessment chapter (page 301) describes several types of people, including those with issues of performance and behaviour. The most common issue here is people who are performing well (such as bringing in sales, or leading product development), but having a disruptive impact on team culture (these are called 'B/C players' in the Talent Assessment chart). Refer to page 301 on how to deal with these. The worst manifestation of this is having a **terrorist** on the team: one person who is determined to undermine and cause problems, possibly because they have a grudge or feel threatened somehow.
Resolutions	It often doesn't take much digging if there is someone like this in the team, people (including the leader) often have a clear view of such individuals. The challenge is facing the problem, as it may be a contentious process, and the risk of losing that individual and their performance may be significant.
Example solutions	• Tough conversations with relevant individual(s) • Removing them from the team
\textit{New joiners}	
Issue	One way growth can impact team dynamics is that it leads to adding new people to the team. New people bring new personalities and behaviours that may not always fit with existing people and habits. This can sometimes create situations of 'them and us' or the 'old and new guard'. Sometimes it is isolated individuals who are struggling to fit in.
Resolutions	Integrating new people into the team is an art. Each person brings something new and contributes to the culture, but also must adapt to how things are done. There is no hard and fast rule for how such situations should be addressed. The key is to make everyone feel that it is 'their team' and that they can both fit into it and/or mould it.
Example solutions	Focus on the onboarding and integration process Feedback and review for more recent people to make suggestions for change Sometimes, a new joiner is just not a good fit, and the firm needs to let the person go

Worksheet

Team Dynamics

SCALE — Business growth made easy

| Name: | Company: | Date: |

"Teamwork is not a virtue. It is a choice – and a strategic one."
- Patrick Lencioni

What's the one characteristic of our team dynamic that we need to improve (ideally must tie in with a Core Value)?

For example *'Having each others' backs'.*

For yourself, in the past period, share behaviours and examples of where you've done things that have contributed to, or detracted from, that characteristic

Contributed to	Detracted from
Example: *I reduced headcount in my team to support extra resource elsewhere.*	Example: *I left another team to go ahead with a project I knew would fail.*

Now do the same thing for each member of the team.

Team member name	Contributed to	Detracted from

Next Steps. Based on what's been shared, what are the top 1-2 specific changes that you or another member of the team need to make?

Exercise

Session Basics	
Name	Team dynamics – building trust
How to communicate	'For us to perform as a team, we have to look at where our dynamic is going wrong, and how to fix it. We're going to do an exercise together that will ask us to give each other feedback. Please come prepared to share, to be frank and honest, and possibly to have some tough conversations…'
Time	60–90 minutes
Format	Roundtable session
Attendees	The leadership team
Preparation	This exercise requires the team to understand in advance what is expected of them; ask them to read this article and consider their thoughts in advance
Objective and outcome	A list of actions or changes we need to take to get our team dynamics back on track
Learning and reading	Pat Lencioni – *The 5 Dysfunctions of Teams* (available as a book, and a Manga story-book version)
Materials	Requires one worksheet (and pen) per person The exercise can be done with Post-Its/flipcharts, or just verbally

Exercise	
Agenda and objective	Discuss and agree how you are going to go about the exercise. Specifically:
Key characteristic	Have a group discussion about what aspect of behaviour is going wrong. Get examples. Get each person to share. Try and link it to one of the Core Values, and create a statement of the type: 'The key characteristic we need to fix is…'
Reflection	Each person fills out for themselves where they have exhibited specific behaviours in the past period that contribute to and detract from that characteristic
Sharing	Agree on how long you will spend on each person (e.g. ten minutes each). With each person, start by sharing the reflection notes written for 1–2 minutes. Then invite the rest of the team to reflect back on specific actions and behaviours they have observed in that person who has either contributed or detracted from the key characteristic

	In this section, it's important that it is not a back and forth. It's OK to ask for examples and clarifications, but avoid defensive comments and rebuttals
Next steps	This is the most important part. What specific changes does the team, or certain individuals, need to take in order to fix the problem

FAQs and pitfalls

What does good look like?

What's a good outcome from this process? The most important aspects are:

- The #1 thing is the list of changes at the end. Make them specific and actionable. Include them in your priorities for the quarter, and follow up on progress.
- Through the feedback process, for people to get an understanding of how their behaviour is affecting others. This should lead to awareness and self-regulation.
- The 360-degree discussion process will show up 'hotspots' that will allow you to narrow down where the dynamic issues are going wrong.

Dealing with conflict

This can be an intense process. It's common for people to get emotional and upset. Sometimes people decide that either the process, or the team itself, is not for them, and walk out. It can take some courage to persevere and get to the heart of the issue.

Often, this exercise will bring to the surface gripes and resentments, which can lead to conflict.

There is a balance to be struck between letting people have their say, and keeping things respectful. A few rules of thumb help:

- Describe the emotion, don't display it. If something has made someone angry, it's OK to say that, but less helpful to actually get angry.
- Describe behaviours and outcomes rather than critique personalities. It is more helpful to say to someone 'When you lost your temper with me, I couldn't work for the rest of the day' than to accuse someone of have 'a short-tempered personality'.
- Separate facilitation from participation. Nominate someone who is not involved to run the session (an external person is best). A neutral voice that people trust allows for an environment that feels fairer and less charged.
- Accept that these things happen. It's a regular thing for teams that are growing fast to have growing pains. Don't beat yourselves up for having rumbles along the way. Just find a way to resolve it.

Personality profiles

Summary

People work in different ways. For a team to perform effectively together, members of the team must understand the personalities and working styles of their team-mates. This is easily done these days with free and low-cost profiling software available to map and understand each person's own style.

Concept

Many years ago, I went to the offices of a large London logistics company, and everyone was wearing lanyards, all backed with one of four different colours. They explained that they referred to four key personality types, and that the lanyards helped because, when people met together, they could immediately see their personality type, and adapt their communication accordingly.

This was a practical and positive example of a team making use of **personality profiles**. Tools like these are now easily accessible online for teams to self-implement, so you can either gain insights at limited or no cost yourself, or hire experts to dive deeper into the subject.

Personality vs Strengths
There is an important distinction between tests for personality traits (characteristics such as introversion vs extroversion) and strengths (such as an ability for data analysis). Here we deal with personality tests only.

MBTI®

Myers–Briggs® is one of the oldest and best-established personality profiling systems. Profiles are constructed across four areas: Mind, Energy, Nature, and Tactics. Each area has two types (listed below), creating 16 possible personality profiles. In addition, there is an identity type which further divides each of the 16 profiles into 'A' and 'T'

Mind Introvert vs Extravert	Introverted individuals prefer solitary activities and get exhausted by social interaction.	Extraverted individuals prefer group activities and get energised by social interaction.
Energy observation vs intuition	Observant individuals are highly practical, pragmatic and down-to-earth. They tend to have strong habits and focus on what is happening or has already happened.	Intuitive individuals are very imaginative, open-minded and curious. They prefer novelty over stability and focus on hidden meanings and future possibilities.
Nature thinking vs feeling	Thinking individuals focus on objectivity and rationality, prioritising logic over emotions. They tend to hide their feelings and see efficiency as more important than cooperation.	Feeling individuals are sensitive and emotionally expressive. They are more empathic and less competitive than thinking types, and focus on social harmony and cooperation.

Tactics judging vs prospecting	Judging individuals are decisive, thorough and highly organised. They value clarity, predictability and closure, preferring structure and planning to spontaneity.	Prospecting individuals are very good at improvising and spotting opportunities. They tend to be flexible, relaxed nonconformists who prefer keeping their options open.
*Identity assertive vs turbulent	Assertive (-A) individuals are self-assured, even-tempered and resistant to stress. They refuse to worry too much and do not push themselves too hard when it comes to achieving goals.	Turbulent (-T) individuals are self-conscious and sensitive to stress. They are likely to experience a wide range of emotions and to be success-driven, perfectionistic and eager to improve.

A model we commonly recommend for use is from the website www.16personalities.com. They provide colourful, easy to understand profiles, with basic ones created for, or affordable deep-dive profiles

Based on the types described above, these are the 16 profiles that emerge:

ISTJ — Hardworking with sound practical judgement.

ISFJ — Devoted caretakers who enjoy being helpful to others.

INFJ — Seek cooperation, enjoy intellectual stimulation.

INTJ — Driven by their own original ideas to achieve improvements.

ISTP — Skilled at understanding how mechanical things work.

ISFP — Seek to create a personal environment that is practical

INFP — Value personal growth, focus on dreams and possibilities.

INTP — Original thinkers who enjoy creative problem solving.

ESTP — Pragmatic problem solvers and skillful negotiators.

ESFP — Have common sense, enjoy helping people in tangible ways.

ENFP — Value inspiration and enjoy starting new projects.

ENTP — Enjoy new ideas and challenges, value inspiration.

ESTJ — Like to run the show and gets things done in an orderly fashion.

ESFJ — Seek to be helpful and enjoy being active and productive.

ENFJ — Skilled communicators, organised and responsible.

ENTJ — Effective planners of people and long range planners.

Exercise

Once each person has created their personality profile online, bring the team together for an exercise to share with each other, bringing their personality profile reports with them.

Session Basics	
Name	Personality profiles
How to communicate	'Understanding one another's working styles and personalities well, it will help us to work effectively together'
Time	60–90 minutes
Format	Workshop session
Attendees	Teams requiring development of their team dynamic. Start with the leadership team.

Preparation	
Objective and outcome	A clear understanding of one another's personality profile, in order to be able to adapt better to one another's working style.
Learning and reading	MBTI® personality profiles are fully explained on www.16personalities.com
Materials	• Each team member fills out their MBTI® personality profile on www.16personalities.com in advance, and bring their profile report • Worksheets and pens

Exercise	
Agenda and objective	Discuss and agree objectives, agenda, and timing of the session
The concept	Share insights and experiences on MBTI® (or other) personality profile systems, and how they can help teams.
Exercise	Each person fills out the sheet, starting with do's and don'ts for communication and working with them, based on their personality profile. Then each person fills out the names of the other team members, and guesses what their personality profile might be.
Sharing	One by one, each team member shares their actual personality profile, along with key Do's and Don'ts for communicating and working with them. Team members fill out their worksheets as each person shares.
Next steps	Discuss and agree any next steps for how these personality profiles might be included into everyday working life in the team.

Worksheet

MBTI personality profile

Name: _____ **Company:** _____ **Date:** _____

Each team member complete their profile here: www.16personalities.com/free-personality-test

Mind **I**ntrovert vs **E**xtrovert	**I**ntroverted individuals prefer solitary activities and get exhausted by social interaction.	**E**xtroverted individuals prefer group activities and get energized by social interaction
Energy Ob**S**ervation vs I**N**tuition	Ob**s**ervant individuals are highly practical, pragmatic and down-to-earth. They tend to have strong habits and focus on what is happening or has already happened.	I**n**tuitive individuals are very imaginative, open-minded and curious. They prefer novelty over stability and focus on hidden meanings and future possibilities
Nature **T**hinking vs **F**eeling	**T**hinking individuals focus on objectivity and rationality, prioritizing logic over emotions. They tend to hide their feelings and see efficiency as more important than cooperation.	**F**eeling individuals are sensitive and emotionally expressive. They are more empathic and less competitive than Thinking types, and focus on social harmony and cooperation.
Tactics **J**udging vs **P**rospecting	**J**udging individuals are decisive, thorough and highly organized. They value clarity, predictability and closure, preferring structure and planning to spontaneity	**P**rospecting individuals are very good at improvising and spotting opportunities. They tend to be flexible, relaxed nonconformists who prefer keeping their options open.
*Identity **A**ssertive vs **T**urbulent	**A**ssertive (**-A**) individuals are self-assured, even-tempered and resistant to stress. They refuse to worry too much and do not push themselves too hard when it comes to achieving goals.	**T**urbulent (**-T**) individuals are self-conscious and sensitive to stress. They are likely to experience a wide range of emotions and to be success-driven, perfectionistic and eager to improve.

Key DO's and DON'Ts when communicating with me

Name	Guessed MBTI	Actual MBTI	Key traits, do's and don'ts
E.g. Annabel	ENTJ-A	ENFP-A	May tend to people please

Feb23 · © Clarity Strategy Ltd DBA Scale 2023 | © MBTI Personalities - https://www.16personalities.com   www.scalecoach.co.uk

Coaching

Summary

How would your company or team manage if you were not around day-to-day? Is that even conceivable for you at the moment? The fact is that it is achievable, but you will have to change certain mindsets and behaviours to make it happen. A key one is the skill and mindset of coaching, so that you can support others to resolve their issues, rather than getting involved yourself.

Key concept

Getting the monkey off your back

> It's such an exciting thing for the business that you can do this without me now.

Message from the CEO of a £60m business, with over 100 team members, to the management team, sharing with them that he would not join them for the team annual planning meeting.

If you manage/lead a team and are finding yourself overworked and stressed, then it's probably because you're more involved in your team members' work that you need to be. For many leaders and managers in an organisation, the key to having more time to work on what's important is to not get involved in the minutiae of their team's work. A popular concept to describe this phenomenon is the 'monkey on the back'. Each time a team member brings a problem to you, it's like they're carrying a monkey on their back, and if you decide to get involved in solving that issue with or for them, then you are taking that monkey from their back onto yours.

And here's the kicker: those team members often really don't want you involved with what they're doing either. They want help to figure things out, but want to retain control, ownership, and autonomy over what they're doing.

So, **how to support team members to solve their own issues**? That is the central question. Succeeding in this depends upon changing certain mindsets, some deeply entrenched, and learning a few new skills. Combined, these are often described as **'Coaching'**.

What is coaching?

At the heart of coaching sits the mindset that **the coachee has the ability to solve their problem**. My first introduction to coaching was in a 'Forum', a regular get-together with other entrepreneurs, as part of the Entrepreneurs Organisation. Each month, eight of us would meet to share the biggest challenges we were facing in our lives at that time. And, each month, two of those challenges would be chosen for a 'Deep Dive' presentation.

When I first started, when a forum mate shared a challenge in this way, my first response was to want to offer a solution. A lifetime of problem-solving had primed me for this response, all throughout my life I had been measured and rewarded by my ability to solve problems.

However, with this group, there was a rule in place that prevented all advice-giving. To be clear: **all** advice-giving (including suggestions, 'If I were you' statements, and even leading questions) was explicitly forbidden. Instead, we were encouraged to do two things: share of relevant, actual experience, and ask good coaching questions.

Here lies the clue to coaching, much of it is about asking questions.

A coach may play multiple roles with a coachee, including:

- **Provider of focus.** Coaching questions typically follow a 'narrowing down' process, whereby a coach is helping a coachee to 'narrow down' to the heart of problem, then questioning the coachee to think through to solutions, and again 'narrow down' to best solutions, and next steps. It verbally plays out the train of thought that we follow to solve problems we face in life (but rarely actually take the time to work through in a systematic way).
- **Provoker of thought.** A great coaching question is often followed by silence. This is because the coachee is stopping to think. It's the most

beautiful sound in a coaching session, when it happens you know you're getting it right. For example, if a coachee lists three big problems in life, simply asking them which they need to fix first forces them to actually think that through.

- **Accountability partner.** A good coaching session always concludes with next steps and actions. A coach is the person that helps in subsequent check-ins ask whether the coachee got them done. Human beings make much quicker progress when they feel they've made a commitment to another human being rather than just to themselves. That's how the programming works.
- **Sounding Board.** A great coaching conversation often involves the coachee vocalising something for the first time. This can be an exhilarating moment; vocalisation is very powerful. It's how we test the thoughts and ideas that are in our minds. Being able to do so in a consequence-free environment allows to see how a thought looks in the cold light of day, to work through which of our many thoughts and ideas have validity, and which do not.
- **Force for action.** Coaching is about more than just thought-provoking questions; it's about focusing the coachee on actions they need to take. Every coaching call must conclude with clear actions and next steps, including follow-up. When maintained as a rhythm this provides tremendous momentum for change. This is how big changes in lives and businesses that had previously only been aspirations actually get done.
- **Challenger.** A Coach will never tell a coachee whether something is right or wrong, but they may ask if a thing is achievable, or in line with existing goals, or whether it has been tested out.

Becoming a good coach takes time. Below is an exercise you can do to practice the skills of coaching. What you will find is that, over time, they will start to influence and affect many of your interactions with your team (and maybe also with family, friends, and colleagues). You will naturally find yourself moving towards a position of support, rather than control and involvement.

Worksheets

Coaching — SCALE | Business growth made easy

Name: _____ Company: _____ Date: _____

1. Opening
- What would be helpful to discuss today?
- What is your biggest stuck?
- Where is your big issue right now?
- What is your #1 thing?

2. Clarifying the topic
- Of all those issues, which is the most important / pressing / bothering you most / causing you the most issues?
- Which issue should we address first?

3. Explore
- Tell me more about it
- How is this important?
- What are your options?
- Where are you at in the decision making process?
- What have you tried so far?

4. Solution
- What are the pro's and con's of those options?
- Which option / solution makes the most sense?
- What would you advise yourself to do?
- What would a great outcome look like?

5. Action
- What does the first step look like to resolve this?
- What objectives can you set yourself around the issues?
- What support or help do you need?
- Where will you be with this by your next meeting?

Notes

Remember – no advice (even hiding in a question), let them find their own solution.

Feb23 · © Clarity Strategy Ltd DBA Scale 2023   www.scalecoach.co.uk

Coachee

SCALE | Business growth made easy

| Name: | Company: | Date: |

| Coach: | Next Meeting date: |

Objective
Define the next steps to take you forward on your #1 current issue.

Preparation
Think about and fill out the answers to the questions below before the meeting.

Agenda
1. Agree time and date of next meeting
2. Progress from last time. How did you get on with the actions agreed? Where are you still stuck?
3. Your #1 issue. Fill out the questions below to think about your issue, then work with your coach on solutions and next steps.
4. Record your next steps & immediate actions.

What's the #1 issue you'd like to discuss today?	
Describe the background and context of the issue. Why is it an issue? What's the impact if nothing gets done?	
What emotions or feelings do you have connected with this issue?	
What is the ideal outcome from the session today?	

Top 3 actions to resolve this issue

1	
2	
3	

Feb23 - © Clarity Strategy Ltd DBA Scale 2023 — www.scalecoach.co.uk

Exercise

Session basics	
Name	'Coaching'
How to Communicate	'For us to enjoy our work, get great results, and not waste time, it's important to get rid of low value or low ability tasks. We're going to get together to understand what's in each other's Sweetspot, and what we can do to eliminate activities that are getting in the way of spending more time there'
Time	90 minutes
Format	Workshop session. (NB: This session does require some confidence and experience with coaching in order to deliver effectively, especially to do the open coaching demonstration. Make sure it is led by someone confident in this area.)
Attendees	Best done in teams that work together including the leader / line manager of that team.

Preparation	
Objective and outcome	Develop a new way of interacting with team members that gives people space to solve their own challenges.
Learning and reading	• The Coaching Habit • Mastercoach
Materials	Printed worksheets and pens

Exercise	
Objective	Share and discuss the objective of the session. Emphasise that this is the beginning of a transition, a change that will require repetition and practice.
Introduce the process	Introduce both of the worksheets: • Coaching worksheet. This contains the series of questions that a coach can ask to help coachee to move through the stages of a coaching conversation. • Coachee worksheet. This contains questions and categories that a coachee can think about when they are preparing a presentation to be coaches.
Open demonstration	Take a volunteer to be a coachee, and do a 10 minute open coaching session in front of the team. Have them choose an actual challenge they are facing (something relatively simple, that can meaningfully be addressed in a short time), and coach them through it. Afterwards, take comments and feedback from the team.

Coaching exercise	• Set the group into groups of three, and establish three roles: coach coachee, and observer. • The coaching activity is run three times, each time rotating the roles, so that everyone has an opportunity to practice each role. • Ensure that there are enough coaching and coachee worksheets for each person to practice each role. • For each rotation, follow these approximate timings: 10 mins on coaching 2–3 minutes for the observer to share observations with the coach and coachee • If you are short on time, then do the exercise in pairs, and run it twice, swapping between the coach / coachee role.
Feedback	Take feedback from the team on their experiences as coaches, coachees, and observers. What were the common challenges, and how did they overcome them?
Next steps	Establish coaching pairs and relationships and set check-in coaching times. Set up a time for a follow-on session to come together and practice these skills again.

Guide and pitfalls

The most common pitfall

The one thing that most people find hardest in this exercise is to **switch their minds off from problem-solving**. When faced with another person's difficult challenge, the immediate, powerful response is to start thinking of solutions.

It's as if there are circuits in the mind that are automatically activated when faced with a described problem. In fact, it's possible to notice when it happens to the listener, because they subtly stop listening. Everyone has the experience of 'listening' whilst analysing the situation and working through solutions in our minds.

This needs to be switched off. It has to be a genuine 'listen without prejudice', just a pure act of listening. Once the coachee has stopped talking, then take time to reflect and think what might be a good next question. Often, simply paraphrasing what you've heard is a great way to help the coachee progress their line of thought.

What if the coachee simply doesn't have the experience or resources necessary?

One of the hardest situations when coaching someone is if they're genuinely stuck and don't have the knowledge or means themselves to solve their situation. What do you do?

The answer is that it depends upon your situation. If you are just a coach in their life, then your task is to support the coachee to work out how to get the information and support they need to solve the situation. What research, outreach, and fact-finding work do they need to do to start finding answers? Who can they lean on? How can they mine their networks and access information?

If you have a wider relationship with the coachee and are in a position to provide or connect them with answers and resources they need, then you need to be assiduous in clarifying when you're changing roles. Whilst in coach mode, it's OK to say: 'At the end of our conversation, I can put my manager/mentor hat on, and see if there are some answers or resources I can provide' and carry on with the coaching conversation.

When you do reach that point, be as explicit as 'I'm going to take my coaching hat off now, and see if there are ways that I can help you with this situation'. At that point, if there are introductions, resources, or experiences you can provide, then that is the appropriate moment.

What if I'm the coachee's manager?

It is more challenging coaching someone if you are also their line manager, principally because they may not be as willing to share as openly and vulnerably to someone they see as potentially having a role of judgement in their life.

The key is to distinguish clearly between different types of conversations. Even if you are the same person who may also give appraisals, it is possible to draw lines between them and coaching conversations, and complete both productively.

Most importantly, you have to live up to the expectations of the role. Being a coach is about not intervening, not solving problems or providing advice. If you stick to those disciplines, the employee usually naturally flows into the role of coachee.

Who can be your coach?

Coaching is quite different from line management. The answer is that anyone with good coaching skills can be your coach. I often call up members of my team (they are all great coaches) when I'm stuck with something just to have them coach me through it, for example, if I'm stuck on a difficult client or commercial issue.

Leadership characteristics

Summary

Are you an effective leader? The ultimate test is in the results of your team. To improve as a leader, one of the best ways is simply to ask. Use this exercise as a tool to understand where your strengths and weaknesses for common leadership characteristics lie.

Concept

There are no good or bad leaders; there are only effective and ineffective teams. The role of the leader is for the team to perform. Therefore, if there are problems in a team, the first place to look is to the leader of the team.

Everyone has their own leadership style, there are many different ways to lead teams effectively. And different leadership styles work for and attract different types of team members. I think of myself as a poor leader, I'm not strong at many of the personal engagement skills I would expect a strong leader to have. I shared this concern with my team one time, and their reply surprised me. For them, they liked working in an environment where they were largely left to operate independently without the need for constantly participating in team activity. The type of environment we have wouldn't be for everyone, but it has attracted a certain type of person.

Are there traits common to all strong leaders? Jim Collins, in his book 'Beyond Entrepreneurship 2.0' suggests that there are seven, which are summarised in this worksheet and exercise.

Worksheet

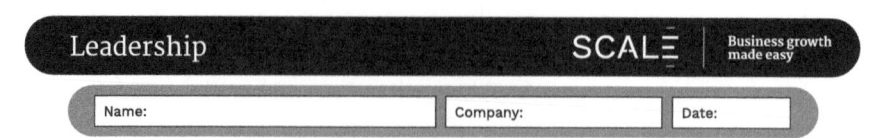

Leadership

SCALE | Business growth made easy

Name: _____ Company: _____ Date: _____

> "Leadership is the art of getting people to want to do what must be done."
> - Jim Collins

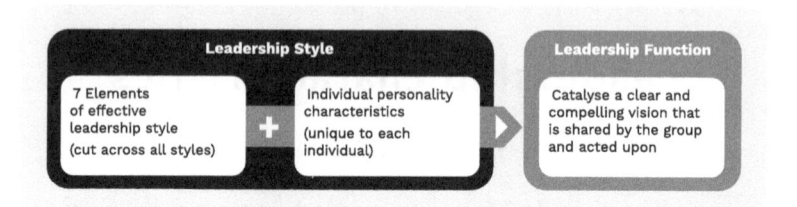

Leadership Style
- 7 Elements of effective leadership style (cut across all styles)
- **+** Individual personality characteristics (unique to each individual)

Leadership Function
- Catalyse a clear and compelling vision that is shared by the group and acted upon

7 Elements of Effective Leadership Style

1. Authenticity
- Be an authentic role model for the vision and values of the company.
- Back words with action. Take strategic decisions based on vision & values.
- What cause do you serve? Lead with Purpose & belief.

Score 0 -

2. Decisiveness
- Be decisive. Don't let analysis prevent a decision.
- Follow your gut. A bad decision is often better than no decision.
- Group decision-making. Delegate decision-making; encourage disagreement.
- Accept responsibility; share credit.

Score 0 -

3. Focus
- Take one shot at a time. Max. 1-3 Priorities. Make hard choices to prioritise.
- Manage your time, not your work. Are you in your Sweetspot?

Score 0 -

4. Personal touch
- Build relationships. Personally invest time in developing relationships.
- Be accessible and approachable. Minimise 'status barriers'.
- Know what's going on.
- Personal touch vs. micro-management.

Score 0 -

5. Hard / Soft People skills
- The importance of giving (mostly positive) feedback.
- Leader as teacher. Develop, don't critique.
- High expectations. Assume people can and want to attain high standards.

Score 0 -

6. Communication
- Communicate vision and strategy. Constant repetition. Use analogies & images.
- Add a personal touch to formal communications (and call a duck a duck).
- Stimulate communication in others.

Score 0 -

7. Ever forward
- Personal development. Improve with each day.
- Keep the energy up. Optimism and tenacity.
- Keep the company moving forward.
- Touch the spirit.

Score 0 -

Feb23 · © Clarity Strategy Ltd DBA Scale 2023 | Adapted from 'Beyond Entrepreneurship 2.0' by Jim Collins   www.scalecoach.co.uk

Exercise

In preparation for this exercise, send the checklist to anyone in the team that you lead, to collect their scores on your leadership characteristics. This may be easier done by a third party, or anonymously, in order to encourage honest answers. Also, fill out the checklist yourself with your own view of your scores.

The exercise is best done with a coach, mentor, or line manager on a 1:1 basis. Review both your own scores and those from the team, and identify together areas for development and improvement (make use of the guide below).

What to do with the results?

The object of the exercise is to find the areas that require development. This is the hard part, as changing your own leadership style is difficult. I'm not great at either 'Hard/soft people skills' or 'Personal touch'. In truth, don't think I'll ever be great at them. So, how do we overcome shortcomings?

In life, there are two types of skillsets:

- **Intrinsic**. The things you naturally do well.
- **Learned**. Skills you've had to overcome natural weaknesses to learn.

Make no mistake: great success in life depends upon focusing on strengths (further developed in the Sweetspot exercise in Chapter 10): that is, those intrinsic skills that you were born with. However, unmitigated shortcomings ('fatal flaws') can be serious barriers to success. If you score low on items on this list, then you are in need of **personal development** techniques in order to improve.

Learn what good looks like

Like all learned skills, leadership skills can be learned. Based on the areas you have scored badly, search out books and training courses that can provide expertise. One of the best resources is to have a coach or mentor to train and guide you on those skills.

For example, one of the CEOs with whom I work, who was promoted to the role, is perceived as having weaker skills in decisiveness. So, he works with a coach, who sits in on meetings, listens to team feedback, and provides reflections on which he can work.

Fake it till you make it

I first learned this phrase in alcohol recovery. Few personal **behaviours** are harder to **re-engineer** that those associated with addiction. Staying sober requires the wholesale change of a range of behaviours, from not meeting with certain people, not going to certain places, and new approaches to admission of fault, dealing with anger, and engaging with people honestly. I can remember many times running through my head, the question, 'How would a sober, responsible person react to this situation?' and simply forcing myself to do that, whatever existing instincts and impulses were telling me.

An extreme example of this comes from **autistic people**. The stereotype of an autistic person is that they have poor social skills. However, you can meet many autistic people who do an excellent job of convincing you otherwise, displaying traits such as engaging conversation, personal interest, and active listening. A lot of this behaviour is learned, and it's called **'masking'**. It serves a vital purpose in our lives – to interact constructively with other people. But it's tiring, cannot be maintained indefinitely, and has to be interspersed with periods of recovery, or else you risk burnout.

Blindspots

If the scores from your team vary significantly from your own, then it may be that you have leadership deficiencies that you don't see. For example, you may think you have a personal touch, but if your team sees otherwise, you may have a blindspot.

Correcting for such biases is hard. It requires regularly collecting honest feedback, as by definition it's something we cannot see in ourselves. One CEO I work with had Decisiveness as a low score from the team, so every 2 weeks we spent 30 minutes reviewing all the decisions he faced and had made, in order to identify where he needed to train himself to spot gaps in this behaviour.

Giving feedback

Summary

Think about yourself, your team, and the state of the business. Are any of them perfect (are any of them even 'good')? No doubt there is room for improvement in all of them. How do you find out, and how do you practically go about making those improvements?

The answer all lies in **feedback** – collecting it, sharing it, and holding people to it. It's the key means by which we identify and deliver on improvements. But it's hard. It takes a difficult mix of courage, compassion, and openness, by all parties. Learn how to develop great skills at feedback.

What do we mean by 'Feedback'?

In a business I was running one time, there was a member of the team who I valued very much. I went to lunch at his house one day to talk about life and the future of the business. As we talked and ate, he looked me in the eye and told me, in so many words, that a key function of the business was underperforming, and that the leader of that team was not suitable for the job. I had not explicitly asked him this question: he took the initiative to share his assessment with me.

I was hugely grateful for it, because this was **feedback**. When I heard him share those words, I knew in my heart that he was 100% right. A part of me didn't want to hear it, not because it wasn't true, but because of the implicit fault on my part, and discomfort in the resolution of it.

I came away from the lunch with two conclusions: to let the underperformer go (which I did), and to always ensure that I work with people like this. Whatever it takes to create a team of people willing to share in this way, it's worth it, because without feedback, there is no hope for improvement, either of ourselves or of the business.

Types of feedback

- **Direction**. In the example above, the feedback was 'upwards': that is, from a team member to the leader of the team. Feedback must happen in both directions.

- **Situation**. In this case, it was also 'reactive': that is, in reaction to an event that has happened or an assessment made. Feedback also needs to happen as part of a regular, structured cycle, such as monthly or annual reviews.
- **Charge**. Finally, this was 'constructive feedback' (i.e. something wrong that needed fixing). Feedback can also be positive – recognition for something done well.

(NB: This chapter on Feedback could equally have appeared in the section on Accountability, we just feel the emotional component slightly trumps the rational one.)

Key concepts – golden rules for feedback

Do it yourself

Giving feedback is tough – it takes courage, can be uncomfortable, and risks the relationship. So, it's tempting to ask or expect others to do it for us. Don't fall into this easy outcome. The message will not be conveyed in the way that you want, and it will hurt your relationship with the person if they are hearing your feedback second-hand.

It is common to coordinate with people, such as an HR manager, on giving people feedback, but if you have something that the person needs to hear, then you are the best person to deliver the message.

Make it timely

If you're giving feedback in response to something that has happened, do it as soon as possible after the event, while the event is still fresh in your minds. Otherwise, the moment will pass, and it will either go unremarked and you lose the opportunity for feedback. Worse still, the next time something similar happens, you will have a harder job unpicking the issue.

For example, one of the teams we work with had a colleague who delivered a workshop to members of the team. It turned out that the content of the workshop wasn't quite what the team needed. But no one mentioned it at the time. It wasn't until weeks later on a group planning session that it came out, and the colleague in question was mortified. Why had no one told him at the time? In fact, it would have been easy for him to fix, but not if he didn't know the feedback.

Make it appropriate

In the story above, one issue with the way that the feedback was handled was that the feedback was both negative and delivered in front of the team. This broke the golden rule of praising publicly and criticising privately.

PRAISE PUBLICLY; CRITICISE PRIVATELY

The strength, or level of the feedback also needs to be in line with the issue or behaviour. Like with children you cannot give a level 10 reaction to a level 5 issue (or vice versa).

Learn to give CPR

The book 'Crucial Accountabilities' introduces a helpful model to apply appropriate feedback. The number of occurrences of a particular behaviour or event is relevant to what feedback is given, and how. It's called **'CPR':**

- **Content**: The first time something unwanted occurs, feedback the content: that is, what happened and the consequence or reaction to it.
- **Pattern**: If something unwanted happens more than once, then feedback the pattern related to the events repeated over time.
- **Relationship**: If the problem continues, talk about the relationship, about how it's affecting us or the wider team.

Sticking to these best practices avoids the scenario where an issue does not get raised, so happens repeatedly, until someone (usually the line manager) erupts in a fit of anger, often at something small.

The magic ratio

Feedback can of course be positive and negative. If something good happens, giving recognition and approval is vital. So which is more beneficial: positive or negative feedback?

An excellent piece of research, published in *HBR* in 2013 (see below) found an illuminating answer to this question. Positive and negative feedback are both necessary and important: it's the ratio that's vital. Research showed that the teams that performed the best had a ratio of just over **5:1** of positive to negative feedback. That means that there were on average over five positive comments for every one piece of constructive criticism.

That might seem like a high ratio, but it comes down to human psychology. Simply put, we are wired to be much more sensitive to criticism than to praise.

What it means is that you have to 'earn' the right to criticism by demonstrating you care enough for the person by praising them in a suitable ratio. The relationship is more nuanced than that though. In fact, people who are performing poorly need a lower ratio of praise to criticism, they need to understand that there is something wrong and that they need to improve their performance.

The point is that the 'neutral' or 'default' point of a balance of praise to criticism – what people receiving it sub-consciously feel is 'about right' – is about 5:1, which means that if your ratio sits below that, people are feeling criticised. https://hbr.org/2013/03/the-ideal-praise-to-criticism

Separate the emotion

If feedback is reactive, that is, in response to something that has happened, the event may have triggered strong emotions in the person giving the feedback. For example, if someone has ignored an instruction, and it happens repeatedly, the line manager giving instructions may get increasingly frustrated.

The key here when giving feedback is to *state the emotion, but not demonstrate the emotion*. So, it's fine to say, 'This makes me feel angry', but demonstrating the actual behaviours and manifestations of anger will be counter-productive.

This is a hard art to master; we are not robots. Sometimes it's worth taking a day or two to process relevant emotions and take the immediate sting out of them. What's helpful is to share the emotion (or display it) with someone else before doing so with the cause of it (I use our HR manager for this purpose). Vent, talk it through, get it off your chest, then raise it objectively with the person who needs feedback.

Separate the person from the feedback

If someone has done something wrong, it means they've done something wrong, not that they are a person that does wrong things. This is much more than a semantic distinction.

I got a lesson in this myself recently. A member of my team, working on marketing, wrote some copy that I felt was weak, that it was too mild and needed more 'punch'. That is a reasonable piece of pushback for a manager to make. However, my mistake was to say that the feedback was too mild because the individual has a mild personality. That is a personal criticism, directed at their character, not at their behaviour, and this crossed a line.

Fortunately, the team member felt confident enough to call me on this. We had a long talk. I apologised profusely, having re-read my email, and fully accepted that I had crossed a line, that this was an error on my part. Which takes us to making sure it goes both ways.

Make sure it goes both ways

Leaders in the business have to give feedback and elicit it from others. This is easy to say and hard to achieve.

The team has to see and understand that the leader of the team is willing to accept error and challenging feedback. The only way to do that is to make a habit of displaying error. This is where the golden rule gets turned on its head:

Self-criticise publicly

If the team see that you have a sincere willingness to take on negative feedback, this will give them the confidence to approach you with more feedback. Words like 'I'm sorry…', 'My bad…', 'I got this wrong…', and 'This was my mistake…' have to be heard in front of the team. A common ice-breaker at our weekly team huddle is 'lessons learned' and I always use it to point out something I have done wrong.

Giving difficult feedback

In a leadership position, one of the most uncomfortable tasks for many is the job of holding people to account, especially if they've behaved badly in some way. There are good and bad ways of going about this.

If someone has done something wrong, it's hard to challenge them for it, even if you're in a situation of power over them. You might be afraid of their emotional reaction, of hurting them, or of them responding with negative behaviour, like undermining you, or even leaving the team altogether. It takes courage.

Think about it on axis from 'Silence' (i.e. not raising it) to 'Direct challenge' (which is pointing out to them explicitly what they've done wrong). They are much likelier to take the feedback if they feel that it is coming from a place of support and care from you, rather than outright challenge and threat.

As an example, take the situation of someone with their flies undone:

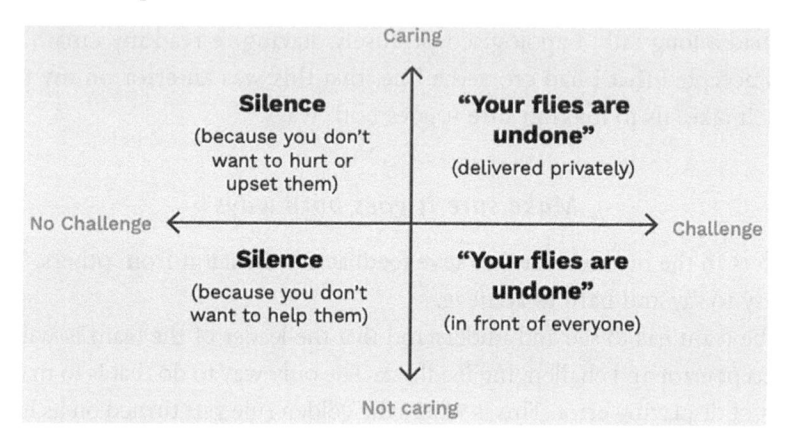

```
                              Caring
                                ↑
            Silence            |    "Your flies are
       (because you don't      |        undone"
        want to hurt or        |
          upset them)          |   (delivered privately)
                               |
 No Challenge  ←───────────────┼───────────────→  Challenge
                               |
            Silence            |    "Your flies are
       (because you don't      |        undone"
       want to help them)      |
                               |  (in front of everyone)
                                ↓
                            Not caring
```

- **Caring and challenging**: Privately/discreetly letting them know their flies are undone
- **Uncaring and challenging**: Publicly, and for everyone's benefit, pointing out their flies are undone
- **Caring and unchallenging**: Not pointing it out, for fear of embarrassing them
- **Uncaring and unchallenging**: Not pointing it out, either because you don't care to help them, or even in the hope that they get noticed and embarrassed

These four boxes apply in all situations involving feedback, and can be understood by the following model:

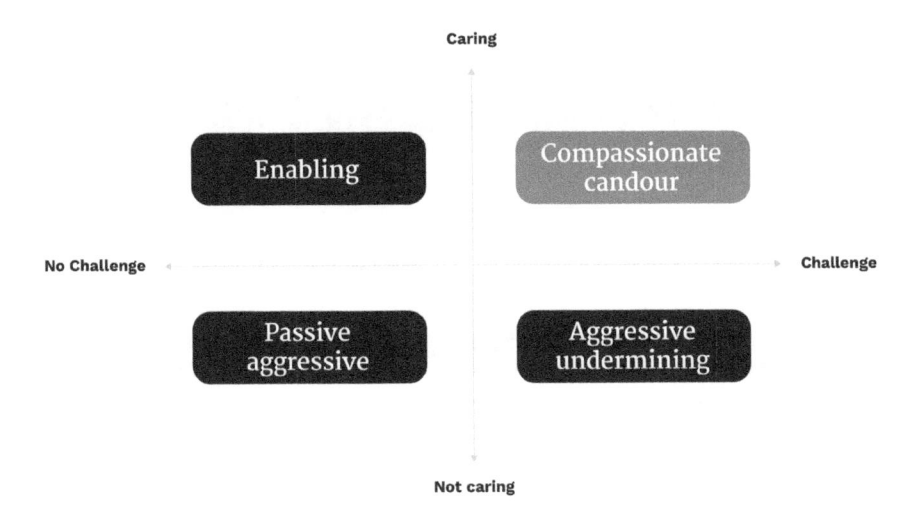

```
                    Caring
                      ▲
                      |
    ┌─────────────┐   |   ┌─────────────────┐
    │   Enabling  │   |   │  Compassionate  │
    │             │   |   │     candour     │
    └─────────────┘   |   └─────────────────┘
                      |
No Challenge ◄────────┼────────► Challenge
                      |
    ┌─────────────┐   |   ┌─────────────────┐
    │   Passive   │   |   │    Aggressive   │
    │  aggressive │   |   │   undermining   │
    └─────────────┘   |   └─────────────────┘
                      |
                      ▼
                  Not caring
```

- **Enabling.** If you show caring but don't challenge, this amounts to enabling of unwanted behaviour, and not only doesn't solve the problem, but will undermine the culture of the team, and leave the door open to more of such behaviour across the organisation.
- **Passive aggressive.** If you don't have a strong caring or empathy for someone, and don't challenge them on bad behaviour either, this amounts to 'passive aggressive' behaviour. Your disproval will show either way; it's just that in this way it is hidden and undermining, and leaves the issue unresolved.
- **Aggressive undermining.** Challenging people in ways driven by a lack of actual caring for that person creates feelings of personal animosity and victimisation, and will lead to a strong negative reaction.
- **Compassionate candour.** Capturing the difficult balance between caring and the willingness to challenge. Making someone understand what they've done wrong, and believe that your challenge to them comes from a place of genuine care and support.

It's worth noting that these are not personality types, it's not about assigning certain people to the four boxes. In fact, we all exhibit all these behaviours and one time or another, with different people. It's about defining and calling the behaviours when they occur.

Worksheet

Giving feedback — SCALE | Business growth made easy

Name: _____ Company: _____ Date: _____

How is feedback working in your organisation? Use this diagnostic tool to assess, and plan improvements. Ask the team to score (0-10) themselves and the team:

Feedback is..	The team	Me
Timely. Little or no gap between event and provision of feedback.		
Self-led. Feedback is given by the person with the feedback.		
Balanced. There is a healthy ratio of praise to criticism. Praise tends to be done in public, criticism in private.		
Planned. Feedback happens in response to events and at regular, planned intervals.		
Caring and Challenging. Feedback given addresses the issue head on, and makes the person feel it's done from a place of caring		
Bi-directional. Feedback happens both ways.		
Specific. Both praise and criticism are supported with examples.		
Not personal. Feedback focuses on impacts and outcomes, not on personality.		

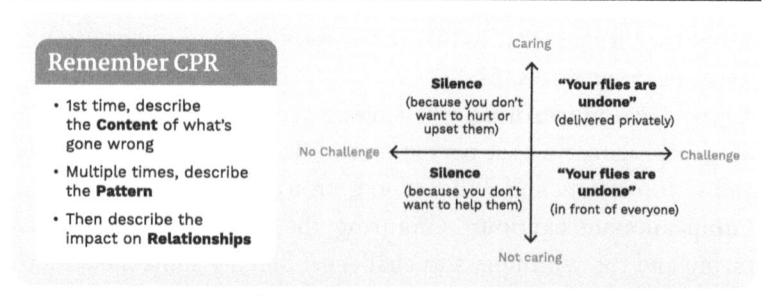

Remember CPR

- 1st time, describe the **Content** of what's gone wrong
- Multiple times, describe the **Pattern**
- Then describe the impact on **Relationships**

Caring / Not caring axis vs No Challenge / Challenge axis:

- **Caring, No Challenge**: Silence (because you don't want to hurt or upset them)
- **Caring, Challenge**: "Your flies are undone" (delivered privately)
- **Not caring, No Challenge**: Silence (because you don't want to help them)
- **Not caring, Challenge**: "Your flies are undone" (in front of everyone)

Next Steps. Based on these scores, which item above should we work on this Q, and what should we do?

Exercise

This exercise is a team diagnosis of what's working and not working with respect to how you give feedback:

- Get the team together for 60 minutes, in order to discuss how we can work and perform as a team by improving how we give feedback.
- Invite each team member to fill out their scores, from 0 to 10, for themselves, and for the team as a whole.
- In pairs, groups, or as a whole team, share the scores.
- Identify where the common areas for improvement are.
- Brainstorm how this can be improved. Refer to the tools and concepts of the article above.

13

SMC 7 – PROFITABILITY

Checklist item

Issue

Our **profitability** is too low, or trending negatively.

Manifestation

Our net profitability is at or trending towards <15–25%.

Summary

A great business should be motivated by a strong sense of purpose *and* a drive to generate profit. There should be no contradiction between these objectives. Profit both provides the resources to further expand and rewards those contributing to it.

Money is fungible – it can move seamlessly between markets and industries, so companies or sectors that deliver low returns get starved of funding, and decline. The net effect of this is that within major industry blocks, there exist **goldilocks zones** of profitability. For example, for standard service companies, this range sits between 15% and 25% net profit rate. Above that rate, competitors quickly spring up and erode margins, below it, investment dries up.

If your profit rate is below target for your industry, in this section, we cover three topics that will allow you to get it where it needs to be.

Key concepts – profitability

They can't change what they don't know

My first piece of advice about profitability is: *share profitability data with your team*. Company owners can be nervous about this, afraid that staff might form resentments, or ask for more money, if they share how much profit the business makes. Believe me, you probably earn less profit than they think you do. Super-coach Andy Bailey of Petra Coach in the United States regularly polls teams that don't get to see company profit data on what they think the profit of the company is. The teams **always** over-estimate, assuming the company is making significantly more than it really does.

The point here though is that you cannot encourage people to improve performance on a number about which they have no visibility. If you're the only person who truly understands the profitability of the business, then for sure you are a bottleneck in improving it. People are, to a surprising extent, happy to accept that different people earn different amounts of money in life, and perfectly willing to work hard to improve a number that may only benefit them indirectly. Good teams take pride in running a business to a good level of profit. Everyone realises it is a key factor dictating how quickly the company (and therefore their opportunities for growth) can expand.

Being honest about profitability

On the face of it, profitability looks like it should be an easy number to work out and report on; however, there are common distortions that can cause the number to be inaccurate:

- **Under-paying yourself.** Surprisingly common amongst entrepreneurs. The 'belt-tightening' ethos of the start-up days lingers well beyond necessity. It's easy to test: if you had to replace yourself with a paid professional, how much would they cost? *Pay yourself that amount.* Anything else is not only unfair on you, but also a distortion of how profitable your company is. I have met many entrepreneurs who, as a result of under-paying themselves, have accepted low prices from their clients because they are under the false impression that their profitability is okay.
- **Paying yourself below the line.** If, for tax reasons, you pay yourself out of dividends (which is a sensible and legitimate thing to do), make sure that the profitability number you are looking at is after these deductions. If you don't, then you will look more profitable than you really are.
- **Including assets for which you haven't paid.** A business can be propped up from outside in many ways. Maybe another business in the group or family provides you with leads for free, or you have access to free office space, or have taken an interest-free loan. Any of these will make you look more profitable than you are. Include a consideration for the true cost of any bungs when you analyse profitability.
- **Stuffing non-company costs.** If you include costs into your P&L that aren't strictly company business, the company will look less profitable than it is. As well as potentially getting you in trouble with the tax man, at a certain point, this bad habit must be dropped in favour of clean management accounts.

If any of the above apply to you, rectify the distortion, at least on a spreadsheet, so that you can get an honest number about your profitability. These can be hard habits to kick, but bear one thing in mind: *one day you will have to sell your company*. There is no way round it, other than going bankrupt or just shutting up shop. No external acquirer will accept distortions in P&L reporting, so the sooner you clean it up, the sooner that day can come around.

In order to improve your profitability and grow your company, you will need the help of others. Most obviously this is the leadership team, but this may also include banks for external funding, government departments for tax grants and support, or auditors for the purpose of participating in and winning competitions and awards. *All of these people need an **accurate** view of profitability*, so if you are serious about scaling, you must leave these small company behaviours behind.

The #1 myth about profitability

Several years ago, I was giving training to a group of smart company CEOs, all running high-growth, mid-sized companies. We were discussing the link between profitability and cash flow, looking at a chart similar to this:

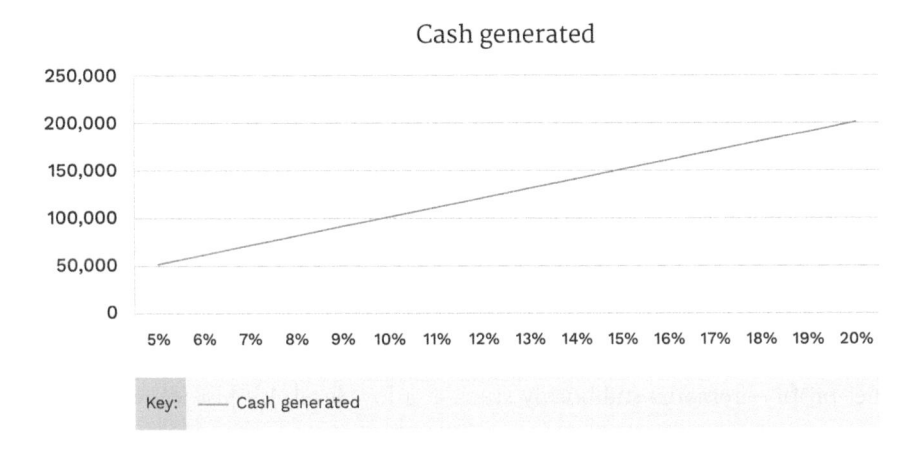

Cash generated

Key:	Cash generated

It makes the (rather obvious) point that the higher your net profit rate, the more cash you generate.

One of the attendees, running a successful manufacturing business, stated definitively that the net profit rate in his industry was: '6% – always has been, always will be', as if this were a given law of his business. We discussed cost-saving opportunities, and it became clear that he was over-paying on his factoring, and by changing supplier, he could add 2% points to his bottom line. So, I asked him 'What would happen now if you 'locked in' this new level of profit – 8%, and let your business carry on growth?' He conceded that this was totally possible, and all it required was the discipline to not go and spend this extra 2% on something else. And, he immediately realised that a company that consistently throws off 8% of profit will generate significantly more profit over time, that can subsequently be reinvested for growth.

What is at play here, once again, is **Parkinson's Law** (referenced also in Chapter 8 about time spent on meetings). It's a quirk of human psychology that we increase 'demand' in line with increase in 'supply'. In this case, it means that we spend according to what we earn (not a behaviour unique to business owners, by the way). So, as company income increases, we increase spending accordingly, maybe opening a nice office full of expensive equipment, or paying everyone various perks and benefits.

Parkinson's Law
The demand upon a resource tends to expand to match the supply of the resource, if the price of the resource is zero.
(The reverse is not true.)

For example:

- The amount spent by a department will rise to meet the budget allocated to them
- The amount of time spent discussing an item in a meeting will expand to match the time allocated for that meeting.

How this plays out in the company P&L is that you get the classic 'parallel lines' shape of historic income and costs. The gap between the two – the net profit – remains stubbornly stuck at a low level. It's just too easy and enjoyable to spend money that we earn…

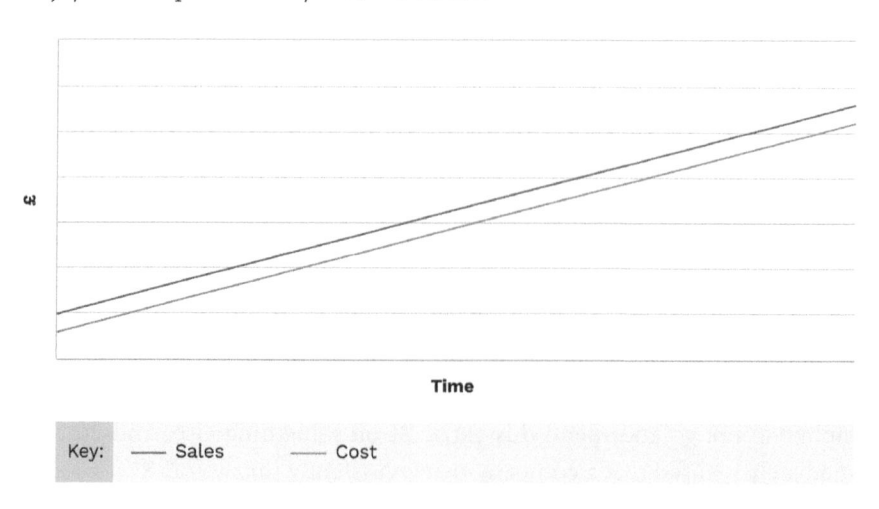

Key: ——— Sales   ——— Cost

This is a book about growth — how to scale a company, so we must ask: 'Why is high profitability good for growth?' Many company owners (much like my friend in the story above) would challenge that the reason they have low profitability is that they are constantly investing for growth. However, there is a difference between running at a low profit rate, and re-investing existing reserves for growth. These are different pools of capital in the business (this is explored in more detail in Chapter 14). It may sound like a semantic distinction, but they are different in important ways:

	Expenses	Reinvested profits
Period/frequency	Recurring	Projects
Measure of success	P&L Performance ratios	Project ROI (over a period)
Objective/purpose	Driving existing top-line revenue	Chasing new/ future growth
Timing and reporting	Pre-profit	Post-profit

As the company grows and financial management becomes more sophisticated, these become separate pools of capital in the business, even under different business entities.

Don't allow the temptation of the thought 'this is an investment for the future' allow you to add to today's cost base.

Here we will focus on how to improve core profitability. Low profitability can come about for just a short list of reasons:

- Your pricing is too low
- Your costs are too high
- Based on a fixed cost base, your sales are too low.

Before we look at these in more detail, it's important for you to understand the impact that changes in each of these areas can have on your bottom line, explored in the next chapter.

Power of One

Summary

Find out how to make 1 + 1 + 1 + 1 = 33 (where '33' means a 33% improvement in your profitability). Financially driven decision-making is key to the development of any maturing business. This exercise gives you and the team the information you need to make key decisions to improve the performance of your business.

Concept

Think like an owner

Development as an entrepreneur requires 'thinking like an owner'.

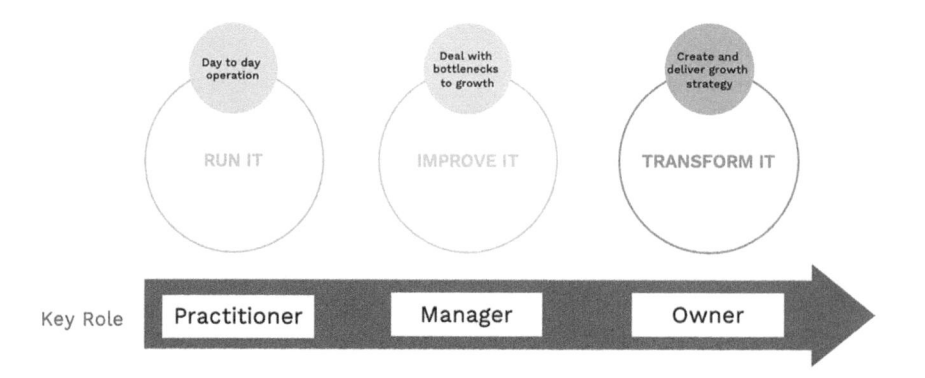

	Day to day operation	Deal with bottlenecks to growth	Create and deliver growth strategy
	RUN IT	IMPROVE IT	TRANSFORM IT
Key Role	Practitioner	Manager	Owner

A key aspect of this is to think of the business increasingly in **financial terms**. This is not to downplay the importance of culture, team, people, customer service, and all the other things that may make your company special. It's that as a company grows, financial decisions simply become more important. There is an increasing responsibility on the owner of the business to get them right, for everyone's sake.

This needs to start with a clear understanding of the consequences of changes in the financial levers of the business. It is remarkable what the power of small, compound changes can be, and being clear eyed about them can have significant impact on your financial decision-making.

Small changes with big impacts

Take a look at this example from a small design agency. They've listed out their current cash and profitability, then worked out what 1% changes to certain key financial metrics would mean to their cash and profit in the following 12 months:

Your Power of One		Net Cash Flow £	EBIT £
Your Current Position		-£ 400,201	£ 532,641

Your Power of One	Change You Would Like to make	Annual Impact on Cash Flow	Impact on EBIT £
Price Increase %	1%	£ 81,464.71	£ 81,464.71
Volume Increase %	1%	£ 19,867.40	£ 19,867.40
COGS Reduction %	1%	£ 61,597.31	£ 61,597.31
Overheads Reduction %	1%	£ 14,540.99	£ 14,540.99
Reduction in Debtor Days	1 day	£ 22,319.10	n/a
Reduction in Stock Days	1 day	n/a	n/a
Reduction in Creditors Days	1 day	£ 16,875.98	n/a
Your Power of One Impact		£ 216,665.48	£ 177,470.41
Your Power of One		Net Cash Flow £	EBIT £
Your Adjusted Position		-£ 183,535.52	£ 710,111.41

This exercise is called 'The Power of One' (developed by Alan Miltz). In this example, even though they're only changing four things by 1%, the total is an improvement of their profitability from £532k to £710k, an improvement of over 33%. It makes 1 + 1 + 1 + 1=33.

The impact on cash is even more significant. As well as the previous four changes, they also look at the impact of 1% improvements in their debtor and creditor days. The total improvement here is over £216k, which is a 54% improvement in their cash position, over 12 months.

How does it help?

Knowledge is power

Most teams, when doing this for the first time, are surprised by the extent of small changes on their cash and profit positions. When everyone understands these impacts, it makes it easier to influence all the small day-to-day behaviours that go to influence these numbers, such as payment terms with suppliers and customers.

Tweak your settings

Working out the 1% numbers allows you to then do target setting for the year. It's a bit like setting the dials on an amplifier, you need to get them set right for the best performance. Maybe you want to sacrifice a little turnover in favour of higher prices, or have a big push on COGS reduction, even if expenses don't move too much? It gives you the information to understand the financial impact of those calls.

Set targets

This a helpful exercise to run towards the end of the year, as it allows you to set targets and budgets for the following year. Including the team in the process allows these decisions to be collective, and agree together where the improvements need to come from.

Make a real difference

We have seen teams make remarkable improvements to their financial performance based on this simple exercise. Teams that were previously losing money now becoming profitable, or teams reaching sustained profit levels that then allowed them to sell the business. It can do the same for you.

Exercise

The exercise below is a simple introduction to a few key financial decision-making frameworks that you need to master.

(NB – this is a simplified version of the 'Power of One' exercise, by Alan Miltz)

Session basics	
Name	'Power of One'
How to Communicate	'Understanding the impact of small changes in the financial performance of the business in certain areas can help us to make good decisions on the financial future of the business'.

SMC 7 – PROFITABILITY

Time	90 minutes
Format	Workshop session
Attendees	Leadership team, especially with finance leadership

Preparation	
Objective and outcome	Understand the implication of % point changes in key areas, in order to create a future budget for the business.
Learning and reading	*Cash Flow Story* by Alan Miltz
Materials	Worksheet. This exercise is best done together using one sheet (either digitally, or printed). For this exercise, you will need your full year P&L for the past 2 years.

Exercise	
Objective	Share and discuss the objectives of the session.
Actuals	Start by filling out the actual figures listed from the P&L, for the past 2 years.
1% changes	Use the formulae provided to work out what the impact of 1% changes would be across the four levers listed.
Discussion	Discuss where you see the opportunities for change and improvement being in the upcoming period.
Targets	Start with Rows 1., 2., fill in target % change first, then the target amount (calculated by multiplying the target % change by last year actuals). Then add the target amounts from 1. and 2. into Target amount on row 3., to work out target sales for the next period. Now work out the target profit rate, starting with % change, then the actual amount, and what that would be the % of sales. Finally, work through the three key cost numbers, to complete the set of targets. For labour, remember it is typically included as a component of overheads, not in addition to it.
Next steps	This is an effective means of creating a draft budget with the finance and management team. Next steps are typically for finance to work with department heads to work out more detailed budgets, based on these headline figures.

Worksheet

Power of 1 — SCALE — Business growth made easy

Name: _____ Company: _____ Date: _____

Come prepared with your P&L's from the past 2 years. First, fill out the actuals:

Item	Last year actual	As % sales	Previous year actual	As % sales
Sales				
COGS				
Overheads				
Labour				
Profit				

How would 1% changes affect numbers (based on last years' numbers)?

Item	Formula	1% change impact
Price increase	1% x Sales	
Volume increase	1% x Sales - COGS	
COGS reduction	1% x COGS	
Overhead reduction	1% x Overheads	

How much do you want to move each dial?
Set a target % change, and work out the target amount (based on last year actual)

	A. Item	B. Target % change	C. Target amount (B. x last yr actual)	As % sales	Notes
1	Price				Av total price increase
2	Volume				Excl. effect of 1.
3	Sales			100%	Sum of 1. and 2.
4	COGS				Take into account 2.
5	Overheads				
6	Labour				What is ideal ratio?
7	Profit				Remember Profit 1st !

Feb23 - © Clarity Strategy Ltd DBA Scale 2023   www.scalecoach.co.uk

Pricing

Summary

The #1 way to improve your profitability is through pricing. Low pricing holds back many more scaling companies than over-pricing. Done well, great pricing can achieve two objectives seemingly at odds simultaneously:

- Improve margins, *and*
- Improve customer conversion rates.

How can this be possible? Classic economic theory dictates that pricing works linearly – prices go up, conversions go down. Fortunately, pricing is nowhere near this simple, there is plenty of scope to improve both.

This section contains some of the key concepts associated with pricing. Different pricing models are suited to different types of products and services. Read through the different concepts and models, and reflect on which might be valid for your products and services, then work through the workshop worksheet with the team.

Key concepts

Rule #1

This is a simple one:

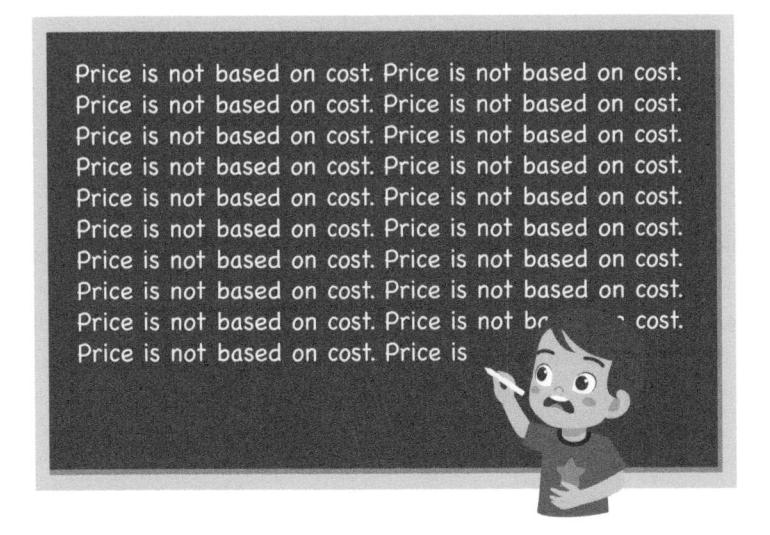

> Price is not based on cost. Price is not based on cost.
> Price is not based on cost. Price is not based on cost.
> Price is not based on cost. Price is not based on cost.
> Price is not based on cost. Price is not based on cost.
> Price is not based on cost. Price is not based on cost.
> Price is not based on cost. Price is not based on cost.
> Price is not based on cost. Price is not based on cost.
> Price is not based on cost. Price is not based on cost.
> Price is not based on cost. Price is not based on cost.
> Price is not based on cost. Price is

Don't make the mistake of just taking cost prices and adding a nominal margin rate to each product or service. Of course this is what your customers would like you to do, but short of actually losing money on each sale, it is about the worst pricing strategy you can adopt.

Let's cover a little theory to understand better approaches.

Turning a pricing triangle into a pricing square

In classic economic theory, the relationship between price and sales is linear, and negative, meaning that higher price causes lower sales. On a chart, this would look like this:

Typically, there is a unit cost below which we stop making money, that is, selling below that price means that we lose money. So, there is a zone, or 'triangle', of potential price points above that price, within which we can make money. Bottom right of this triangle denotes a 'high price – low volume', and top left is 'low price – high volume'.

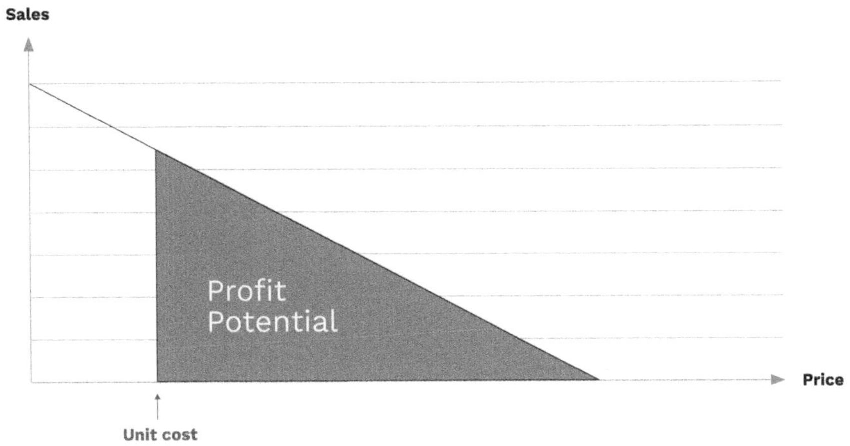
Sales
Profit Potential
Price
Unit cost

Picking up one nominal price point within this triangle ('our price' on the chart below) means foregoing two opportunities:

- *'Passed up profit'*. Customers who would have bought profitably, but at a lower price, and
- *Money left on the table'*. Customers who would have bought the same product at a higher price.

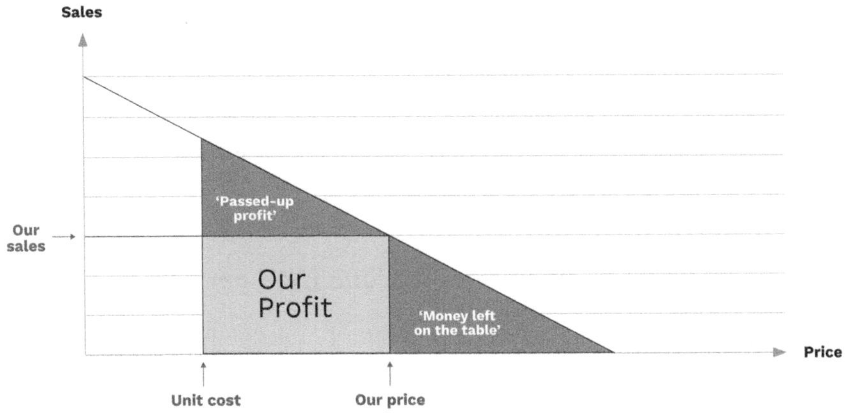
Sales
'Passed-up profit'
Our sales
Our Profit
'Money left on the table'
Price
Unit cost
Our price

The way to avoid these missed opportunities, and the conclusion to draw from this model, therefore, is that effective pricing depends upon being able to sell to **different customer groups at different price points**. This concept is key to the understanding of effective pricing.

This example comes from a German cinema chain that changed their pricing to offer differential pricing based on the number of visits within the period. You can see from the diagram how this has 'filled out' their price 'rectangle' into something resembling a pricing 'triangle'.

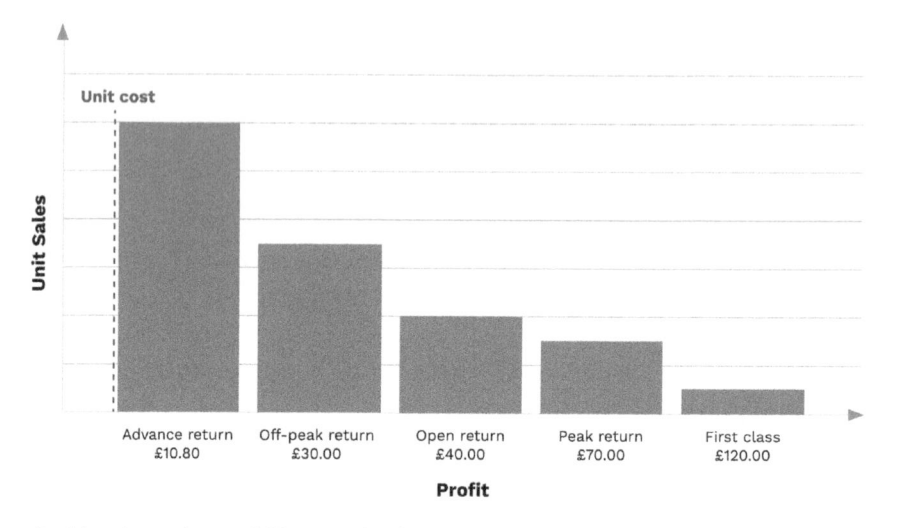

[Chart: Unit Sales (y-axis) vs Profit (x-axis), with "Unit cost" marked as a horizontal reference line. Bars from tallest to shortest:
- Advance return £10.80
- Off-peak return £30.00
- Open return £40.00
- Peak return £70.00
- First class £120.00]

(*Models and examples provided here are taken from various books by pricing guru Hermann Simon, such as 'Confessions of the Pricing Man'.*)

Much of the pricing strategy therefore is about realising ways to achieve the outcome of **different prices for different customers.** Let's look at a few.

There is no such thing as 'one item one price'

In the real world, there is rarely a concept of 'one product'. Regardless of whether you sell products or services, they are rarely discrete to the point of single, indivisible products. Take coffee, for example. Which of the products below counts as 'coffee'?

The level of price depends upon the perceived value of that customer group. This is a complex notion that can include all sorts of emotive and rational consideration on behalf of the client, from brand, convenience,

Price per cup

| 3 pence | 9 pence | £2.25 | £2.85 |

benefit, and even just how they're feeling when they make the purchase. Take a look at these (2019) price points for a cup of coffee from different brands.

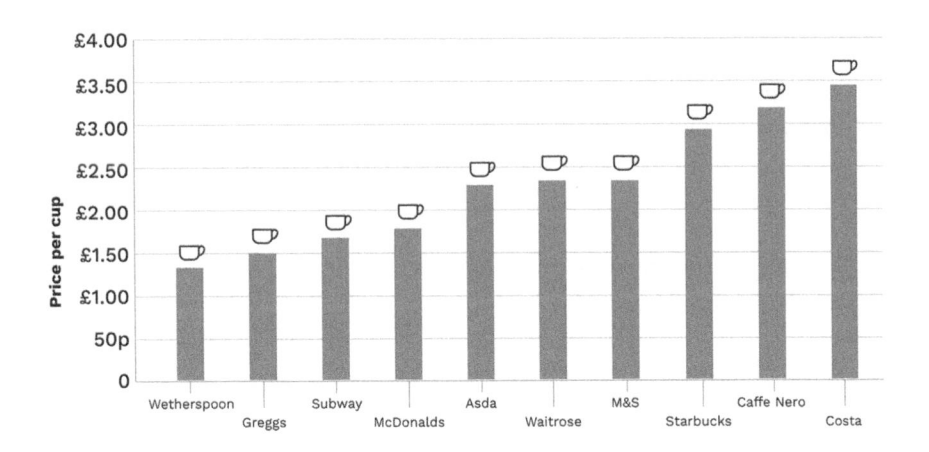

[Bar chart showing price per cup by brand: Wetherspoon ~£1.40, Greggs ~£1.50, Subway ~£1.70, McDonalds ~£1.80, Asda ~£2.35, Waitrose ~£2.40, M&S ~£2.40, Starbucks ~£2.95, Caffe Nero ~£3.25, Costa ~£3.50]

Most products and services have numerous variants and variables to them, that make direct 'apple to apple' price comparisons very difficult. A lot of price guarantees contain the weaselly words 'if you find *the same product* cheaper elsewhere, then we will...', because they know that most products and services differ in some way or another.

The same item can have different prices

Even in the situation where a product is uniform and clear-cut, it can still be sold for different prices. Take, for example, a can of drink. Everyone is clear on what this product is, and how much it costs, and yet willing to accept different prices for it, depending on where it's being purchased.

Chart: Price of 0.33l can by location

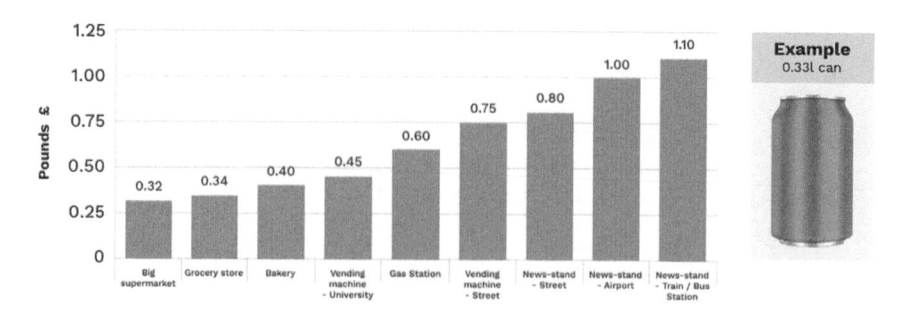

Location	Price (Pounds £)
Big supermarket	0.32
Grocery store	0.34
Bakery	0.40
Vending machine - University	0.45
Gas Station	0.60
Vending machine - Street	0.75
News-stand - Street	0.80
News-stand - Airport	1.00
News-stand - Train / Bus Station	1.10

Example: 0.33l can

The masters of this are airlines. Again, as customers, we have become familiar with the concept that an identical product – same seat on the same flight, can be sold for different prices, depending on when it's purchased, and how many have already been sold. We understand that they operate a pricing system based on demand, not on the cost of service delivery.

> If I have 2,000 customers on a given route and 400 prices, I am obviously short 1,600 prices.
>
> Robert Crandall
> CEO of American Airlines

Prices can vary for the same product or service for numerous reasons. Here are some common ones:

- **Sales channels**. If you sell through intermediaries, such as retailers or wholesalers, some incur additional cost, have different target market, so can justify different prices.
- **Customer groups**. Some customers can afford to pay more, even for the same product. Students can be a viable customer group, but they will expect a discount.
- **Location**. The sandwich at the mountain restaurant will always cost more than the one in the valley.
- **Volume**. Whether a single person surcharge or volume discount, the same item will have a different cost depending on how much is purchased.
- **Time of purchase**. Never offer a discount to someone in a hurry.

What other variables do you have that merit different prices for the same item?

The pinnacle of this pricing method is the auction. In an auction situation, buyer and seller both accept that there is no fixed price for what is being sold, simply variables on demand. Google uses this to great effect in the selling of their ads, this is not some antiquated methodology, but in active use today.

My therapist uses a similar method which is: 'Simply pay me what you think it's worth'. She offers no guide price, and I have no idea whether I pay more or less than her other clients. Studies have shown that this exotic method on average leads to higher average spend than advertised, fixed prices.

Range pricing

Customers want choice. But not too much choice. Human psychology provides interesting guide-rails as to how to go about range pricing. For whatever reason, the goldilocks zone of choices in a range is three. Retailers are experts at this, where it is known under the moniker 'Good – better – best', here are numerous examples of this range architecture:

Product	Brand	Prices (index)	
Chocolate (1 bar 100g)	Tesco Ms Molly's		£0.33
	Dairy Milk		£1.25
	Green & Black's		£2.00
Ice cream (1 litre)	Asda		£1.75
	Carte D'Or		£3.50
	Häagen-Dazs		£4.80
Crisps (6x 25g)	Tesco		£1.00
	Walkers		£1.75
	Kettle Chips		£2.35

This is by no means limited to traditional retail. Software companies have adopted this architecture in a big way.

Set the price boundaries

A huge advantage of having a range is that you get to set the reference points that customers will use for making purchase decisions.

Take, for example, this range of wines in a restaurant:

Rotwein– Vino Rosso – Red Wine – Vin Rouge			
Alliotto Lunelli	13% Vol.	0.75l	19.50€
Primitivo Passo del Cardinale	14% Vol.	0.75l	24.50€
Sabazio Rosso di Montepulciano	13% Vol.	0.75l	29.50€
Tacco rosso Negramaro	14.5% Vol.	0.75l	38.50€
Ronchiedone Ca dei Frati	14.5% Vol.	0.75l	38.50€
Insoglio del Cinghiale	13.5% Vol.	0.75l	42.50€

What do you think happens to the average transaction value when it changes to this?

Rotwein– Vino Rosso – Red Wine – Vin Rouge			
Alliotto Lunelli	13% Vol.	0.75l	19.50€
Primitivo Passo del Cardinale	14% Vol.	0.75l	24.50€
Sabazio Rosso di Montepulciano	13% Vol.	0.75l	29.50€
Tacco rosso Negramaro	14.5% Vol.	0.75l	38.50€
Ronchiedone Ca dei Frati	14.5% Vol.	0.75l	38.50€
Insoglio del Cinghiale	13.5% Vol.	0.75l	42.50€
Brunello di Montalcino Biondi Santi	13% Vol.	0.75l	110.00€
Tignanello	14.5% Vol.	0.75l	120.00€

The addition of the two expensive items causes the average customer spend to increase. This is not because people are buying many of the very expensive bottles of wine; it's because their reference point of affordability has changed. Their view of the 'typical price' of a bottle of wine has increased, so they change their purchase behaviour accordingly.

I was recently looking at birthday gifts for a friend who drives a Rolls Royce. I found a Rolls Royce picnic hamper that looked nice, until I checked the price – over £40,000. If I take the reference point of this item as other picnic hampers, priced at a few hundred £, it looks outrageously over-priced. However, if you're buying a car for £400,000 and you see an extra that is £40,000, your frame of reference is quite different. It still doesn't feel 'cheap', but it may feel relatively 'affordable' vs. the main event (especially if you equate value with specialisation of your expensive car).

Bundling

So far, we have been looking at prices for 'single items', but in the real world, pricing is rarely so discrete. Even in the example of the cup of coffee above, you may pay extra if you want a special milk, or earn some kind of a discount if you 'bundle' it with a pastry.

Take a look at this example. In the first situation, a bank account is advertised at £1 (the example actually comes from the United States in US$), and a bank account with a credit card at £2.50. You can see that 41% of customers chose just the account, and 59% the account with the credit card, for an average spend of £1.89.

In the second scenario, the only thing that was changed was the addition of another price point, which was for the stand-alone credit card at £2.50/month.

		Share of sales	ARPU
Bank Account	£1 / month	41%	£1.89
Bank Account with Credit Card	£2.50 / month	59%	
Bank Account	£1 / month	?	
Credit Card	£2.50 / month	?	?
Bank Account with Credit Card	£2.50 / month	?	

How do you think the share of sales and Average Revenue Per Unit changed after this addition?

		Share of sales	ARPU
Bank Account	£1 / month	41%	£1.89
Bank Account with Credit Card	£2.50 / month	59%	
Bank Account	£1 / month	17%	£2.24 +19%
Credit Card	£2.50 / month	2%	
Bank Account with Credit Card	£2.50 / month	81%	

That's a 19% increase in average spend for doing nothing more than including another price point. This example demonstrates the power of pricing so clearly. It really is an example of money for nothing. No product development was required for this increase, no expensive marketing campaign, or lengthy training of sales teams. Just the addition of one item on a product flyer, and revenues are increased by almost a fifth, with no extra costs.

Much strategy around bundling rests upon the logic of the cost of acquisition of a customer. Given how much it costs to acquire a customer, once you have them with their wallet open, it pays to cross-sell them to as many other products as possible, even if those products are not sold at full price. You will still make more money than going out to acquire another customer. We are all familiar with how bundling pricing works from fast food restaurants:

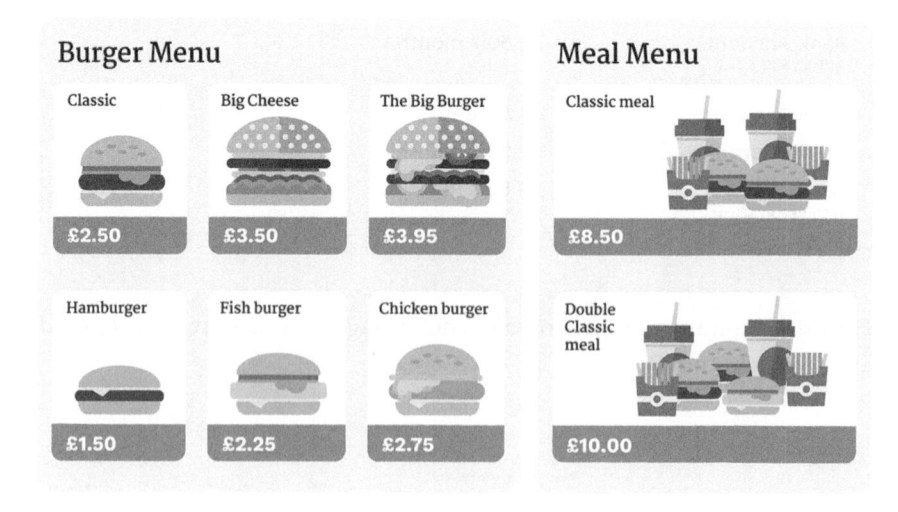

Burger Menu

Classic	Big Cheese	The Big Burger
£2.50	£3.50	£3.95
Hamburger	Fish burger	Chicken burger
£1.50	£2.25	£2.75

Meal Menu

Classic meal	£8.50
Double Classic meal	£10.00

Add-ons

The related, but opposite, cousin to bundling is the add-on. The industry with form in this area is cars. We are all familiar with the situation of liking the look and price of a particular model in the showroom, only for the final product to end up painfully higher, given all the add-ons that the salesperson suggests on adding.

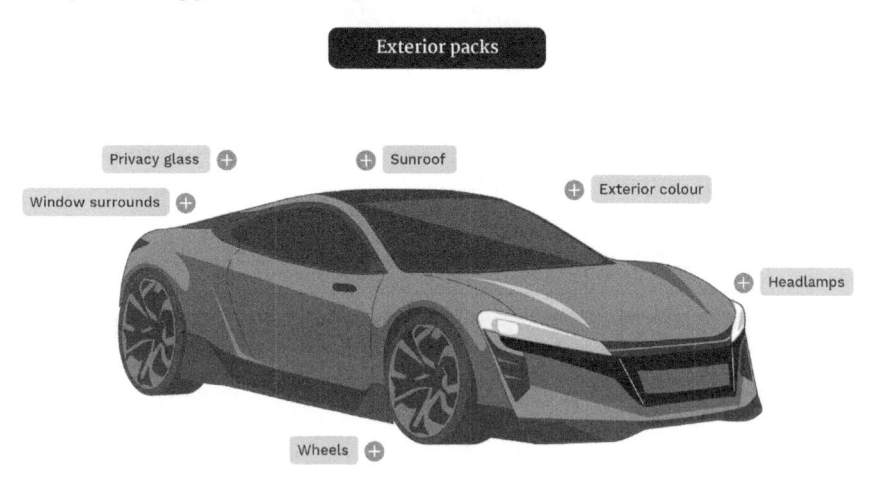

Inflation

One final point to remember about pricing is that if you are not regularly raising prices, then you are by default reducing them, as the constant force of inflation acts to reduce the value of what you're paid in – currency.

Worksheet

Pricing strategy
SCALE | Business growth made easy

Name: _____ Company: _____ Date: _____

1 Price over market share

Where are you now & what do you want? What options do you see? Value? Perception? Segments? New products/services?

Price \ Market share	Low	Market share	High
High			
Price			
Low			

Options	Price +/-	Share +/-

2 Price choice

What could you do to offer different price options for similar products and services?

Product / Service	Price	Lower option	Higher option

3 Product ranges

Could you offer a higher or lower priced option in the same category? Using partners or affiliates?

Product / Service category	Lower option	Your price	Higher option

4 Pricing technique mix

Technique	Margin impact	New method
Competitive		
Multi-Dimensional		
Bundling		
Add-On		
Exotics		

Feb23 · © Clarity Strategy Ltd DBA Scale 2023 | Original document used with permission · Copyright 2011 Gazelles, Inc.   www.scalecoach.co.uk

Exercise

Session basics	
Name	'Pricing'
How to Communicate	'If we improve our margins, we can make life better for the whole business – improving both our margins and our customer conversions'
Time	90 minutes
Format	Workshop session
Attendees	Leadership team and senior managers in sales, marketing, and product development

Preparation	
Objective and outcome	Improve margins and conversions through using pricing best practices to improve how we price.
Learning and reading	*Confessions of a Pricing Man* Herman Simon
Materials	Printed worksheets and pens

Exercise	
Objective	Share and discuss the objective of the session. We're looking for a list of actions and changes we will make over this quarter to improve conversions and margins.
Price vs. market share	Confirm understanding of the two axes: • Price/margin. Are we, relative to the competition at a high/medium/or low price or margin point? • Market share. Within our defined market, is our market share low/medium/high? • Have each attendee on their worksheet plot first where they think you are now, then draw an arrow to where they think we should be. Discuss as a team, and agree on the direction of travel for the business.
Price choice	Have each participant record their ideas, then brainstorm together the opportunities for selling the same goods and services at different price points, for example through different sales channels, to different customer groups, or at different purchase times or volumes.
Ranges	What opportunities do you have to create ranges of your products for different customer groups? Have participants write down their own ideas, then compare, and discuss. Compile a 'good-better-best' range architecture that would work for your products.
Other pricing techniques	Have each participant reflect and record their ideas for further pricing options, then discuss as a team. Which would be the ones that would increase margins and conversions for the business?

Next steps	Pull together the ideas from the discussions, and agree on what steps you will take over the next 3 months and set targets on sales, margins, and conversions for the new price points agreed.

Cost control

Summary

Consistently growing profitability means keeping a handle on costs whilst revenues continue to rise. This requires discipline, and there are some tricks and techniques that can help to maintain it.

Key concepts

Profit first

Based on your Power of One assessment, you may have decided that you have costs that could be reduced. If cost control is a challenge for you and your company, a valuable approach to this challenge comes from Mike Michalowicz's book *Profit First*. The trick is to re-frame the profit formula of the company. We all know that company profit works according to the formula:

Profit = Income – Costs

But we can think about the formula differently:

Costs = Income – profit

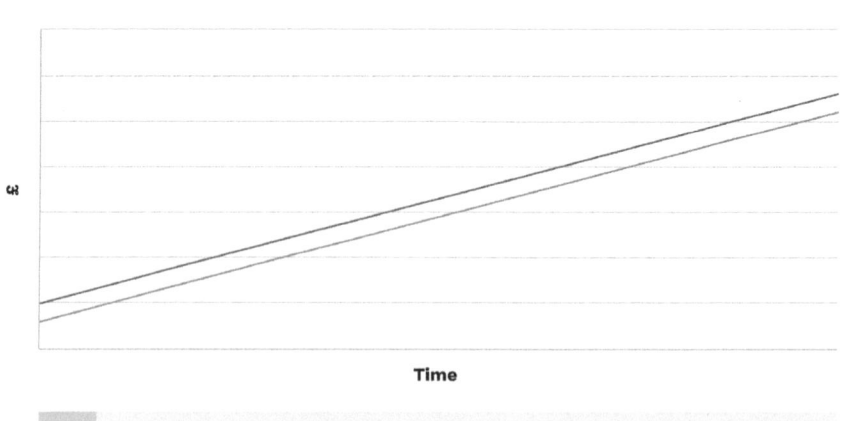

Key: —— Sales   —— Cost

Time

That is, set a fixed target profit rate in the business and only spend according to that rate.

This approach is for dealing with the common syndrome whereby, as a company grows, spending simply increases in line with sales growth, and you get stuck always just making the same money (either as a %, or worse, as a fixed amount).

This occurs as a result of Parkinson's Law (explained in detail on page 150), whereby we psychologically adapt what we allow ourselves to spend, based on what we earn. Setting a target profit rate, and only allow ourselves to spend around that fights against this tendency.

Granny accounting

Michalowicz suggests setting that money aside somewhere where you can't touch it. This means setting up separate bank accounts to put set asides for things like personal earnings, taxes, profit, and expenses, even automatically deducting it into those accounts.

This is called 'granny accounting' as it's akin to the method old people used to employ by putting cash in specific envelopes for items such as rent, and having the discipline to not raid those envelopes for other expenditure.

Not everyone needs such a level of intervention, but we have seen it work very effectively for those who just can't control the urge to spend. I have a friend in Australia who pulled himself out of bankruptcy simply by applying his technique.

Controlling costs

A helpful exercise coming from this concept is a **recurring cost review**. It's very easy to build up a long list of recurring costs over time, such as software licences, publication subscriptions, memberships, and a long list of items that stay on the cost ledger, but fall into disuse. Resolve these by printing out of all your costs for the past 3 months, and take 3 coloured markers, 1 colour for each of:

- Required to keep the lights on
- Necessary or important
- Nice to have (but could live without).

Immediately cancel anything that isn't category 1 and react to anything that causes shouts from the team over the next 2 months.

14

SMC 8 – CASH

Checklist item

Issue

Our **cash** position is too weak, or trending negatively.

Manifestation

- Cash reserves at or trending towards <3 months expenses.
- More growth is leading to less cash.

Summary

The first law of entrepreneurial gravity famously states that **'Growth sucks cash'.** It does not have to be this way, however. Many companies have a positive 'cash conversion cycle' (CCC), that is, the more they grow, the more cash they generate.

Cash is important in a business in just two ways:

- Running out of it is a 'hard line', that is, a barrier we cannot cross, and
- More of it allows us to reinvest for growth.

What is 'cash'?

This may sound like an odd way to start a section titled 'Cash'; however, it's important to be clear on what it means. 'Cash' in this context refers to 'working capital', that is, the money we have on hand for the running of the business.

This is distinct from 'Profitability' (covered in Chapter 13). Though the two are intrinsically linked, they are different challenges, with different solutions. Whereas profitability concerns whether we are making money on paper, cash flow is all about whether that paper profitability is being converted into actual sources of usable funds for the business.

In this chapter, we cover:

- Understanding the five dials of cash flow, to ensure you always have healthy reserves of cash
- Having a positive CCC, to ensure that the more you grow, the more cash you generate.

Dials of cash flow

Summary

A healthy business needs to be built on solid financial fundamentals, which in turn requires understanding what 'normal' or 'good' look like in managing the money side of the business. For example, how much money should you take out of the business, how much to reinvest, and how much for growth? The dials of cash flow break down the movement of money in the business into five components and explains what targets to set for yourself for each.

Key concepts

Understanding the five dials

There are several 'forces' that affect cash in a business, and each can be thought of as a dial on a dashboard. At any given time, a dial can be moved, or left alone. The first foundational rule that must guide our tweaking of these dials is that we cannot run out of cash:

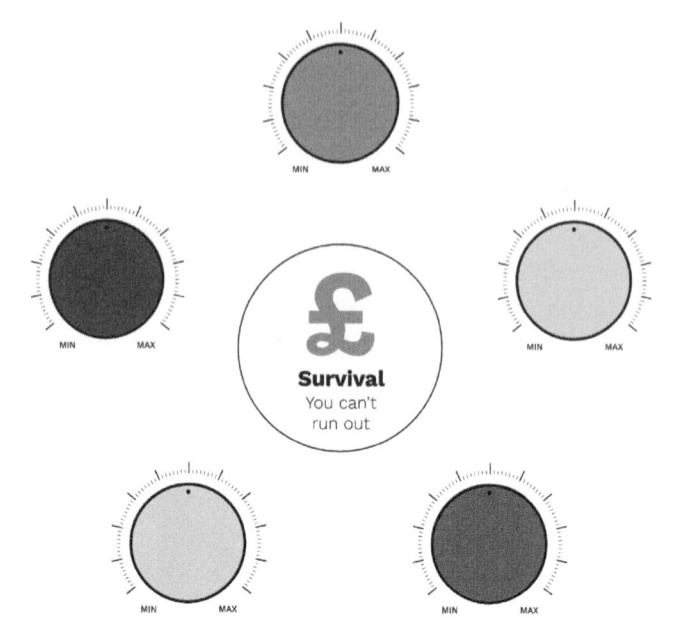

Survival
You can't run out

Let's look at what these five key factors, or dials, are:

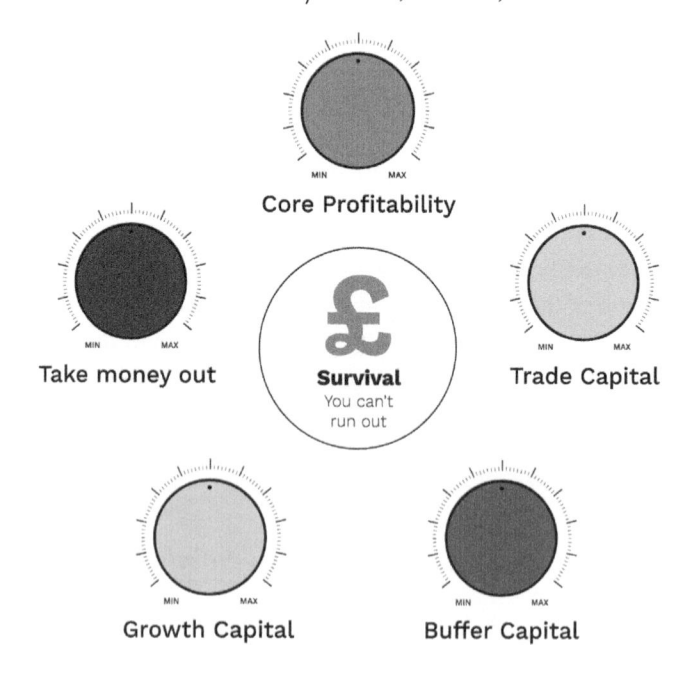

Core Profitability

Take money out — **Survival** You can't run out — **Trade Capital**

Growth Capital — **Buffer Capital**

SMC 8 – CASH   281

Item	Definition	How to find/calculate it	Impact it has	Impacted by
Core profitability	The net profit rate of the business	Net profit rate, from your P&L	Profitability has a direct impact on cash, namely, the more profitable you are, the more cash you generate	Key levers are pricing and cost control
Trade capital	Based on your payment terms w customers and suppliers, do you get paid before or after you have to pay out?	Cash Conversion Cycle (covered in detail on page 285)	Significant impact on cash. A positive CCC allows you to generate more cash as you grow (and vice versa)	The net balance of payment terms with customers and suppliers, as well as any trade financing, and stock turn
Buffer capital	Cash reserves, including day-to-day balance and set-asides, to cover running costs, shocks to the business, and set-asides for commitments such as taxes	Cash on hand, and any cash reserves in set-aside accounts. All included on the balance sheet	Too much set-aside sucks cash from other uses, not enough leaves you exposed in the event of shocks	Funds left in the main operating account(s), as well as decisions on transfer to set-aside accounts
Growth capital	Retained profits that can be allocated to investments	Cash reserves from retained profit	Invested well, will deliver growth, and further cash, to the business	Funds allocated for growth, and the return on investment (ROI) of growth projects
Taking money out	The amount of money you choose to take out of your business	Your salary and dividend payments	How much money you take out affects your quality of life, and how much cash there is left in the business for investment and growth	How do you decide to pay yourself fairly

Where to focus?

Making changes to any of these dials has an impact on your cash situation. What is most helpful from this model is to understand *'what good looks like'*. Following the guidelines below as a best practice on how to manage your cash will ensure that:

- You never run out of cash
- You always have funds to fuel growth
- You live within your means
- You and other owners get fairly and properly rewarded for the performance of the business.

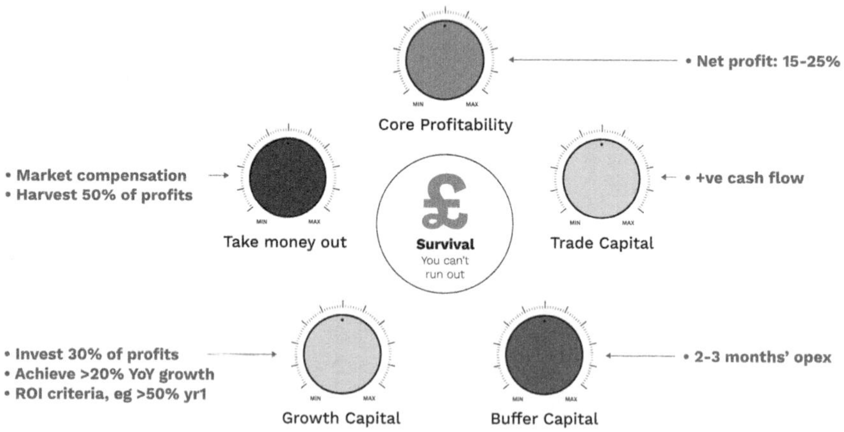
• Net profit: 15-25%
Core Profitability
• Market compensation
• Harvest 50% of profits
Take money out
Survival
You can't run out
Trade Capital
• +ve cash flow
• Invest 30% of profits
• Achieve >20% YoY growth
• ROI criteria, eg >50% yr1
Growth Capital
Buffer Capital
• 2-3 months' opex

What 'good' looks like:

- **Core profitability**. The business should run at above standard industry profit rates. Net profit rates vary by industry, but for a service business, this should be a net profit of >15–25% (explored in more detail in Chapter 13).
- **Trade capital**. The simple benchmark here is that you must have a positive Cash Conversion Cycle: that is, more sales generate more cash in the business (work on this in the exercise in this section on CCC).
- **Buffer capital**. Two key rules:

- Always have 2–3 months full operational costs on hand in the business. You never know when a shock will hit the business.
- Make sure you have cash for any upcoming significant payables, particularly tax, put in a separate set-aside account, where they don't get touched.

- **Growth capital**. Invest 50% of retained profits into growth initiatives, in order to achieve at least 20% compound growth. Ensure that every such project has clear rules on ROI, such as 50% payback within 12 months.
- **Take out money**:
  - Pay yourself a market salary.
  - Pay out the remaining 50% of retained profits, in order to reward the owners/shareholders of the business.

How do you perform against these benchmarks? Which are the areas you would work on first in order to improve your situation? Follow this exercise to decide if and where you need to make changes:

Worksheet

Exercise

- Stack rank the five in order of which you think requires the most focus now
- List out the actions in order to make improvements in the top 1–2 from the stack ranking
- Agree on next steps.

CHECKLISTS – DIAGNOSING BOTTLENECKS

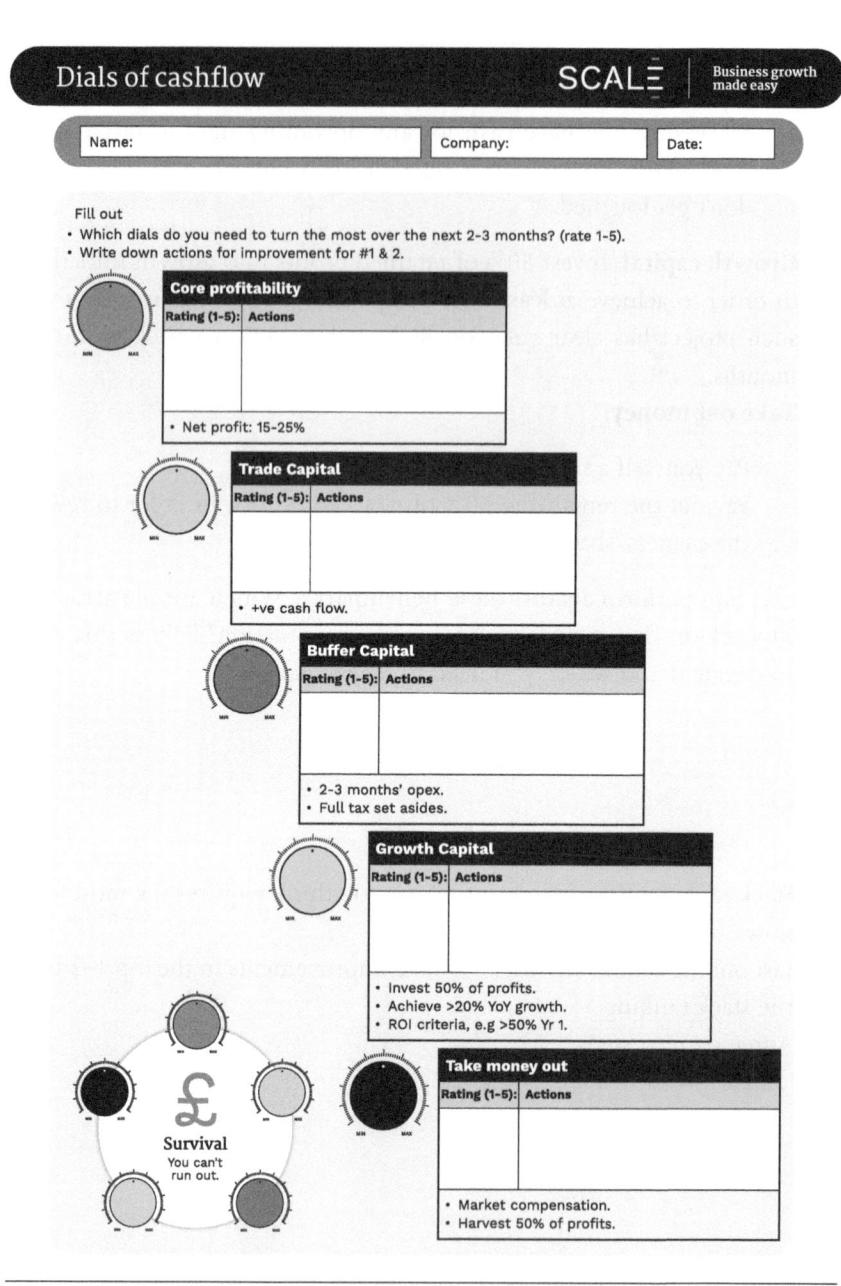

Dials of cashflow

SCALE — Business growth made easy

Name: Company: Date:

Fill out
- Which dials do you need to turn the most over the next 2-3 months? (rate 1-5).
- Write down actions for improvement for #1 & 2.

Core profitability
Rating (1-5):	Actions

- Net profit: 15-25%

Trade Capital
Rating (1-5):	Actions

- +ve cash flow.

Buffer Capital
Rating (1-5):	Actions

- 2-3 months' opex.
- Full tax set asides.

Growth Capital
Rating (1-5):	Actions

- Invest 50% of profits.
- Achieve >20% YoY growth.
- ROI criteria, e.g >50% Yr 1.

Take money out
Rating (1-5):	Actions

- Market compensation.
- Harvest 50% of profits.

Survival — You can't run out.

Feb23 - © Clarity Strategy Ltd DBA Scale 2023   www.scalecoach.co.uk

Cash conversion cycle

Summary

Understanding the Cash Conversion Cycle (CCC) comes down to one core question: **do you get paid before you have to pay out?** The answer to this question is very important for the growth of your business. If the answer is no, then the more you grow, the more you will deplete cash reserves, until they become a bottleneck on growth. The extent to which you answer 'yes' to this question (and it can be measured in days) will determine the levels of cash reserves you have to reinvest in the growth of the business.

Key concepts

What is the CCC?

The CCC is actually a series of cycles, the sum of which describes how long it takes (in days) for a £ invested into the business to come back in cash. A CCC can be either positive or negative: that is, you may have to put money in first, or you get paid first. This 'tipping point' is really important.

There are a couple of definitions of the CCC, the first is a 'full CCC' including elements of the business that can impact the CCC, then there is a narrower accounting definition, that I will summarise for you below.

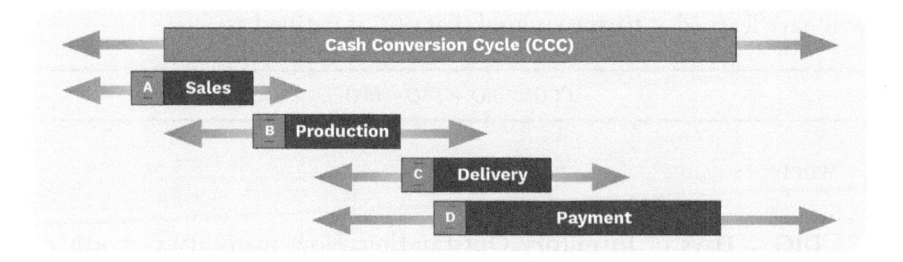

'Full' CCC

The full CCC is made up of four component cycles. They are of varying importance to different companies. For example, if you are a service business with no inventory, then your 'Production' cycle will not be so relevant. These cycles often happen **concurrently**. For example, you may start your billing cycle before you have completed your delivery cycle (in fact, it is good practice to start it as early as possible!):

- **Sales cycle.** From starting to make investments in lead generation, such as pay-per-click marketing, or sponsoring an event, how long does it take to close a lead and sign them as a customer?
- **Production.** Cash committed to the purchase of inventory and production of your product. How long it takes from the payment of inventory until final goods are ready for delivery. This cycle is of course particularly relevant to companies that sell physical goods.
- **Delivery.** In a physical goods business, this is the time taken to get the goods into the client's hands and signed off, including any install times. For a services company, this cycle is how long it takes to deliver your service, so from project initiation to sign-off.
- **Payment.** This starts when you invoice a client and takes as long as it takes until the cash reaches your bank account. In some businesses, such as retail or online businesses, this cycle is essentially instantaneous, because the customer pays upfront, and there is no billing cycle.

Accounting definition

If you speak to your finance department, they will be familiar with the concept of the CCC, but will not equate it with the diagram above. They will have learned at finance school that CCC is defined as:

$$CCC = DIO + DSO - DPO$$

where:

- **DIO = Days of Inventory Outstanding.** How many days' worth of sales of inventory you hold. The higher this number, the more inventory you have, and the more cash it is tying up.
- **DSO = Days Sales Outstanding.** A measure of your accounts receivable. Can be understood as the average of how long it takes for you to get paid.
- **DPO = Days Payable Outstanding.** A measure of your accounts payable. Can be understood as how many days, on average, it takes you to pay your suppliers.

This is an important and valuable number to understand and track as part of your CCC.

How to improve your CCC?

The #1 suggestion I would make is to encourage you to **share cash flow data with your team**. I had a client in China many years ago, a British design agency. They wanted their team in China to believe that they were a much larger agency than they really were, so they did not share cash flow data with the team. This had the desired effect, the team out there believed that they were part of a large, well-funded business, and they behaved accordingly.

Within 3 years, a profitable British small and medium-sized enterprise export business decided to close up shop in China. Why? Because they were fed up having to subsidise cash flow from London. In fact, in the months after closing down the business, a wave of cash ended up flowing back to the U.K. company.

What had happened was that no one (except a stressed-out General Manager) was prioritising cash flow. Cash flow is as much the results of *many small decisions* spread across a team as it is of significant central ones. Everyone impacts cash flow in a team, they all make decisions that have financial impact. So, in order to influence and guide those decisions, they need to understand the real cash flow situation. This is more of a statement of confidence than pretending that you have bottomless pockets. Every team we have ever worked with has taken a sensible and grown-up response to having cash flow data shared with them, even if the data are alarming.

Shortening your CCC

On the worksheet, you can see that the improvements are listed in three categories. Here we describe each, and share examples on how teams have made improvements in each of these areas.

Shorten cycle times

The quicker cycles get completed, the more the CCC improves:

- **Sales cycle**. Improving your sales best practices by developing and implementing a Sales Playbook (described in detail here: Sales Playbook) will allow you to reduce your sales cycle time.

- **Production**. Improvements tend to be found in three key areas: Production, Supply chain, and Inventory. In particular, we see teams working to reduce inventory levels, for example, by analysing inventory turn rates for different items and updating ordering accordingly, and selling or returning surplus or non-sale stock.
- **Delivery**. This tends to be a long cycle time in service companies, such as those providing consulting services. As well as business model changes (see below), often what we see teams doing is focusing on improving their recording of use of time, and speed of cycles to be able to move to billing, such as recording work done more quickly so it can be billed.
- **Payment and billing**. We have seen teams take a wide range of actions in this area, including:
    - *Relationships*. Getting to know client accounts payable teams and developing close relationships with them is a huge benefit to getting paid on time. For example, our clients know they will always receive something pleasant for the team, such as cards, calls, and treats like biscuits and doughnuts if they pay on time, and they love it.
        - *Break payments down*. If you wait for project completion, or month end, or lengthy milestones before invoicing, that slows down getting paid. One team we work with improved their CCC significantly simply by requiring all their project teams to submit progress invoices fortnightly.
        - *Deposits and upfront payments*. When initiating projects, the amount committed by the client upfront has a big impact on CCC, so needs to be maximised. We often work with service companies where they take no upfront payment at point of sale or initiation of a project, they simply issue a purchase order. This is a significant missed opportunity. It's always reasonable to expect a client to start paying once a project kicks off.
        - *Escalation procedures*. Payments is a constant game of cat-and-mouse. It's an uncomfortably zero-sum part of business. For any business that relies upon non-automated customer payments, it's vital to have a team chasing payments, that

they have accurate data, and a strong internal routine for the tracking and chasing of payments. Inevitably though, there will be clients that fall behind, and it's key to have a clear escalation procedure internally, so that increasingly senior people can take up the issue with a mirror ladder of people on the client side.
- Financing. If you work in an industry where customer payment cycles are such that you are forced to live with long-payment terms (such as selling to retailers), it is possible to have sales financed by intermediaries, especially if your customers have a good credit rating, through services such as factoring. This really does need to be a last resort, however, as factoring is famously the crack cocaine of business, in that once you start to rely on it, it is almost impossible to wean yourself off.

Eliminate mistakes

Mistakes in any of these cycles will lead to a delay in payment, so ensuring accuracy is an important way to improve the CCC. For example, if you have consultants on a team, and their logging of hours contains errors, then any re-work required on that is all time lost with regard to getting in cash.

Business model

Some business models have better CCCs than others, so changing your business model can have a big impact on CCC. One team with which we work made a transition to offering digital rather than consulting solutions, and a huge benefit was that digital solutions get paid upfront, whereas consulting is typically paid in arrears, so this cash benefit quickly re-earned them what they had invested in the digital product.

Professor John Mullins of London Business School, in his book 'The Customer-Funded Business' emphasises that the best way to get funding for any business is from its customers, and suggests five types of business models that achieve the following:

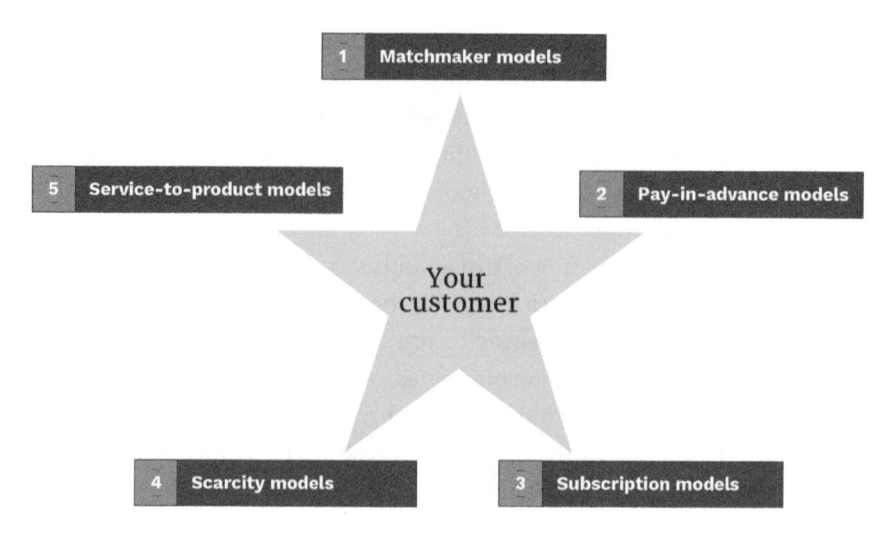

```
         1  Matchmaker models

5  Service-to-product models           2  Pay-in-advance models

              Your
              customer

     4  Scarcity models        3  Subscription models
```

(Reproduced by permission of John Mullins)

- **Matchmaker**. Be the platform upon which transactions happen, and take payments upfront (e.g. e-bay, Harley Therapy).
- **Pay-in-advance**. In return for some kind of benefit (e.g. low prices, or bespoke design), design a business model that requires payment (or a significant deposit) in advance. Dell computers is a great example of this, which turned around the PC industry.
- **Subscription**. For example, rather than charging by the hour as a consultant, charge fixed month subscriptions, paid in advance (this is how Scale Coach work).
- **Scarcity**. Have clients club together to acquire something that may be scarce, such as 'flash sale' companies. Many crowdfunding platforms exist on this premise too, that enthusiastic customers will be willing to fund growth and expansion of companies that they literally do 'buy into'.
- **Service-to-product**. Many companies start as a service model, then pivot to offering a more standard product. This is how Microsoft got started, designing bespoke software for hardware manufacturers, before creating its own product, MS-DOS.

Worksheet

Cash conversion cycle

SCALE | Business growth made easy

Name: _____ Company: _____ Date: _____

Cash Conversion Cycle (CCC)
- A: Sales
- B: Production
- C: Delivery
- D: Payment

Work out your 'Accounting CCC'

Days of Inventory Outstanding (DIO) = _____
Days Sales Outstanding (DSO) = _____
Days Payable Outstanding (DPO) = _____

CCC		DIO		DSO		DPO
	=		+		−	

Do your payments in occur before or after significant payments out? Identify where improvements must be made.

		Shorten Cycle times	Eliminate mistakes	Improve Business Model & P/L
A	**Ways to improve your sales cycle**			
1				
2				
3				
4				
5				
B	**Ways to improve your make/production & inventory cycle**			
1				
2				
3				
4				
5				
C	**Ways to improve your delivery cycle**			
1				
2				
3				
4				
5				
D	**Ways to improve your billing & payment cycle**			
1				
2				
3				
4				
5				

15

SMC 9 – ORGANISATIONAL CULTURE

Checklist item

Issue

Organisation Culture. People not behaving or performing in line with the culture or performance we desire.

Manifestation

- Inconsistent behaviours across the organisation are creating drama, dispute, or issues with performance.
- Struggling to attract the right talent.
- Poor team retention and/or engagement.

Summary

When a team is performing well, the members are bound together by a common set of behaviours that act like a glue. The wrong behaviours are naturally singled out and eliminated. A 'way of working here' emerges that is special and unique, and attracts more of the right kind of people.

Achieving this kind of cultural advantages requires a defined code, or a set of values or behaviours (go to section Culture/Core Values on page 75 if you do not have these set yet) and maintaining and bringing them to life in active ways on a day-to-day basis.

This section describes how you can use these Core Values to create a truly unique culture:

- Bringing Core Values to life across the business, including questions to use to test candidates.
- Use Talent Assessment Chart to apply Core Values to team assessment, and create a team of 'A Players'.

Bringing Core Values to life

Summary

Once Core Values have been defined, the work then really starts to bring them to life, which can take time to fully embed. A focus on bringing Core Values to life is what will make your business feel different, to work in, and also for people who interact with you. It's what will allow you to attract and retain like-minded people and make a real difference.

Key concepts

A values-based business

I always enjoy every time I visit HISBE in Brighton. They're a small chain of supermarkets, dedicated to a new way of working that puts sustainability front and centre. When you enter the shop, you notice vegetables that may be knobbly and imperfect-looking, but are large, fresh, and natural. Large hoppers store dry goods that you take away in your own container, and every range contains local options. It's an example where Core Values have not just been set, but are lived every day. This is what the business is built around.

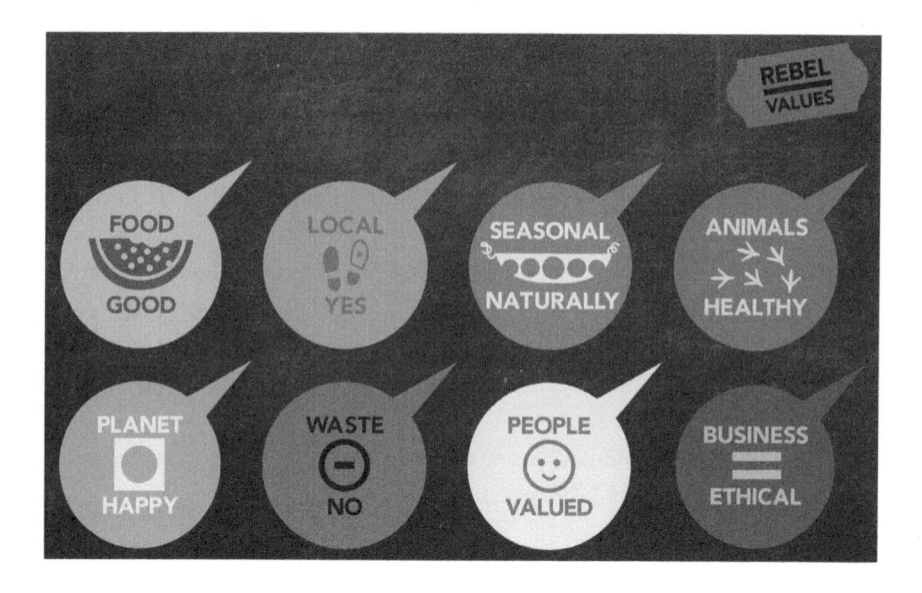

[Rebel Values graphic: FOOD GOOD, LOCAL YES, SEASONAL NATURALLY, ANIMALS HEALTHY, PLANET HAPPY, WASTE NO, PEOPLE VALUED, BUSINESS ETHICAL]

Achieving this has taken the co-founders Ruth and Jack over 10 years. It's a cumulation of many day-to-day decisions, each framed through the question, 'Is this in line with our Core Values?' It's required trade-offs and sacrifices, such as parting with people, or letting go of potentially lucrative opportunities. But it's created something unique, that you can feel both as an employee, and as a customer of the business. It's what makes them stand out.

Building out your Core Values

If you have a set of Core Values defined, but feel like they're not alive, the place to start is to build out the details that sit around each Value. The short statements or phrases that initially define the Core Values are open to interpretation, so need to be defined in clear and specific ways. It is helpful to define them in terms of the following two factors:

BEHAVIOURS

Specific behaviours are associated with each Core Value. It's worth taking the time to think not just of the behaviours that are in line with the Core Value, but also those that aren't. The point of Core Values is not about appealing to everyone. Here is an example from our Scale Coach Core Values, taken from our first Value – Intense Moments. Notice how we make a point of including sections of what it doesn't mean, and why it might not be for you. Remember, there always has to be a price paid for something to be meaningful...

Intense moments

What it means

- Permission to go deep (not just permission, encouragement)
- It's a privilege to experience intense moments with people (each other, and with our Members).
- We're there for the 1%, to talk about what's important (not just what's on people's minds).
- If it's not intense / important, then why bother? Life's too short not to go after real change and ambition. We work in the space that lets that happen [and we love it].
- Small talk optional 😊
- For us, a good day is one where we've gone deep with someone, made a profound difference, touched a soul, created a deep connection.

What it doesn't mean

- Judgement. We do meet people where *they're* at, what *they're* ready for (push *their* boundaries, not ours). You can identify, and even raise, a shortcoming or failing someone has, without being in judgement of it.
- Have blanket permission. Trust needs to be established with people.
- We tell people what to do: 90% coaching, 9% reflection, 1% advice.
- We can't have fun.

Practical Examples

- Coaching and workshops leading to life-changing moments.
- Holding the silence.
- Tears, soul2soul looks, 'Ah-ha's', big picture thinking.

What price to do we pay / how can it feel negative?

- 'Intensity' isn't for everyone
- Exhausting / overwhelming?

How would the opposite be good?

- Relaxed
- Chummy, chatty, bubbly

QUESTIONS

If you were to interview someone to ascertain whether they would be a fit with the Core Value, what questions would you ask? What examples might you look for in their life, to see if there is a fit with the Core Values or not?

Bringing them to life

Once the Core Values are defined with plenty of detail, there is then a long list of actions you can take to bring them to life every day.

Here are a few examples:

> ### Examples
>
> These are examples of tools and techniques teams have used to bring CV's to life. Can be used for core purpose and BHAG too.
>
> - Ice-breakers at huddles (share actual stories).
> - Posters on the walls.
> - Screensavers.
> - Wifi / other passwords.
> - Theme a Q or a retreat.
> - Always reference CV's in praise and criticism.
> - Include in staff survey.
> - 1st item in new staff induction.
> - Create a CV handbook.
> - CV explanatory videos.
> - CV swag.
> - Appoint CV heroes and celebrate them.
> - Create a CV reminder automation.
> - Include in interview questions.
> - Fire people for serious or consistent transgression.
> - Use the talent assessment chart model.

You can find others by asking around other entrepreneurs, there are even YouTube videos with fun examples of teams living their Core Values.

Worksheet

Bringing core values to life

Name: _____ Company: _____ Date: _____

Once you have core values defined, it's important to use them throughout the organisation, to 'bring them to life'. A key is to describe example behaviours, and also to craft questions to ask at interviews and staff assessments.

Core values	Behaviour / Story	Question
e.g. 'Closer to the customer.'	e.g. 'The time when Ashley drove all night to deliver the part to the customer.'	e.g. 'Tell us about a time you did something to delight a customer?'

Examples

These are examples of tools and techniques teams have used to bring CV's to life. Can be used for core purpose and BHAG too.

- Ice-breakers at huddles (share actual stories).
- Posters on the walls.
- Screensavers.
- Wifi / other passwords.
- Theme a Q or a retreat.
- Always reference CV's in praise and criticism.
- Include in staff survey.
- 1st item in new staff induction.
- Create a CV handbook.
- CV explanatory videos.
- CV swag.
- Appoint CV heroes and celebrate them.
- Create a CV reminder automation.
- Include in interview questions.
- Fire people for serious or consistent transgression.
- Use the talent assessment chart model.

Exercise

Session Basics	
Name	Bringing Core Values to life
Time	60–90 minutes
Format	Workshop session
Attendees	A cross-section from across the organisation, particularly anyone involved in developing the culture of the team

Preparation	
Objective and outcome	A list of action items that will bring to life the Core Values in the organisation over the next period
Materials	Hand out the printed worksheets and pens

Exercise	
Objective	Each person share/write down the objective of the session: 'to share ideas and agree actions to better bring the CVs to life'
The exercise and key concept	Explain how the exercise will work. A key part to bringing CVs to life is to define them, using stories and examples. Then we need to discuss and agree on actions we can take.
Brainstorm	Each participant fills out the exercise sheet. Start by writing out the Core Values, then filling out actual stories and/or behaviours representing real examples of CV behaviours. Finally, add questions that could be asked, for example, at interview or when decision-making, to establish whether the CV is being demonstrated or not.
Idea sharing	Discuss and share ideas for the behaviours and questions. Agree on a final list of ones to be used and disseminated.
Brainstorm action ideas	Review the list of ideas at the bottom of the worksheet. Discuss and share ideas in the team about other actions that could be taken to better bring the CVs to life.
Action list	Define clear actions, owners, and deadlines (who's going to do what, by when) to get all the agreed items done.

Tips and pitfalls

This guide will help you to really bring your Core Values to life.

Focus on key areas

There are certain parts of the organisation where strong implementation of CVs will deliver enhanced benefits, where they can be drawn upon as a practical and specific tool. Here we collect examples and stories where teams have applied CVs in specific ways:

Area	Examples
Recruitment. Interview and selection exercises to select for the Core Value behaviours that will fit with your culture	Interviews built around explicit sets of questions to probe demonstration of Core Value behaviour
New staff onboarding. Setting the expectations for behaviour from the start, building training of CVs as the first thing done with new team members	Day 1: Core Value walkthrough with the CEO, full of stories and examples
Recognition. Whenever praise or recognition is given within the team, doing so by drawing on the Core Values displayed	Core Value champions of the month/quarter and Core Value recognition badges for the winners
Conflict resolution. When things flare up between teams, using Core Values can guide how to approach resolution	Conflict mentors to guide resolution based on Core Values
Assessment. Using CVs to ascertain what help and development each member of the team needs	Talent Assessment Charts (see the Section Talent Assessment Chart)
Office environment. Make the CVs prominent in the physical and digital workspace	Postcards handed out to all team members with the Core Values explained
Meetings and huddles. Using key, repeated communication points to emphasise CVs	Weekly huddle ice-breaker always tied to CVs
Letting people go. Sometimes, the help people need is to be free to go elsewhere	CEO being explicit to the rest of the team when someone is let go due to behaviour not in line with Core Values. This is probably the single most effective tool to appreciate the significance of Core Values
Decision-making. When faced with big decisions, including choices of partners to work with, asking whether it's in line with Core Values is a key decision point	When rolling out a new product, decisions around design and pricing explicitly reference Core Values

Model it

As the leader of the organisation, the best way to embed Core Values behaviour within a team is to model and demonstrate the behaviours for which you're looking. For example, as we were introducing a new culture into our business, built around a determination to become a 'Teal' organisation, one habit we needed to embed was to fully devolve decision-making. There is a process in Teal organisations called the Advice Process for making decisions, which involves writing up the decision to be made, sharing it, then asking advice from all team members affected, or with insight into the decision. The only way to get the behaviour introduced into the team was for me to go first, so for several weeks, I was the only one to bring my decisions to the team in this way until others gradually picked up the habit.

Sometimes, this also means being honest with the team when we fail to demonstrate such behaviours. Make a big deal of it if you do something yourself that doesn't live up to a Core Value; show the team that the expectations apply to everyone, starting with you.

How are we doing?

It is helpful to regularly score the organisation (as well as individuals) on performance in line with the Core Values (don't worry about it being subjective, that is unavoidable, it is still valuable to do). In the Quarterly Planning workbook, you will find an exercise for the team to do this every Quarter at QPD.

This can often highlight discrepancies between what the leader of the business sees as working/not working, and what others see. Often, a large part of the benefit of the exercise is to identify and share differences in scores, as it requires people to share what they see, and can bring to light examples and areas where we may be doing better or worse than we thought. For example, the leader of the organisation may feel that the whole team have been 'Caring about the Customer', but team members may have many examples and stories of parts of the business where that is not the case.

What action is most impactful?

There is a saying to the effect that the Core Values won't really be alive until you've let someone go for not behaving in accordance with them. There is truth to this, for two reasons:

- People undermining Core Values have a huge negative effect, through influence and undermining.
- The team won't fully trust you to support Core Values unless they really believe you're behind them.

These can be very difficult decisions to make, especially with people who are high performers. This is highlighted in the next section, called Talent Assessment Chart.

Repetition

This discussion and exercise, unlike the original setting of the Core Values is one that needs to be had repeatedly. There will always be ways that you can work to bring behaviours closer in line with Core Values.

Talent assessment chart

Summary

Imagine if your whole team were both performing and behaving well. That's what it's like to have a team of A Players. It's like a current that lifts you along, rather than having to drag others behind you. The Talent Assessment Chart exercise is a practical way of creating such a team.

Key concepts

Applying Core Values to team assessments

A key practical application of Core Values is in team members' assessments. If the team understands that their opportunities within the organisation are linked to their behaviours with relation to Core Values, it is a powerful influencer of behaviour.

The opportunity is to create a team where you only have 'A Players'. To understand what we mean by 'A Players', let's look at the Talent Assessment Chart:

The Talent Assessment Chart maps an individual's performance across two axes: performance in their role, as measured by their KPIs, and behaviour in line with Core Values. Mapping these out on the chart puts them into one of four boxes, which dictates your response to them:

CHECKLISTS – DIAGNOSING BOTTLENECKS

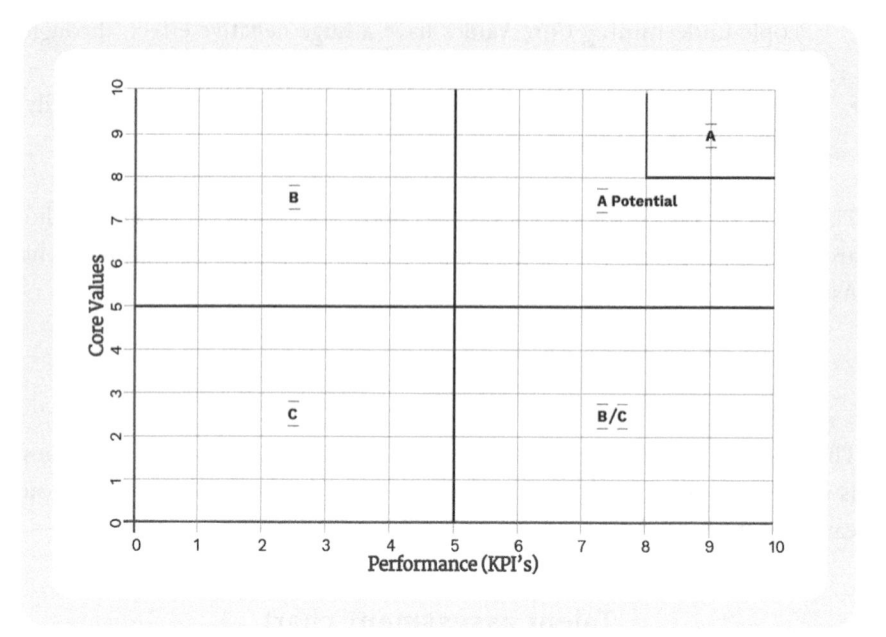

[Chart: A 2D grid with x-axis "Performance (KPI's)" from 0 to 10 and y-axis "Core Values" from 0 to 10. Plotted points: B at approximately (4, 8); A Potential at approximately (7, 8); A at approximately (9, 9); C at approximately (4, 3); B/C at approximately (7, 3).]

A Players

The name of the game here is about **retention**. These are the people you want to stick around, and to be in positions of influence and responsibility. Compensation, reward, incentivisation, promotion, expansion of role, and investment in development programmes are common areas of support for A Players.

B Players

The key here is to turn B Players into A Players, which is all about **improving their performance**. This requires understanding the reasons for lower performance and working on them. Coaching is a common tool used here (see Section on Coaching). It may be that the person requires skills training, isn't being managed correctly, or doesn't have the right tools for the job. Sometimes people have things going on in their personal lives that take time to resolve. It's great when B Players are able to up their game. However, there needs to be a time limit on this. If, in 3–6 months' time, they're still not performing, then it's time for a difficult conversation about their future in the team.

B/C Players

These are the difficult ones. Again, we want them to become A Players, but this transition is more difficult, as we're dealing with more fundamental changes, those of attitude and behaviour. It's also difficult because these people are performing well, for example, they may be a star salesperson, or leading an important development team. It takes courage to challenge such characters, as it may lead to considerable short-term pain if that person leaves or the relationship significantly sours. *B -> A transition is much easier than B/C -> A transition.*

The first action with B/C players is to have the **difficult conversation**, to make them aware of the difficulties they are creating. B/C players are sometimes unaware of the extent of the disruption they're causing, or even if they are, they are not used to being challenged for it. There has to be an element of challenge to this conversation, an explicit expectation that behaviours must change. If that does not work, then you face the challenge of letting them go from the business.

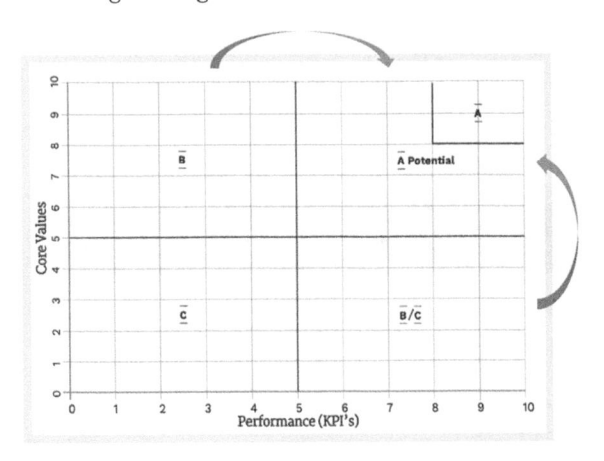

> B -> A transition much easier than B/C -> A transition

C Players

The most common conclusion with C Players is that the best place for them to develop is somewhere else. Occasionally, there are examples of C Players who are behaving so because they are in the wrong role, or have something significant going on in their personal life. These are the exceptions, however, and it's usually an **exit conversation**.

Don't let C Players hang around. Not only will they drain your time and energy, but they send a message to the rest of the team that underperformance and bad behaviour are tolerated. A great way to lose A Players is to keep C Players around.

CHECKLISTS – DIAGNOSING BOTTLENECKS

Worksheet

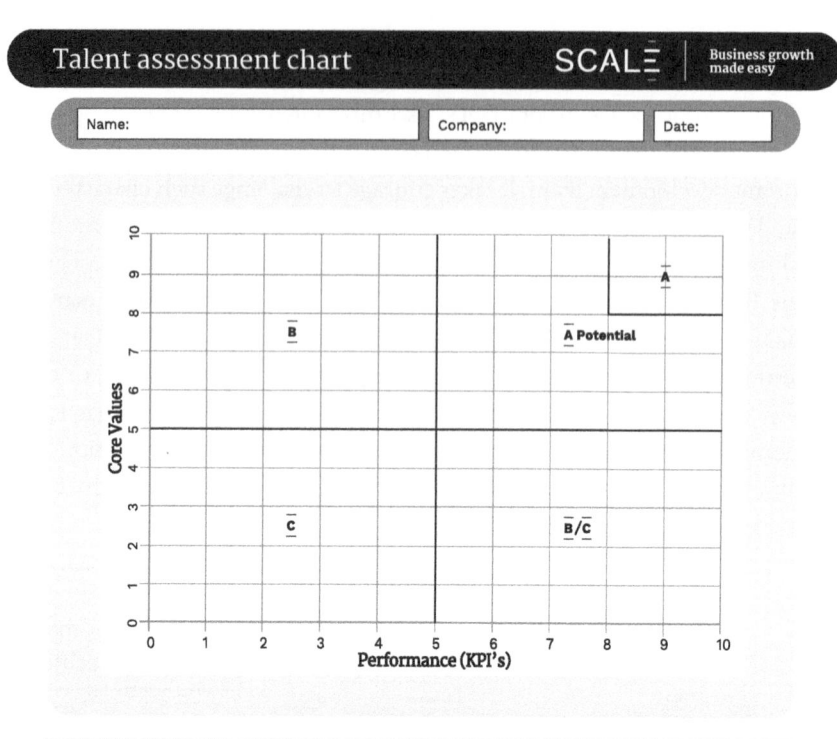

Talent assessment chart

SCALE | Business growth made easy

Name: | Company: | Date:

Chart: Core Values (y-axis, 0–10) vs Performance (KPI's) (x-axis, 0–10)
- A: (~8.5, 9.5)
- A Potential: (~8, 7)
- B: (~3, 7.5)
- C: (~3, 2.5)
- B/C: (~8, 2.5)

Team Member Initials	Performance Score	Core Value Score	Rating (A, B...)	Action Plan (For Next Planning Period)

Feb23 · © Clarity Strategy Ltd DBA Scale 2023 | Adapted from Topgrading by Bradford D. Smart, Ph. D. © Topgrading with permission | www.scalecoach.co.uk

Exercise

1. List of the team member for assessment
2. Score each person for KPI/Performance and Core Values behaviours
3. Place their initials on the chart, and mark whether they are A, B, B/C, or C
4. Discuss and agree the best support that can be provided to each person, based on where they are placed.

Tips and pitfalls

How to rate people?

It's highly beneficial as part of the scoring system to describe in simple terms what a particular score means. For example, a four-point scoring system we often see used for assessment to Core Values is:

1. Does not regularly exhibit CV behaviour, and negatively affects others' behaviour
2. Does not regularly exhibit this CV behaviour
3. Regularly exhibits this behaviour
4. Regularly exhibits this behaviour and positively influences others to do the same as well.

If people doing the assessment are clear on what each score means, then you will get better consistency of scoring, and more objective results.

'I only have A players'

This is the one we see quite a lot, where all team members end up in the 'A-player' box. It may be that you genuinely have a team where everyone is performing well and really demonstrating Core Values. If so, good for you. More often, however, it is due to generous scoring, and in fact there are significant discrepancies within the team. If you are concerned that 'assessment inflation' has occurred, then the easy solution to this is simply to 'move the lines'.

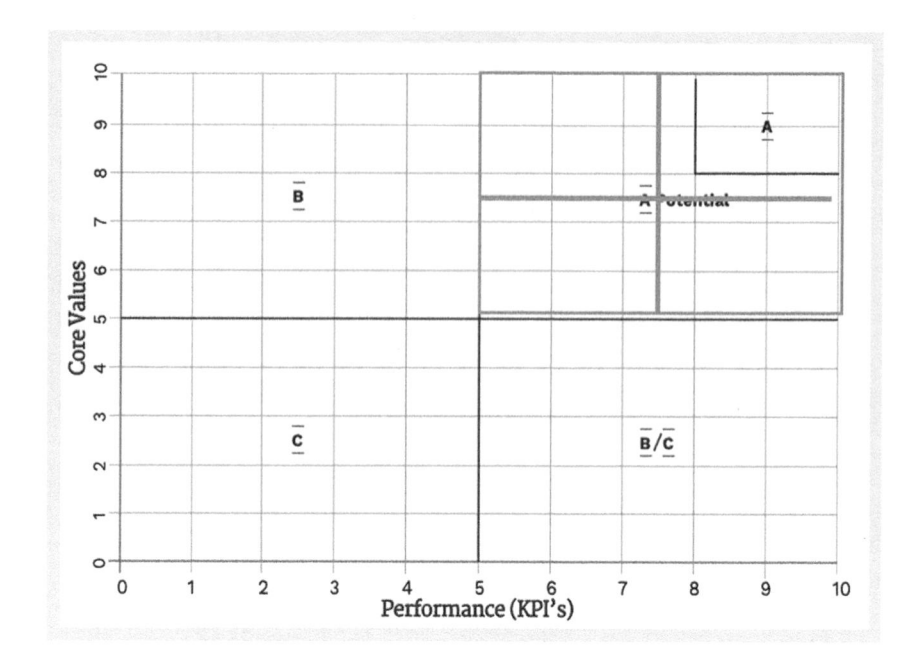

[Chart: Talent Assessment Chart with Core Values (y-axis) vs Performance (KPI's) (x-axis), showing positions A, B, C, B/C, and A Potential zone]

If you split the A-player box in the top-right-hand corner into four, then this will create an updated Assessment Chart that you can then use to resolve according to the guidance in the exercise.

Other forms of Talent Assessment Chart

The chart described above covers two axes for assessing team members, creating a two-dimensional grid. There are other variables that can be used for assessment, such as:

- **Skills**. Does the person possess particular skills of value and relevance to this role? Are there skills they need to work on and develop?
- **Potential**. Does this person have the potential for development? Could they be developed to more senior positions in the organisation?

Once you have more than two variables, it's more common to represent results as blended scores rather than a visual chart.

16

SMC 10 – SYSTEMS AND PROCESSES

Checklist item

Issue

We have **Systems and Processes** letting us down.

Manifestation

Key processes and/or systems are causing excessive cost, delay, drama, or lack of clarity and communication.

Summary

When businesses grow, processes break (another law of entrepreneurial gravity). Optimising all processes all the time is not feasible, so improvement needs to be done on a Pareto principle basis, by stack ranking key processes in the order of the pain they are generating (Covered in the Process Accountability exercise).

Resolving process issues requires two key skills: the mapping of the process to understand and improve it, and the ability to set checklists in order to deal with common fail points (Covered in the Process Resolution exercise).

Process accountability

Summary

If processes are causing problems in the business, the first things to do are to narrow down which processes need fixing first, who's going to do so, and what the measures of success for improvement in that process need to be. Use the Process Accountability tool to resolve these together with the team.

Key concepts

Pareto power – picking priority processes

A team we work with, when doing their Scale Model Checklist, had answers clustered around 'Cash conversion', 'Processes', and 'Busy-ness'. When we explored the heart of the issue, we realised that there was a core of a few key processes within the finance team that, if solved, would make life better for everyone.

This example speaks to the first concept to take to heart when approaching process improvement – the Theory of Constraints (explained in Section on The Scale Model Checklist), which is that you have to identify: **'Which process (es), if resolved, would make life better for everyone?'** This is a diagnostic process to work out where to apply effort. A great rhythm is to work on one key process per quarter.

You cannot, and should not, look to fix all of your processes at once. The idea of having every process in the business carefully mapped and operating smoothly like an oiled machine is tempting (to some at least). But it is a mirage. The reality of operating processes in high-growth companies is that there is always a degree of mess involved. **Processes only need to be good enough to do their job effectively** (there are no extra points for elegance), and they often require re-work and upgrading as the organisation continues to grow anyway.

The trick is to harness the **Pareto principle** – the 80/20 rule – which 20% of your processes are leading to 80% of the problems? We need to ask ourselves 'If we could only fix/work on one key process, which would it be?' Related to this is the important question of **accountability**. Who on the leadership team is accountable for the key processes in the business, and how is the **performance** of those processes measured?

Accountability

The first stage in fixing a faulty process is to **identify who owns it**. This can be a tricky thing to establish, as many key company processes can be cross-functional: for example, how you onboard a new client or a new team member. This is why the exercise is called the Process Accountability Chart (taken from the Verne Harnish book *Scaling Up*).

Once it's clear who owns it, the next step is to clarify how the **success of the process is measured**, which means assigning what KPI or performance metric tells us if the process is operating well or not.

CHECKLISTS – DIAGNOSING BOTTLENECKS

Worksheet

Process Scorecard

SCALE | Business growth made easy

Name: Company: Date:

1. Identify 4 to 9 processes that drive your business.
2. Assign someone specifically accountable for each process.
3. List Key Performance Indicators (KPIs) for each process (better, faster, cheaper).
4. Tick the top 3 process you think need work on this quarter.

1 Name of Process	2 Person Accountable	3 KPI's (Better, Faster, Cheaper)	4 Top 3

Feb23 · © Clarity Strategy Ltd DBA Scale 2023 | Adapted from vBG20/01 · Copyright 2020 Gazelles   www.scalecoach.co.uk

Exercise

Session Basics	
Name	Process Accountability
How to communicate	'Let's decide which of our processes we need to work on improving this quarter, and who is accountable for their performance'
Time	60–90 minutes
Format	Workshop session
Attendees	Leadership team

Preparation	
Objective and outcome	Set accountability and performance metrics for the key processes in the business, and decide which requires immediate improvement
Materials	Printed worksheets and pens

Exercise	
Objective	Discuss and agree on the objective and agenda of the session
The exercise and key concept	Review the worksheet and the key concepts from this section: • Pareto principle – 20% of processes causing 80% of problems • Accountability. Assign owners and performance metrics to key processes
Accountability	Each person fills out the company's top 4–9 processes, who is accountable for each one, and KPIs to measure that process' performance
Discussion	Share answers and agree on a final list for the three columns
Top process to work on	Discuss and agree which process is the priority for focus in this quarter. Discuss cost, drama, delays, and impact on the rest of the business
Actions	Once agreed, the process owner must commit to the group on how they plan to go about improving the performance of that process during the quarter, and their anticipated performance improvement

Process resolution

Summary

Once you've identified which process to work on, let's look at how to go about delivering improvements to performance.

Processes are like Marmite – some people love working on them, and for some it's a headache they'd rather not approach. The challenge we all face with processes, however, is that they are 'second-level work', that is, it's taking time out of day-to-day work to work on the system rather than in it.

Process improvement work faces several challenges:

- It's hard to apply to yourself
- Requires time out of day-to-day work
- Fear of getting it wrong
- Fear of not being future-proof
- How much of the process to fix
- Interplay with IT systems
- Will it stick?

Concerns like these can often cause us to avoid working on process improvement, or perennially delay that work. Again, we need an agile mindset. Accept that you will never achieve a perfect process that will work indefinitely. Identify the few key problems we're looking to solve with this round of improvement, and set the objective to just solve those.

Key concepts

Process mapping

To improve a process, you first need to understand it. In most circumstances, the best way to do this is to draw a 'map' of the process. This is a visual representation, in the form of a flow chart, of the way that the process *actually* works (not how it's supposed to work).

This starts by defining the **brackets** of the process – where does it:

- Start (the trigger), and
- End (completion point)?

For example, for a new staff onboarding process, the trigger might be confirmation from the recruitment team that an offer letter has been signed. The completion point might be that the staff member has successfully passed their 3-month probation checkpoint.

Once the brackets are clear, the team needs to map out and agree on the key **steps** in the process. The best way to achieve this is generally to bring together all the people that participate in the process, and together compile a complete view of the process.

One thing to confirm is what is meant by steps to the process. These are often represented by different symbols on a process map and can include items, such as tasks, decision points, and start/stop points. Here are some commonly used process mapping symbols. Start by agreeing which symbols you will use to represent the elements of your process.

Process mapping symbols

Symbol	Meaning	Symbol	Meaning	Symbol	Meaning	Symbol	Meaning
⬭	Start / Finish	▭	Task / Activity	◇	Online activity	⇒	Flow
▱	Data input / output	▥	Sub-process	⌓	Delay	⊂	Stored data
⬜	Manual input	⏢	Manual task	▽	Manual filing	▯	Document
⌭	Electronic storage	◁	Online activity	○	Process connector	⬡	Preparation

The actual mapping can be effectively done using **Post-It notes**. If you are meeting in person, this means writing them out and using a wall. If virtually, then virtual whiteboard software like Miro or Jamboard is very effective for this.

The key is to do it **silently**. I know this sounds strange, but it is the most efficient approach. Each person writes out the stages in the process of which they are aware, and when collating them all on the wall, where different people have described the same step, those get put together. What emerges is an overall view of the full process.

Here is an example of a hiring process mapped out:

Hiring interview process with swim lanes

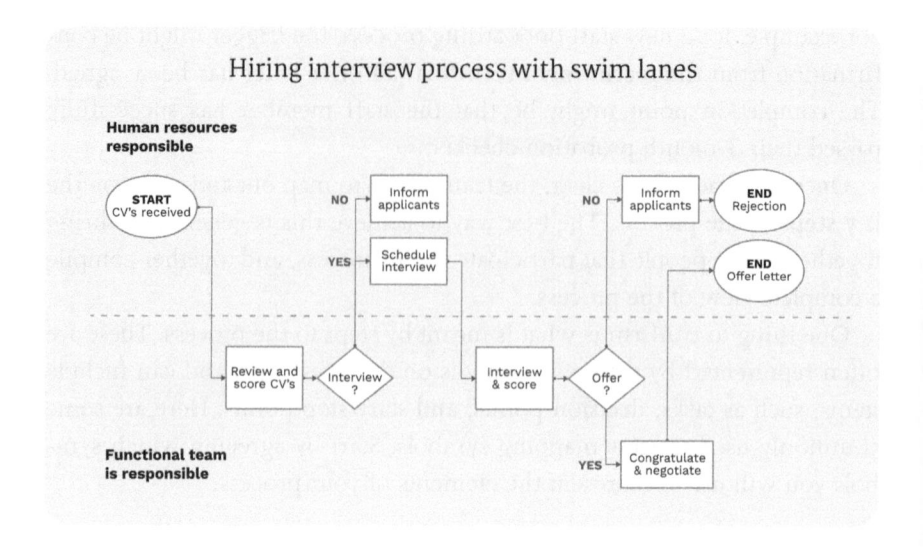

Human resources responsible

START CV's received → NO → Inform applicants
            → YES → Schedule interview
                        ...
            → NO → Inform applicants → END Rejection
            → END Offer letter

Functional team is responsible

Review and score CV's → Interview? → Interview & score → Offer? → YES → Congratulate & negotiate

The final stage of this is to mark up where the process is **failing**. What are the points that are causing excessive cost, delay, error, drama, or variation? This gives you a list of key points in the process to start working on improvements.

Process improvements

There can be many ways to improve a process. This mnemonic guides you to a few key ones:

- **B**ottleneck
- **A**utomation
- **C**hecklist
- **E**limination.

Bottleneck

Is someone or something a bottleneck? Examples include:

- A decision-maker. Maybe an approval or decision point that always takes time
- Access to a key piece of equipment or software

- A key contributor. Without this person or teams' help or input, the process gets stuck.

Consider how that bottleneck could be widened or eliminated. Maybe set a fixed time for batch approvals, delegate approval/decision points, or acquire equipment or licences to accelerate things.

These changes often require placing trust (and controls) with the team, so that they can get on and run the process efficiently. Another common solution to such constraints is to set regular meetings or habits in the diary to work through items.

Automation

Increasingly, processes are hard-wired into **software systems**. If you run a sales process, it is often intractable from your CRM. Anything to do with finance goes through accounting or ERP software.

So, to a large extent, the software is the process. This can be a limiting factor if the process cannot be flexibly changed, but it is also an opportunity. Good software can be an enabler by **automating** key steps. For example, a finance team might set their accounting software to automatically send reminders to late-paying customers.

The great opportunity here these days is for **'zero code' software**. It is becoming very easy for anyone to be able to code and update processes and automations in software these days.

Hubspot is a common example that marketers use to automate the process of sending out content to engaged prospects in a funnel. Our favourite is platforms such as monday.com. Here is an example:

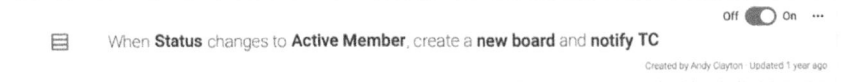

> When **Status** changes to **Active Member**, create a **new board** and **notify TC**
>
> Off ⬤ On
> Created by Andy Clayton · Updated 1 year ago

What this automation does is every time we have a new client, when it is flagged by the salesperson in the relevant screen as 'Active', an onboarding checklist is automatically created and notified to the relevant Team Coach, who manages that client.

You probably have many such examples of small time-savers that do the heavy lifting of repetitive or easy-to-forget tasks. Challenge the team to find such productivity workarounds.

Checklists

When looking at failure points in processes, it's helpful to reflect on how **human memory** works. Atul Gawande is a well-known surgeon in the United States. He was troubled by the high failure rates in surgeries. It seemed curious to him that highly trained doctors, experts in their fields, would often have serious negative outcomes from their surgeries for trivial reasons, such as forgetting hand-washing, or not having the right tools and materials ready.

He spent time in the airline industry, understanding how they achieved such high levels of safety and consistency. He learned that their secret is **checklists**. Not huge, exhaustive checklist, but short, practical ones that were used whenever a key junction, trigger, or decision point occurred in a process.

He then applied such simple checklists to surgeries in his own hospital, resulting in huge improvements in surgical success rates. His experiences and learnings are recorded in his excellent book *The Checklist Manifesto*. The key learning is that human memory is great at certain things, such as remembering faces, processing images, and movement coordination. But it's very bad at retaining lists. This is why it's a sign of intelligence (not stupidity) to go to the supermarket with a shopping list, it's a recognition of a fundamental weakness of the human brain.

This insight is of huge importance when addressing many process failure points. For example, take new customer onboarding, a process that occurs in many businesses. Account managers need to take new clients through a repeated set of actions with each new customer. Failure to cover any item will lead to problems down the line, either for themselves, the customer, or other teams such as finance and accounts. The answer, of course, is to have a well-designed checklist triggered at this vital point in the process. Below is an example from a building materials company in Scotland that has a checklist for exactly this purpose:

Once you start to take this approach, you will be amazed how many process problems can be solved.

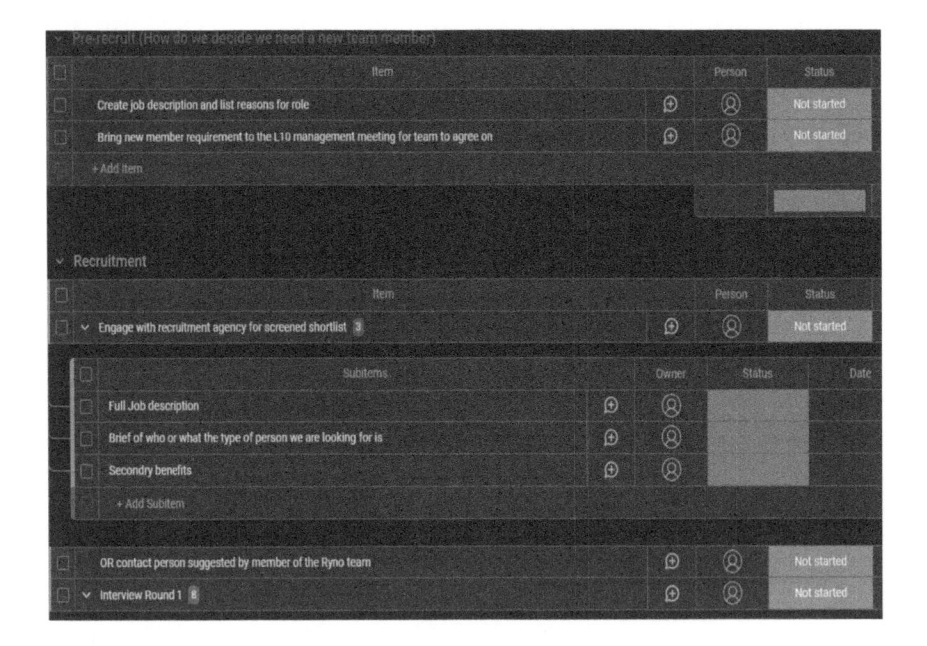

Pre-recruit (How do we decide we need a new team member)			
Item		Person	Status
Create job description and list reasons for role	⊕	⊙	Not started
Bring new member requirement to the L10 management meeting for team to agree on	⊕	⊙	Not started
+ Add item			

Recruitment				
Item		Person	Status	
Engage with recruitment agency for screened shortlist 3	⊕	⊙	Not started	
Subitems	Owner	Status	Date
Full Job description	⊕	⊙		
Brief of who or what the type of person we are looking for is	⊕	⊙		
Secondry benefits	⊕	⊙		
+ Add Subitem				
OR contact person suggested by member of the Ryno team	⊕	⊙	Not started	
Interview Round 1 8	⊕	⊙	Not started	

Elimination

Waste is a common enemy of good process. Are there steps that can be eliminated that would make things move more smoothly? Are there unnecessary sign-offs or authorisations? Is there re-work that could be eliminated by getting something right first time?

For example, one team we work with found that if they had a template sample agreement to share with leads early in their sales process, they could completely eliminate this step later down the line. Another found that by adding one payment clause to standard contracts and training sales teams on it, their finance team were able to eliminate a long and costly chasing process that had developed.

Often, the solution to elimination of steps requires people from different teams to come together, as the solution to one team's pain may lie in the hands of another team to solve.

Worksheet

Process resolution

SCALE | Business growth made easy

| Name: | Company: | Date: |

Resolve your key process that is failing. Focus on how it's currently **actually** working

1. Define the process

Process Name	Process Owner	Key success metric(s)

Start point / trigger	Completion point

2. Map it

As a team, use post-its to silently map out the key process steps (from trigger to completion)

3. Failure points

Use coloured dots to highlight weak points in the current process, that are causing cost, delay, drama, or failure.

4. Resolution

Agree your top 3 resolution actions. Refer to the list for ideas.	Process failure resolution options:
1	• **Bottlenecks**. Is a person, resource or step a bottleneck to be resolved?
2	• **Automation**. System or software triggers or workarounds to reduce or eliminate human error.
	• **Checklist**. Use a checklist to improve recall and accuracy.
3	• **Eliminate**. Are there steps that don't add value? Remove them.

Exercise

Session Basics	
Name	Process resolution
How to communicate?	'We need to find significant improvements in this process to improve accuracy, and reduce cost, variance, time, and drama'
Time	60–90 minutes
Format	Workshop session
Attendees	Key individuals who operate the process

Preparation	
Objective and outcome	A set of specific actions that will significantly improve the performance of this process
Learning and reading	*The Checklist Manifesto*, by Atul Gawande
Materials	• Printed worksheet and pens • Post-Its and wall space

Exercise	
Objective	Discuss and agree the objective and agenda of the session
Define the process	Set the parameters of the process, according to the boxes on the worksheet
Map it	Have each person involved in the process draw out the key steps of the process. Silently stick them all on the wall until the full process is clear and agreed
Failure points	Use coloured dots or a clear mark (give each person three) to identify the key failure points. Narrow them down to the top 3
Brainstorm	Discuss and agree on ideas for improvement to the process (refer to BACE for guidance). Agree on the top three changes for resolution
Actions	Define who will do what by when in order to deliver those changes. Agree on when you will re-convene to review progress

17

SMC 11 – COLLECTING CUSTOMER FEEDBACK

Checklist item

Issue

We're not collecting **Customer Feedback** effectively.

Manifestation

Lack of usable data on customer satisfaction, or how we're delivering on our customer promises.

Summary

Collecting customer feedback well allows you to achieve three wonderful things:

- Quickly pick up on and save customer relationships that are going wrong
- Understand whether you're having the impact you want on your clients and why
- Use feedback data as proofs during sales, to increase lead generation and conversions.

In particular, the third point is one that companies often miss when designing their customer feedback, which is a huge missed opportunity.

Key concepts

Focus on 'Promise Test' questions

In order to design customer feedback well, the starting point needs to be your 'USPs' (refer to Unique Selling Promises section), that is, the few key promises you make and keep to your client base. Questions must be designed to test whether these promises have been achieved or not. This allows you to then use these data to prove delivery to potential new customers.

At Scale, we make a point of using the tools we provide, and to be a model to our Members. This is an example of our Annual 'Impact Report', showing our survey results from 2021.

Impact Report 2021 — SCALE

Each year we gather data to measure the results our member companies have experienced.

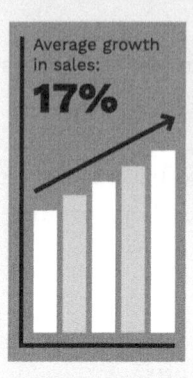

Average growth in sales: 17%

"If you are serious about growing a solid business with a good foundation, Scale has the right tools and brains to support you all the way."
Christoph Wondraczek
Founder, The Hamlet

Increase in team engagement: 27%

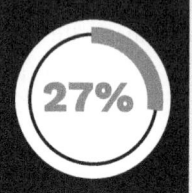

35 NPS — NET PROMOTER SCORE

"To get the most out of Scale, engage as fully as possible with the process."
Ken Kelly
CEO, The Furniture Practice

Average growth in profitability: 19.6%

"Do it. It's great to align your leadership team and get them on the same page to identify the key areas of focus for the business."
Ben Goldsmith
UK Director, ANZUK Education

"It is a great tool to keep the team aligned and connected."
Hassan Alkhiyami
COO, QNIE

In 2021 Scale members had a combined sales of >£400m

www.scalecoach.co.uk

From the 2021 survey, we had one worrying piece of feedback, which we immediately dealt with (and to this day, they're still a Member), and compiled all the data into this report, which we regularly use in sales and marketing-related conversations (and, yes, here is no exception).

Keep it short

We often see companies frustrated with low fill-out rates by clients, and too much data from surveys that are filled out to draw useful insights. This is because they're asking too many questions in their customer feedback surveys. The origin of this issue is usually to do with committee meetings where everyone's idea gets included in the questionnaire. There's often a bias towards 'let's keep it in, because it would be good to know the answer'. This instinct comes at the cost of making the survey too long.

There is only one way round this, and it is to ruthlessly wield the editing pen. Get it down to a list of fewer than seven to eight questions (including hygiene questions), that can be answered in 2–3 minutes.

It helps to ask, **'Are we already asking something similar?'** This applies particularly to questions measuring satisfaction. If you find yourself with numerous questions such as 'Did we meet your expectations?' 'How would you rate the service from our team?' 'Would you recommend us to others?' and so on, limit it to just one.

The example of the Impact Report above was achieved by asking seven questions:

- One Satisfaction question (the Net Promoter Score)
- Three Unique Selling Promise (learn more about these at 'Unique Selling Promises') test questions (regarding change in team engagement, sales, and profit)
- One Hygiene question ('fill in name and surname')
- Two Qualitative questions ('What would you say to someone considering using Scale?' and 'Any other comments or feedback for us?').

So, **keep it short**.

Satisfaction vs. delivery questions

In addition to the number of questions, we often see problems with the types of questions asked, the most common issue being focusing too much on questions that measure different forms of customer satisfaction, rather than measuring delivery on Unique Selling Promises.

Here, the key filter is: '**Is it measuring an outcome?**' If it's not related to the delivery of a USP (for example: 'how much time did you save from using this solution?'), then bin it.

At the heart of these challenges lies an emotional need: '**are we just asking because we want to be liked?**' This is the most natural instinct in the world, but it's not helpful. Scientists have to operate not by looking to prove that their theories are right (which would be emotionally pleasing), but by testing how they might be wrong. This is at the heart of empiricism. And so it is with feedback. Avoid the temptation of asking versions of 'Did we do a good job/did you like us?' and look to test whether the job got done or not.

Measuring absolutes vs. perceptions

The ideal is to measure client success with absolute data, that is, objective measures of whether the client achieved the promises you made. Sometimes this is possible: for example, the ThirdWay Group here were able to collect rental yield data from their client projects, to create a very compelling picture. The chart measures rental yields across the city, in the district of the project, and of the building itself:

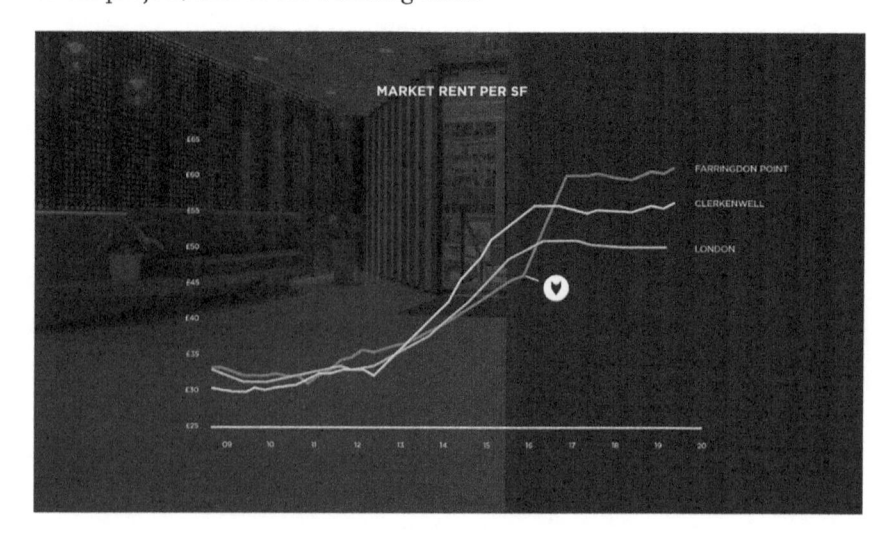

More often than not though, this type of hard client data is hard to come by. For example, if you offer a service that promises to reduce the number of fines a client receives due to system failures (this is taken from a real example), the client may understandably be reticent to share these data with you.

So, how to solve this issue? The best alternative is to collect **perception data**. In this example, it means asking rather than 'what value of fines did you receive before using our system, and what value do you receive now', you can ask alternatives such as:

- 'What is the % increase or decrease in fines since using our system?'
- On a scale of 1–10, how much has our system contributed to a significant reduction in fines?

Much as it would be preferable to have original data, if it's not obtainable, go for perception questions instead.

When to get started?

It's better to get started with an imperfect set of questions than to not start. This is a classic example of where the concept of moving ahead with a 'Minimum Viable Product' applies (mentioned in Chapter 11). I have seen many teams where the customer survey has lounged for years in development hell. Don't let perfect be the enemy of good.

Worksheet

Collecting Customer Feedback
SCALE — Business growth made easy

Name:	Company:	Date:

Quality customer feedback provides:
- Opportunity to pick up on and immediately resolve customer problems
- Understanding of where the business is and isn't delivering and having impact for customers
- Proof data for sales & marketing
- Culture of accountability for client delivery

1. The Process. Decide how you are going to collect customer data:

Item	Options / Examples	Answer
When will you collect customer data?	• Project completion • Regular intervals (e.g. Quarterly, Annually)	
Which customers will you collect from?	• All active customers • All live projects	
Who will do it?	• The service delivery team • Separate customer support team	
How will it be collected?	• Survey tool • Personal email	

2. The questions

- Minimise Type 1 & 2 questions, focus on Type 3
- Survey should take no more than 2-3 minutes to fill out, so max 7 questions (inc. hygiene q's)
- Most questions should be quantitative, with max 1-2 qualitative

Item	Options / examples	Answer
Type 1. Hygiene	• Name, email, project manager. *(Keep to an absolute minimum)*	
Type 2. Satisfaction	• NPS. 'How likely, on a score of 1-10, would you be to recommend us to friends / family / colleagues' *(Avoid asking multiple variants of satisfaction Q's, e.g. 'Did we meet your expectations?', 'Did you get the solution you were looking for?'...)*	
Type 3. Promise Delivery	• 'Rate xxx before, and rate xxx after working with us' • 'How long did it take / how much did it cost / how many leads were generated before?'; 'How much / many now?'	
Qualitative	• 'What would you say to someone considering our products / services?' • 'What could we do to improve our scores with you?' • 'What feedback do you have for the team?'	

3. The data

What to do with the outcomes:
- Immediate follow up of negative feedback. Solve the problem, save the relationship.
- Use Brand Promise delivery data in sales & marketing (e.g. 'We increase team engagement by 46%')
- Include data outcomes into KPI / metric dashboards

Exercise

Session Basics	
Name	Collecting Customer Feedback
How to communicate	'We need to understand whether we're delivering on our promises to our customers, and understand their satisfaction'
Time	60–90 minutes
Format	Workshop session
Attendees	Typically customer service or sales teams
Objective and outcome	Define a full process for how we will collect customer feedback, including who will be responsible for it, the process they will follow, and the questions to ask
Materials	Bring any existing customer feedback surveys and corresponding data for review. Handout the printed worksheet and pens

Exercise	
Objective	Discuss and agree on the objective and agenda of the session
The exercise and key concept	Review the worksheet and the key concepts from this section: Limit the number of questions Ask about promise delivery Get started
The process	Work through, discuss, and agree on the key questions from 'The Process' section of the worksheet
The questions	Brainstorm and agree on the questions that will go in the survey, by working through 'the questions' section of the worksheet
The data	Discuss and agree on how the data from the feedback will be collated, analysed, and reviewed
Actions	Review the action items from the workshop, to define specific actions (who needs to do what by when) in order to start collecting customer feedback. Set a start date when feedback collection will start

18

SMC 12 – SALES AND MARKETING FUNCTIONS

Checklist item

Issue

Our **sales and/or marketing** functions are underperforming.

Manifestation

- Not generating enough leads (of the right quality), or
- Not converting them consistently enough to support growth.

Summary

A great strategy is of no use if you don't execute well in these two key functions. Sales and marketing can be broken down into key components:

- **Branding and messaging.** Translating your strategy into external messages and visuals that will resonate and appeal to your target markets.

- **Lead generation**. Develop marketing channels that will allow potential customers to find you and connect with you for the first time.
- **Conversions**. A sales function that quickly and consistently closes results in revenue.

This section introduces tools that allow you, possibly together with experts or consultants, to develop the functions to pull this off, including:

- **Brand Map**. A branding and messaging framework to create usable brand messaging tools.
- **Marketing Channels**. Developing marketing channels and funnels to generate leads.
- **Sales Playbook**. Creating a sales manual to help salespeople consistently convert leads.

Brand map

Summary

It's time to get creative. The thinking on your strategy is done, now it needs to be communicated to the outside world. The statements you come up with as part of your strategy likely will not be the ones you use in external communication, which consists of a wide range of images, slogans, colours, and graphics. The key to developing these is to think about the 'personality' of your brand – if you could ascribe it human characteristics, what would they be?

Key concepts

Marketing messaging

How to convert strategy into actual messages? Assuming you have your strategic plan complete (if not, go to Chapter 4 to learn how to create it), it needs to be turned into specific, usable messages and visuals for external communication. There are lots of potential tools for external communication, such as:

Website content	Slogans	Logo
Flyers & brochures	Brand colours	Advertising copy
Banner ads	Typeface & fonts	Icons & badges

They need to be consistent, and engagingly convey your desired strategy and positioning to your target audience.

From strategy to brand

How to take a strategy and turn it into a brand? They are closely correlated, but distinct:

Strategy	Brand
Behind the scenes, not publicly visible	Explicitly visible to the outside world
Combines needs of company and market	Speaks to the needs of the market
Emotive and rational	Typically has emotive appeal
Can cover one, or multiple, brands	One brand per positioning (typically analogous to one product set or target market)

Many companies opt to **hire a design agency** for this work. This is often a good option, as they have the creative skills and design capacity to generate the materials required. However you do it, to get a good outcome, it's important to understand and follow a strong process.

The heart of the process of getting from strategy to brand is to develop your brand **'Personality'**. Teams use different words, such as 'soul', 'tone', or 'attitude', but the essence is attributing to your brand *human personality traits*. For example, you may want people to feel that your brand is 'approachable', 'inspiring', 'down to earth', or 'humorous'. These are examples of the kind of characteristic adjectives to go for.

Once you have that personality, then you set your creative teams to work on producing the actual communication tools you require, such as ads, graphics, slogans, colours, and fonts.

If you represent multiple sub-brands in your business, for example, for particular product sets, or certain target markets, each brand will require its own identity and relevant visuals.

Bear in mind that even the same product or service sold in different markets may have to be branded differently. For example, when Pizza Hut launched in China in the 90s, it was as a premium dining restaurant, quite different from the fast-food positioning in home markets.

Picking your personality

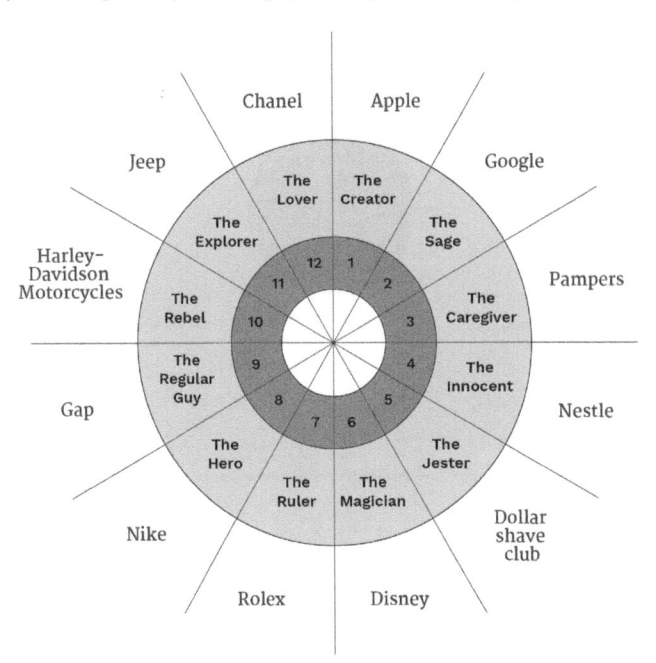

Establishing a description of a personality overlap with areas of **psychology**. A popular system used in this context is of **personality archetypes**, originally developed by Swiss psychologist Carl Jung, and seized on by marketeers around the world since. It draws on ancient mythology and story-telling to portray 12 personality 'archetypes'. Each archetype has certain traits which characterise it. Here they are, with examples of well-known brands associated with each:

It's worth spending some time understanding these in more detail, especially as each of these archetypes is further divided into five sub-archetypes (so a total of 60), for a further level of refinement, which are listed here:

https://element5digital.com/what-are-branding-archetypes-and-how-do-they-work/

These are well-worth exploring, for example, our brand archetype is a sub-brand of Magician, known as 'Engineer'. Magician archetypes are all about transformation (we help companies transform). In the case of Engineer brands, it's about achieving that transformation through some proprietary process or technology. As a result, our website (www.scalecoach.co.uk) has the look and feel of engineering schematics, and we emphasise the transformation that occurs when you apply the magic of what is in our black box, for example, in this image:

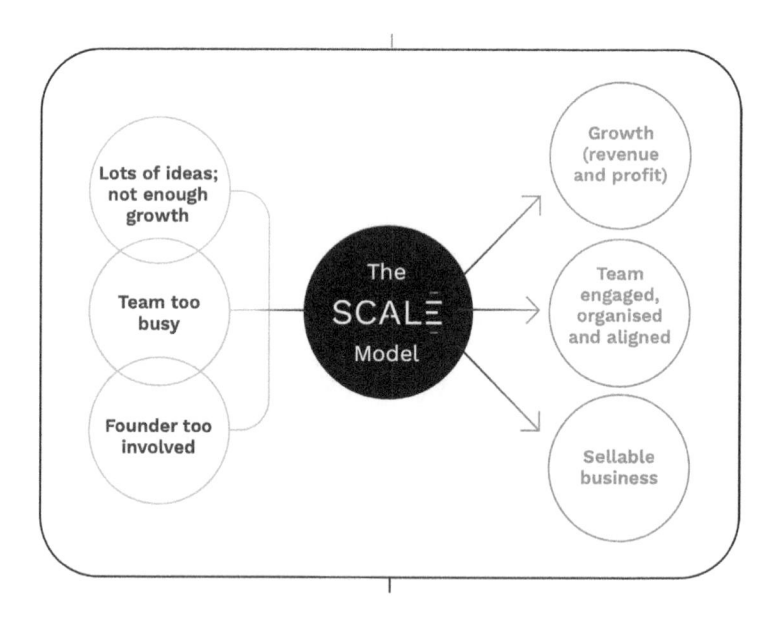

To help you figure out which archetype you might be, this quiz is helpful: https://brandpersonalityquiz.com/

Worksheet

Brand map

Name: _____ Company: _____ Date: _____

Brand Archetype

Which archetype would best describe the brand?

(Brand archetype wheel showing 12 archetypes: The Lover (Chanel), The Creator (Apple), The Sage (Google), The Caregiver (Pampers), The Innocent (Nestle), The Jester (Disney), The Magician, The Ruler (Rolex), The Hero (Nike), The Regular Guy (Gap), The Rebel (Harley-Davidson Motorcycles), The Explorer (Jeep), with Dollar shave club also shown)

Brand Personality

If the brand was a person, what top 3 words would you use to describe them?

-
-
-

Build out the brand

Based on the archetype and personality, answer the following questions.

What external communication tools need to be developed?	
What colours, images or other brands evoke the brand?	
What statements or slogans represent the brand?	

Exercise

Session Basics	
Name	Brand map
How to communicate	'We have to translate our strategy into a clear brand personality and external communication messages'
Time	60–90 minutes to brainstorm brand map and ideas of messages
Format	Workshop session
Attendees	Marketing and sales teams
Objective and outcome	Brainstorm ideas for external branding and communication messages for the brand
Materials	• Important to bring outputs of the strategic plan • Worksheets, pens, and flipcharts/Post-It notes

Exercise	
Objective	Discuss and agree on the objective and agenda of the session
Key concept	Discuss and agree on the concepts of strategy vs. brand, and what is understood by core idea, USPs, and brand personality
Exercise	Individually fill out the three parts of the brand map. Share ideas and brainstorm. Record ideas on flipcharts or Post-Its, and discuss favourite ones
Messages	Fill out and discuss the key external messages to be developed, and ideas for visuals and slogans
Next steps	Agree who needs to do what over the upcoming period, to develop the brand and external messaging visuals and statements required

Marketing channels

Summary

A key challenge to getting your message out to the wide world is knowing where to share it – what marketing channels to invest in.

Key concepts

Marketing as artillery

Marketing has two key functions in a business:

- Generating **leads** for new business.
- Turning strategy into **message**. Communicate the positioning to the outside world and provide materials and support to improve conversions.

A military analogy is helpful here. If you are an army looking to take enemy territory, you need two components to your attack: 'infantry' – boots on the ground to occupy territory, and 'artillery' – cannons and air strikes that soften up the enemy, to increase the effectiveness of the infantry.

Functions like sales and Business Development are the infantry. They meet with potential partners and clients to negotiate deals. Marketing is the artillery that supports them. Potential partners and clients will do research on you: they'll look at the website, read your articles, and scrutinise and assess your brand – the functions of marketing. These supporting elements have a huge impact on the success of conversions in sales.

There is a magic number here. If a prospect has come across positive messaging about you from three separate sources, then the chances of conversion increase significantly. As a result, marketing is a balance of being spread across enough channels to hit that magic number, whilst not spreading resources so thinly that they are ineffective.

For the reasons above, sales and marketing are often one department, or managed by the same person, as there is enormous complementarity between the two functions.

Marketing as infantry – generating leads

In one key regard, though, marketing is also infantry – lead generation. Using the tools of external communication to allow potential clients to find you and give them that first connection to you and your brand. This generates leads that the sales function can then work to close.

There is a diverse range of channels used to achieve this, like a constellation of different activities. Common ones include:

Cold calling	Flyers	Referral partners
Social media	Organic search	Customer referral
Paid search	Trade shows	Events
Partner websites	Ads	Memberships / Networks
Walk-in traffic	Marketing partners	Organic search

A key challenge for marketeers is to work out which channels will have the best chance of generating leads for the business.

Defining lead generation channels

The way to defining optimum lead generation channels is to think about potential customers, and where they go to find information relating to what you sell. For example, they might checkout certain websites, read articles or watch videos by influencers, or attend an event. Each of these points is a potential channel for you to communicate with them.

The first step, therefore, is to think about and record this target customer information-gathering process.

Choosing where and how to communicate

Once you've mapped that out, you can decide which are the primary channels you can use for communication, and what information and communication tools you might employ. As you think about this process, it's also important to reflect on the stages a potential customer goes through when collecting such information. It typically follows three steps:

- **Awareness.** Potential buyers at this stage are looking for information related to their needs and pain points, and whether this industry might be able to help them. They're not yet familiar with industry jargon and require information phrased in terms they understand. Common materials at this stage include White papers or industry research/analyst reports.
- **Consideration (or Comparison).** This phase is about a buyer's evaluation of different methods available to them. They start comparing different types of solutions and benefits available in this market and are starting to pick up some industry terminology. Common content might include product comparison guides.
- **Decision.** At the final stage of information-gathering, the potential buyer is deciding on a specific tool to purchase or a vendor to work with. Information that benefits them at this stage includes materials to gain confidence in their decision, such as vendor/product comparisons, case studies, and free trials.

Finally, marketing teams will build and maintain funnels, to track progress and generation of leads in the channels chosen, such as attendance at events, hits to websites and landing pages, or interaction with content. These funnels are designed with **calls to action** (CTA) in mind at each stage, so that potential prospects are always being encouraged through to the next stage of interaction.

Worksheet

Marketing

SCALE | Business growth made easy

Name: _____ Company: _____ Date: _____

"Half of our marketing budget is effective. We have no idea which half."

Channels

Think about your Core Customer. Where are all the places where they might obtain information related to the products and services you sell? Write them in order of the customer journey (e.g. 'First they might ask... , then they would search on website...").

1	2	3	4	5	6

Each of these is a potential channel of communication for you to connect.

List out the top 3.
Describe how you can develop each as a channel of communication.

1.
2.
3.

Funnels

For each channel, describe the key steps in the funnel to creating leads.
At each stage describe the Call To Action.

1. CTA			
2. CTA			
3. CTA			
4. CTA			
5. CTA			

Feb23 - © Clarity Strategy Ltd DBA Scale 2023   www.scalecoach.co.uk

Exercise

Session Basics	
Name	Marketing channels
How to communicate	'To improve our lead generation, we must identify our top target channels, and build funnels to generate leads from them'
Time	A 90-minute workshop is enough to map out the channels, funnels, and calls to action (CTA). Channels and funnels then need to be built and tested, which is a constant, ongoing process in any business
Format	Workshop session
Attendees	Marketing and sales teams
Objective and outcome	Identify key channels for customer communication, and how we will build funnels to take advantage of them
Materials	• Post-Its are great for mapping the process • Worksheets and pens • Bring any lead generation data you have

Exercise	
Objective	Discuss and agree on the objective and agenda of the session
The exercise and key concept	Review the worksheet and the key concepts from this section. The benefits of: • Sharing best practices • Defining steps and CTAs in the sales process • Understanding where in the process we're not converting • Building out the materials together to improve those conversions
Customer journey	Each person writes out their understanding of the key steps a potential buyer goes through in uncovering information relating to our industry, products, and services. Transcribe these to Post-It notes, and as a team silently (i.e. no talking or discussion) stick them on the wall until the team has agreed on the key steps
Top 3 channels	Discuss and agree which of those customer information points represent the three best opportunities for us to communicate with them
Funnels	For each of the three chosen, build out a funnel of stages of communication with the potential buyer. Ensure that there is a specific CTA for each one
Next steps	Agree who needs to do what over the upcoming period, in order to build out and test these funnels

Sales Playbook

Summary

Are all the people selling in your business doing so in a similar way? Or, is there a wide variation in selling performance? If there is variation, then it's vital to get everyone who sells on the same page, by developing and training through a Sales Playbook. It contains all your unique set of best practices of what works when selling in your business.

Key concepts

Defining 'Sales'

How is 'Sales' viewed in your business? Is it at the core, what everyone loves to do (maybe even more so than actual delivery)? Or is there a stigma about it, is it something viewed as a necessary evil, so that people can get on and do more client work? We've met companies at both ends of this spectrum.

Let's be clear what we mean by 'Sales'. Most businesses have some kind of marketing function, whose role it is to generate leads (or 'prospects', 'deals', or 'opportunities', or whatever term you use), for example, from a website, events, or from partners.

Sales take these leads, qualify whether they might be a good fit, and if so, close them into business, in the shortest possible time (NB. If you are a totally online business without any human sales processes, this chapter will be of limited value to you).

So, sales is generally distinguished as having a start point (lead handed over from marketing), and an end point (signing up a new customer).

Sales metrics and tracking

A characteristic of sales is that measurements and metrics are clear and easy to understand and track (and vital to success). Key ones include:

- **Conversion rate** from lead to customer (# signed clients/# leads, in any given period)
- Average **time of closing** (Average of sign date – lead handover date, in any given period)

- **Cost** per sale (sales costs/# of clients signed)

In a sales team, it's worth noting that each of the metrics above can be worked out on a per person basis, to create **league tables** of performance, a vital way to learn who is (and isn't) delivering on sales. These numbers can also be worked out for the **individual steps** in the sales process.

Sales leadership

Sales is a team sport. As such, it benefits from having a good captain, and sticking to certain good habits and disciplines. If you run a sales team, there are a few key things to continually manage and maintain:

- **Regular Sales Meetings**. Managing the sales Meetings is a vital component of sales leadership. It generally comprises two components:
    - Tactical review of the **Sales Funnel**. Ensuring accountability is clear for each lead, and that there are next steps defined for each lead in the funnel.
        - **Upskilling** of the sales team. Training and sharing best practices, communicating new policies, team bonding, and motivation.
- Tracking and sharing of **sales performance data**. Understand and deal with variances in performance within sales teams. These may be related to individual capabilities, or relate to challenges associated with different customers' groups, products, or geographies which need to be understood and accounted for (for example, through updates in pricing, or the product set).
- Management of **recognition and incentive** schemes associated with sales. Designing a system that best fits how your team needs to sell, for example, with respect to individual vs team incentives, or ratios of base to performance-linked compensation.
- Constantly improving the **sales process**. Finding opportunities to remove steps or improve conversions through process improvement: for example, by collecting answers in advance by survey, or slimming down contract templates.

- **Teaching of sales as a skill.** Sales has a body of knowledge associated with it that is important for people involved in sales to understand and master. There are great books and training courses, and within a team, mentoring and coaching make a big difference.
- Management and use of **sales software**. Typically, a CRM system. Teams must use their software correctly to ensure clean data. Such software often has opportunities for upgrading, or linking with other software, to make sales teams life easier, such as accounting software for billing and contracting, or time tracking software for logging time.
- **Representing** sales. As a key function of the business, sales must be strongly represented at the leadership team, to ensure resources and attention are focused on ensuring continual progress of the function.

The single best thing the leader of a sales team can do for their team is to provide a strong **Sales Playbook** (often called 'Sales Manual' in the United Kingdom). See the exercise below on how to develop this vital tool.

Where does sales sit in the organisation?

In the development of many companies, growth of the sales function is led by an individual, who grows a stand-alone sales team. In this model, once clients are signed up, they are then handed over to the relevant customer service or operational departments.

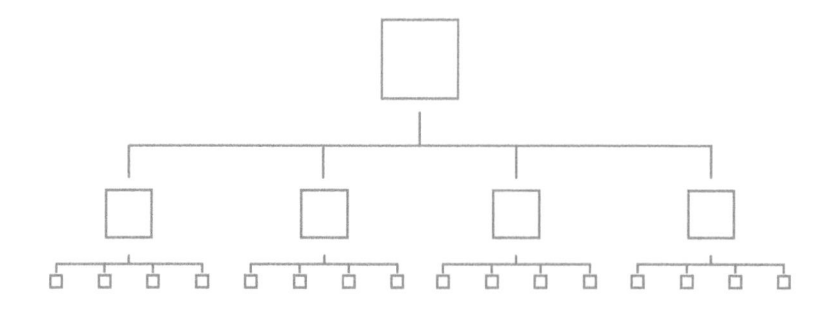

Command
A traditional top-down structure.
The conections that matter are between
workers and their managers

However, this structure can become a limit to great customer service, and to growth. Some of the best teams with whom we have worked marry a central sales leadership and best practice function, with a dispersed sales team, with the salespeople themselves spread across cross-functional teams (this model is explained in more detail under Team Structure).

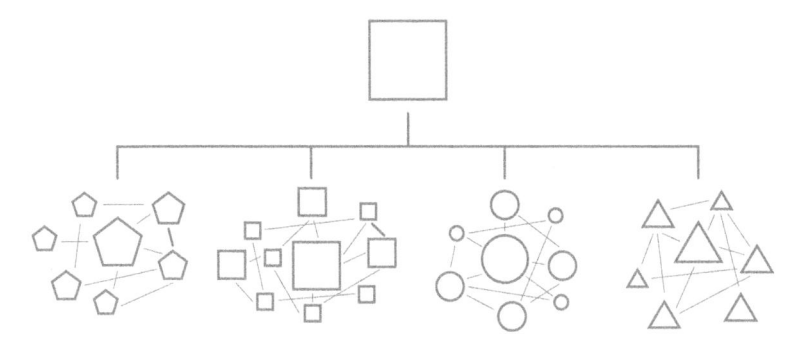

Command of Teams
Small teams operate independently
but still within a more rigid superstructure

This model has significant benefits from a sales perspective:

- **Focus on a target customer group.** When companies create cross-functional team structures, they must decide on what the new teams should focus. This might be on geography, product line, or customer type. The team therefore has a specific market focus, so the salespeople can specialise. They understand the particular needs of that market segment and can optimise in it.
- **Easy handovers.** For a customer, it can be very frustrating to build up a rapport with a salesperson who takes the time to understand your needs, only to have to re-do it with someone from a different department when you sign a contract. Having cross-functional teams reduces friction from such handoffs, as they are not inter-departmental, but within the same team.
- **Coordination with downstream team.** As a salesperson, there are often items that you need to coordinate with operating departments on, for example, if you need drawings or designs for a pitch, or if you need to run a trial for a client. If everyone is on the same team, this kind of cooperation is so much easier, which improves sales conversions.

Sales Playbook

If I were to ask two different salespeople in your business how they actually go about selling, would they give me the same answer? For example, would they be aware of the same buying personas, or using the same closing scripts? Or, is each of them doing it their own way? If so, then presumably some of them are making a better job of it than others?

A Sales Playbook (or Sales Manual in the United Kingdom) is a record of all the best practices that your best salespeople are using to close leads. It compiles these into one place for training and sharing, so that the whole team is learning from the best tools and techniques.

Sales process

The first thing to do is have a clear, common understanding of how many **steps** there are in your sales process. For example, maybe you start by researching a client, and if they look promising, you decide to move to the stage of arranging a first call. Each stage in this process must have a **CTA**, that is, a key decision point on your part or theirs, that decides whether the lead moves to the next stage, or gets disqualified as unsuitable. In this example, the CTA was 'lead looks suitable, move to arranging call'.

Taking this example forward, if you then have a first call with the lead, it's important to understand your CTA to the next stage. Let's say, from experience, you know that clients' next step is typically to have a site visit, then you have one of two outcomes to the call: either the lead does not want to move to a site visit, in which case they are disqualified from the funnel, or they do agree to a site visit, in which case they move to the next stage of the funnel.

This rigorous process of **disqualification** must continue throughout the sales process. One of the largest sources of waste in many growing businesses is time spent on sales with customers who won't eventually buy. It's vital to have the means to understand which leads must be removed from the funnel, so that scarce sales resources can be focused on those most likely to buy.

At any moment, all salespeople need to be focused on getting their live leads not to the end of the funnel but to the next CTA. This is an important concept to master.

So, the first stage of creating your Sales Playbook is to map out each of the stages of your sales process, with a clear CTA at each stage.

Sales best practices

Once you understand your stages, you can then work on developing and sharing the best practices in the team to maximise the % of leads that go to the next stage. Make sure you include at least the following ones at the relevant stages of your sales cycle in your Sales Playbook:

- **Vetting**. At the early stages of contact with a lead, it's typical to start with research to better understand whether they may be a good match. An excellent technique here to use is **surveys**. If a client has an interest, have them fill out a short survey asking key questions that will indicate whether they might be a good fit or not, in advance of arranging a first call. In a previous company of mine, we used the results of such surveys and matched them to an 'Ideal' and 'Red Flag' list.

Item	Ideal	Red flags
Company size	Company with a trading turnover between $5–100m.	• One man bands & start-ups • Large blue chip corporations that already have a significant presence in China.
Need or Opportunity in China	Company who have a clear opportrnity, project, or activity in China that is stuck in some way due to operational challenges. Will have done some research, and have some working familiarity with business in China.	• Variants of: "We hear China's really hot right now, do you think our product would work?"
Location	Basedin a Western country, with experience exporting to other markets.	Based on China, with lots of experience and access to local agents.
Contact details	Comapny email; Company has well presented website, that matches the description presented to us.	• Personal (e.g. gmail) address - No company website (or 'not working')
Interest in LNP	Has an understanding of our services, and keen to meet / talk.	No response, or misunderstanding of what we do.
Channel	• Personally recommended by a known and trusted partner. • Followed our online nurturing pathway, having found us with targeted keywords, and read multiple pieces of content.	The following channels can deliver low-quality leads: • event attendees • business clinic walk-ins • certain keywords searches, such "how to get money out of China"

- **Customer personas/avatars**. These are detailed descriptions, including demographics, personality, and needs of key customer types. Ensuring that each salesperson has a clear understanding of these few key

target customer personas makes them much more effective in focusing on those most likely to convert (Go to Section Core Customer to learn how to develop such persona/avatars)
- **Great questions**. Questions sit at the heart of a successful sales process. Salespeople must understand which ones are the most effective in your business, so the Playbook must include your effective questions. There are three 'hero questions' that stand out as necessary in most sales conversations:
  - The not shying away from money question. A version of "Do you have the budget to cover the cost of this?"
    - The uncovering objection question: 'What concerns or issues would you have to starting on xxx date?' Drives out what real objections they have to buying.
    - The Closing Question: 'Assuming we can deal with xxx issue, would you be prepared to start on yyy date?' How to deal with objections to get to close.
- **Objections handling**. It's helpful to list out the common objections your leads have, and what works for dealing with them. A great way of handling objections is whether you have certain 'USP' Promise Guarantees (explained in more detail here: Unique Selling Promises), such as a price promise, a satisfaction guarantee.
- **Power statements**. Your company has certain achievements or gongs, the statement of which enhances your credibility in the eyes of leads. Examples include awards you've won, prestigious clients with whom you've worked, market rankings, media appearances or citations, or published works. The best are proofs of delivery of your USPs (described in more detail here: Unique Selling Promises).
- **Buying signals**. Leads will convey their intent to buy (or not to buy) in certain ways, not all of which are obvious. Actions like asking about price, start times, kick-off process, or for an agreement are all clear ones. Sales teams need to be taught what the common buying signals are in your business, and that the absence of them is cause for disqualification.

- **Closing statements**. 'ABC – Always Be Closing'. It can take confidence and experience to close effectively, which is why teaching how to do it, and sharing best practices for how it works in your market is vital: a key determinant of sales success.

Other items to include in a Sales Playbook

There are other valuable items commonly included in a Sales Playbook:

- **Company strategy**. Salespeople are on the front line of execution of strategy. It's vital for them to understand how the company is positioned, and how it's differentiated from competitors. This means they need to have a strong understanding of company strategy, so it's an important element to include in the Playbook training applicable to them.
- **Process training**. Salespeople always have certain processes they must follow, such as the correct use of the CRM system. They need to be regularly trained in order to ensure quality data and avoidance of errors.
- **Templates**. It's extremely helpful to have templates of scripts, PowerPoint decks, flyers, emails, and all relevant documents that salespeople can efficiently use for communication with leads. Increasingly, these can be automated through the effective use of CRMs.

Worksheet

Sales playbook — SCALE | Business growth made easy

Name: _____ Company: _____ Date: _____

Best practice

Ensure your sales-people are all working off the established best practice for sales in your business.

At each stage, a key Call To Action is to 'Disqualify as unsuited', or move to the next stage of the funnel.

Stages in the funnel	Name What you call a prospect at this stage.	Call to action Key action to complete with the prospect to move to the next stage.	Time How long does it typically take?	Success % The typical conversion rate.
Example	Lead	Disqualify, or have our name added to the tender.	2 weeks	45%
1				
2				
3				
4				
5				

Examples of sales playbook content

- Personas / core customer avatars
- Core Foundation & Core Values
- Qualification criteria ('red flags' & 'ideals')
- Call / meeting scripts and agendas
- Effective questions
- Email templates
- Power statements. Gongs or points of credibility (e.g. blue-chip clients, awards...)
- Presentation formats & templates
- Common buying signals
- Objections handling
- Closing scripts & techniques
- Client testimonials
- Guide to the sales meeting
- Recommended / required reading & books
- Training on tools e.g. CRM system.

Exercise

Session Basics	
Name	Sales Playbook
How to communicate	'To improve conversions and cycle times in Sales, we need to ensure that everyone selling is following the same set of best practices'
Time	60–90 minutes. This is enough to map out the key stages of the process, and the calls to action (CTA). To build out the full script of the Sales Playbook and train it through to the sales team is often the work of one to two quarters (and requires ongoing maintenance and updating after that)
Format	Workshop session
Attendees	Sales teams!
Objective and outcome	Map out our sales process and key CTA, so that we can build out a Sales Playbook and identify where we need to make improvements
Learning and reading	• *The Sales Bible*, Jeffrey Gittomer. • *Hyper Sales*, Jack Daly
Materials	• Post-Its are great for mapping the process • Worksheets and pens • Bring all the sales conversion data you have

Exercise	
Objective	Discuss and agree on the objective and agenda of the session
The exercise and key concept	Review the worksheet and the key concepts from this section. The benefits of: • Sharing best practice • Defining steps and CTAs in the sales process • Understanding where in the process we're not converting • Building out the materials together to improve those conversions
The sales process	Each person writes out their understanding of the key steps in the sales process. Transcribe these to Post-It notes, and as a team silently (i.e. no talking or discussion) stick them on the wall until the team has agreed on the key steps to the sales process
Calls to action	Discuss and agree what the specific Call to Action for each step is, and add them to the wall
Time and success rate	Use data to work out the time taken and conversion rate for each stage in the funnel. If you don't have data, make best guesses. Then identify which stages require focus first

Brainstorm	For the stage agreed upon, brainstorm as a team, ways to improve conversions or cycle times. Share best practices that work, and brainstorm new ideas. Record best means
Plan the Sales Playbook	Agree how you will structure and record your Sales Playbook, and how you will include the outputs from the workshop. Assign clear accountabilities and objectives for who will take which parts forward, and when you will check-in next to review progress

Part IV

BONUS TOOLS

19

MAXIMISING COMPANY VALUE

Summary

Growing the value of a business has the twin benefits of creating a business that allows you to sleep better at night and increases the chance that the business will outlive you. This requires focus beyond just growth, developing elements of the business that are hard. Use this simple tool to diagnose where you need to start building the business for real value and allow you to leave a legacy.

The problem

Many business owners work hard to grow their businesses, to generate greater sales and profits. Sooner or later though, they end up realising that this approach – focusing principally on growth – is not enough.

For example, take two businesses, with the same sales and profit, but one with entirely recurring revenue, and one having to wipe the slate clean and make new sales each month. From an investor's perspective, these two businesses will have very different values. This is an example of **shareholder value** vs. simple size.

I learned this lesson the hard way. I had a business for several years that I enjoyed, felt a strong sense of purpose for, and that was consistently growing year after year. I never gave much thought to exit or how I would hand it over. But personal circumstances overtook me, and I found myself in a position to have to sell it, without the company really being ready. The sale didn't realise the full value of that business, and within 6 months, the brand was gone, the team dispersed, and the clients all folded into the acquirer.

We all reach a point in life where we have to think about legacy – what are we going to hand over when our work is done? Sometimes this happens when we're old enough to retire, and sometimes, as in my case, much sooner. Even if this date is a long way off, the things that an investor would look at in your business are the same ones that will grow value for you – it's about maximising the company for **shareholder value**, which is important, because:

- it allows you to pass on the business, and leave a legacy that outlives you
- allows you to realise value (i.e. make money) from years of risk and investment
- if shared, can do the same for your team (and motivate them towards the same outcome)
- the actions to improve shareholder value bring benefits that can be summed up in the phrase 'allow you to sleep well at night'.

So why don't more entrepreneurs have a stronger focus on building shareholder value? What we see again and again are the following reasons. Do any apply to you?

- **The voice of shareholder value is a minority.** The owner(s) of the business may be the most influential and powerful people in the

company, but their voice often gets drowned out by day-to-day demands of the market, customers, and staff.
- **Lack of understanding of what drives shareholder value**. Most entrepreneurs only sell their business once in their lives, so they don't have the knowledge and experience to understand what investors look at and value in a company.
- **Lack of capacity to work on it**. Projects to drive shareholder value often fall into the 'Important but not Urgent' category. For entrepreneurs, it is hard to get out of the gravity well of working in the business and not on it.
- **The actions to really grow shareholder value are hard**. Many of the things on the list are really difficult to achieve, to the point where they may feel 'intractable'.
- **Fear of talking about 'exit'**. Any conversation whose ultimate purpose is to work towards the exit of the Founder brings anxiety, both for them and the team. It can be difficult to message such initiatives as being for the common good.

How to fix it? – The shareholder value checklist

Let me be clear – it takes years to really grow shareholder value. Even if you have the notion to sell the company 'in a few years' time', the process of development must start **now**.

If done right, some of the initiatives you choose will take time and may require significant investment to achieve. For example, transitioning to recurring revenue, or diversifying away from a single point of failure are really tough things to achieve if not there already. The key is to keep setting objectives and planning out projects each quarter. That habit breaks down an 'insurmountable' objective into achievable sprints.

What will happen during this journey, is that your mindset will shift from being a manager of your business, to being an owner/investor. You will start to realise that investing back into the business in key areas will end up paying dividends, and you will start to see each project in terms of ROI, with the 'R' being measured in shareholder value.

Worksheet

Shareholder value checklist

SCALE — Business growth made easy

Name: _____ Company: _____ Date: _____

> "Hard things are hard because there are no easy answers or recipes. They are hard because your emotions are at odds with your logic. They are hard because you don't know the answer and you cannot ask for help without showing weakness."
>
> — From **'The Hard Thing About Hard Things'** by Ben Horowitz

Improving the scores of the items on this list will significantly improve the value of the business.

Score the company for current performance across each of these items. In each case, score how close company performance is to the description.

1. Recurring revenue
- All revenues come from subscriptions, long term contracts, or recurring fees (rather than one-off projects).

Score 0 – 10

2. Brand recognition
- The brand is awarded, or recognized as 'the gold standard' or #1 for something valuable in the industry.
- The brand is 'top of mind' amongst potential customers in the industry.

Score 0 – 10

3. Board accountability
- An independent Board is in place, with oversight on strategy, budgets, and owner compensation. Board members are known and respected in the industry.
- Accounts are audited by a reputable, well-known auditor.

Score 0 – 10

4. Financial performance
- The company is consistently growing revenues by >20% year after year, and delivering 15-25% pre-tax profit.
- The cash conversion cycle is positive i.e. increase in topline revenue increases cash levels.

Score 0 – 10

5. Key points of failure
- The business has no place reliant upon 'one thing' (e.g. few customers, sales channels, or products) the loss of which would threaten the business.
- There are no key people the business could not afford to lose.

Score 0 – 10

6. IP
- The business owns Intellectual Property of value (e.g. patents, trademarks, unique inventions, or software) which are registered and protectable.
- The products, services, and processes of the business are standardized to the point of being a structural advantage.

Score 0 – 10

7. Leadership team
- The leadership team is rated as the best in the industry; you would enthusiastically re-hire each member of the leadership team.
- The leadership team have 'skin in the game' – i.e. stand to gain and lose financially based on the shareholder value of the business (not just profit).

Score 0 – 10

8. Strength of the 'Management operating system'
- There is a clear strategy in place, commonly understood across the team, and consistent routines in place for delivering on this strategy.
- Software systems and operational disciplines provide clear reporting on metrics and progress tracking.

Score 0 – 10

Next Steps. Based on these scores, which item above should we work on this Q, and what should we do?

Exercise

Session Basics	
Name	Shareholder Value checklist (SVC)
How to communicate	'Together we're going to look at and tackle some of the challenging issues which, if solved, would allow us to build a business we can all be proud of, and that can leave a legacy'
Time	30–60 minutes
Format	Workshop session
Attendees	Senior leadership, especially those with an ownership stake in the business
Objective and outcome	Key areas of focus in order to improve the shareholder value of the business
Materials	Handout the printed worksheets and pens

Exercise	
Objective	Discuss and agree on the objective and agenda of the session
The exercise and key concept	Explain that at some point the business will have to be valued. To that end, it's important to understand what an investor would look at, so we're going to score ourselves on those areas. Improving in these areas will also allow us to have a better business and sleep well at night
Checklist	Each participant writes a score (out of 10) for each item on the checklist
Compare numbers	Compile the numbers into one spreadsheet, and work out the averages. Ask around particularly high/low numbers, and draw out stories and examples to understand them
Focus area	Discuss and decide which item on the list would benefit improving/working on first. It may be the one with the lowest score, or may not. The key criterion should be achievable, with a positive impact on shareholder value
Priority project	Set a clear objective around the focus area for that period (e.g. the next Quarter). Then plan out the execution of the project to deliver the objective, including assigning milestones, actions, and deadlines to specific individuals
Action list	Define any further actions, owners, and deadlines outside of the priority project, based on the session (who's going to do what, by when) to get all the agreed-on items done

Pitfalls, guidelines, and FAQs

Will it freak the team out?

Entrepreneurs are often reticent to focus team discussion explicitly on shareholder value, because of the direct implication that the business may one day get sold. This can make people feel uncertain about the future, or that they may end up abandoned by the current owners.

Even if that is not the reality of the situation that the owners simply want to ensure that the business becomes inherently more valuable, with no intention of near-term sale, the fallout is often the same. There are several approaches to take:

- **Be explicit about a timeline.** If you think it's 10 years out, or 5, or 3, or whenever, clarify and align that expectation with the team
- **Limit participation.** Create a sub-group of leaders within the business, and run the session behind closed doors and confidentiality

Include them

If you want people to behave like owners, then make them owners. The easiest way to align incentives around shareholder value is to make people shareholders.

It also pays to take others on the journey with you, having key members of the team (or even the wider team) incentivised by shareholding rather than just sales or profit aligns incentives, and creates a sense of ownership.

This may be an option scheme, or directly making key people shareholders in the business. Either way, the more you think like an owner, the more likely it is that you will include others on that journey with you.

Research has shown repeatedly that this is one of the best ways to hold on to key team members. Ownership in a business and the potential of significant returns on an exit event are powerful anchors for people to stick around.

Repetition

This tool and process is one for the long run. Some things, such as getting Board Accountability, can be realistically achieved within one quarter. Most will take longer. So, you need to repeat this process every 6–12 months, and as you improve these scores, you will massively grow the value of your business.

Why isn't this included in the Scale Model checklist?

It used to be, but no one ever chose it, so it appears as a standalone chapter.

20

PLANNING SURVEY

Welcome page

To continue building your organisation, we need your valuable and candid feedback. Please take the necessary time to thoroughly read the questions and provide thoughtful answers based on your perspective of the organisation. This survey is not about a specific individual or department. We're looking for your input about **the company as a whole**.

There are no right or wrong answers. Your feedback will be carefully considered and will remain anonymous unless you request otherwise. All of the survey responses will be combined and presented as a single report. Please set aside at least 30 minutes to complete the survey in one focused session.

Survey questions

1. **Wins and great things.** What happened in the organisation during the last period/quarter, or coming up the next period/quarter, that deserves attention or celebration? Especially share any news from your team or department that is relevant to the entire organisation which they may not know about.
2. **Feel of the team.** Looking back over the past period/quarter, how is the 'feel' of your team and/or the organisation? Please include any positive or negative feedback that is relevant to the entire organisation.
3. **Lessons learned.** During the past period/quarter, what are the losses, struggles, and disappointments that occurred, and more importantly, what did you learn from those events that should be shared with the entire organisation?
4. **Outstanding players.** From your perspective, who are the team members that have stood out this period/quarter as outstanding players? And why do they deserve recognition?
5. **Planning for the next period/quarter: company priorities.** What are the three things that the COMPANY must do in the next period/quarter to move the organisation forward? Take the necessary time to think about the next period/quarter and what are the most important things for the organisation to accomplish. Think beyond just your department.
6. **Planning for the next period/quarter: individual priorities.** What are the three things that YOU must do in the next period/quarter to move the organisation forward? Take the necessary time to think about the next period/quarter and what are the most important things for YOU to accomplish. Be specific with your answers. We ask you to begin thinking of these now and we'll finalise them on the day of planning. Bring your thoughts with you and you will build upon them during our session.
7. **Comments.** Would you like to add anything additional that you would like to see from the Scale team to make your planning day a better experience overall?